Preface

When I was teaching Introduction to the Hebrew Bible to college students, I used to begin the first class by placing a beautiful handmade wooden box in the shape of a heart on the table before them. I would ask them what they saw, and they would say, "A wooden heart." I would then open the box and take out its contents—also a wooden heart, but in the form of an intricate three-dimensional puzzle, composed of scores of carefully made pieces of wood. I would then ask the students what this object was, and they would again say, "A wooden heart," but I could already see in their faces a glint of incipient discovery. I would then ask them which heart they thought was more beautiful, and most of them would point to the solid box. Finally, I would ask them which of the two they thought more interesting, and all of them would indicate the puzzle.

The point of my little demonstration was to introduce an aspect of biblical study which is applicable to almost any narrative portion of the Bible, but particularly to the Pentateuch. The Pentateuch is a combination of the box and the puzzle. On the surface, it is a beautiful work of art— uncomplicated and whole. But inside, it is a complex puzzle composed of innumerable interlocking pieces. I believe that both the fascination *and* the beauty of the Pentateuch are enhanced when we recognize both its puzzle- and its box-like structures.

The following study is an attempt to understand the Pentateuch both in terms of its final form (the box) and its internal complexity (the puzzle). That much more weight is given to the former than to the latter derives from the previous imbalance in Pentateuchal criticism, as the following Introduction will explain.

The origin of this book lies in lectures delivered to hapless students at Princeton Theological Seminary, and in the interest shown by a colleague (Chris Beker) who not only came to hear those lectures beyond the call of his duties, but also encouraged me to put them into some published form. At the same time, another colleague, George Stroup, stimulated my interest in narrative as the primary medium for theologizing, and introduced me to the stories of Flannery O'Connor. A few years later, and in a different place, Malinda Maxfield helped me through the narratives of Homer and Dante, Virginia Wray led me more deeply into the mystery and manners of O'Connor, and Kent Brudney helped me sharpen my own prose—and helped all three of us remain sane. This book is dedicated to these former colleagues in gratitude for their probity and compassion, their intelligence, and, above all, their humor.

I am also indebted to the National Endowment for the Humanities for a College Teachers Fellowship which supported nearly a full year of revision of the manuscript in 1984.

There are probably few congregations which will put up with arcane academic pursuits by their ministers in the midst of duties which are often far more important, and far fewer which will provide a month free of those duties for such pursuits. I was fortunate enough to find one. I thank the Council and members of Parkway United Church of Christ.

Occasionally I have noted Hebrew words when I thought they might be helpful for some readers. I have used a rough phonetic transliteration rather than a technical one to aid in hearing the sound of the words. I have not attempted to eliminate the male language for God in references to the biblical text. While I have great sympathy for those who would do so, the character of Yahweh (and Elohim) is, after all, predominantly male in the Pentateuch. What we do with that in terms of systematic theology is another matter. Finally, I am grateful to Ms. Julie Galambush for her careful and insightful editing of the manuscript.

Thomas W. Mann

For J. Christiaan Beker, George Stroup,
Malinda Maxfield, Virginia F. Wray, and Kent Brudney

Abbreviations

AnBib	*Analecta Biblica*
BA	*Biblical Archeologist*
Bib	*Biblica*
BZAW	*Beihefte zur ZAW*
CBQ	*Catholic Biblical Quarterly*
EvTh	*Evangelische Theologie*
IDB	*The Interpreter's Dictionary of the Bible*
IDBSup	*Supplementary volume to IDB*
Int	*Interpretation*
JAAR	*Journal of the American Academy of Religion*
JBL	*Journal of Biblical Literature*
JPS	*Jewish Publication Society*
JQR	*The Jewish Quarterly Review*
JR	*Journal of Religion*
JSOT	*Journal for the Study of the Old Testament*
JSOTSuppl	*Supplements to JSOT*
KD	*Kerygma und Dogma*
NAB	*The New American Bible*
TTod	*Theology Today*
VT	*Vetus Testamentum*
ZAW	*Zeitschrift für die alttestamentliche Wissenschaft*

Contents

INTRODUCTION

The Hebrew Bible is traditionally referred to by the acronym "Tanak," which stands for the Hebrew words Torah, Nevi'im, Ketuvim, or, in English, Law, Prophets, and Writings. This sequence of words reflects the sequence of literary materials that constitute the Hebrew Scriptures: the Torah, often called the Pentateuch because it contains the five books of Genesis through Deuteronomy; the Prophets, containing the books of Joshua through Malachi; and the Writings, containing Psalms through Chronicles. This order will seem strange to Christians, whose Bible follows an arrangement that, in essence, places the writings in the middle rather than at the end. Nevertheless, for both Christians and Jews, Scripture begins with the Torah. For Judaism we could remove the article and say that "Scripture begins and ends with Torah," inasmuch as the rest of the Hebrew Bible—especially the prophetic books, but also to some extent the "writings"—can be understood as interpretive extensions of the Torah, rather than as portions of equal weight. Thus *all* of Scripture becomes, in some sense, Torah, i.e., "guidance," and Judaism itself may be designated as the Way of Torah.[1]

On the other hand, to say that "Scripture begins with Torah" from a traditionally Christian perspective, means that Scripture *begins* with guidance (more commonly translated "law"), but only with the purpose of pointing to "something greater" (Matt. 12:6), namely, the gospel of the New Testament. Thus not despite but precisely because of its relativizing of the Torah, the New Testament in many respects would be incomprehensible without some understanding of the Torah. In short, those who want to know what it is to be a Jew or a Christian must at some point read the book of the Torah.

The tripartite division of the Hebrew Bible into Torah, Prophets, and Writings is by no means a recent invention. Not only does the New

Testament refer to "the law of Moses, the prophets, and the psalms" (Luke 24:44), but the Prologue to the book of Ecclesiasticus (Sirach), from about 130 B.C.E., provides a similar division. The further back into history we move, of course, the less precisely can we date the crystallization of the Torah. The reference to Ezra's recitation of "the book of the Torah of Moses" in Nehemiah 8:1–8 would seem to place the formal designation of the Pentateuch at least as early as c. 450 B.C.E., after Israel's return from exile in Babylonia. It is even possible that this designation took place almost one hundred years earlier, during the exile itself, but at this point the discussion becomes mostly speculative.[2]

Whenever the Pentateuch received its present shape as a literary unit, it was the result of a surgical procedure. While its separation from the Former Prophets (Joshua through 2 Kings) may seem perfectly natural (e.g., the Pentateuch deals with Israel's history from the creation up to the occupation of the land), in fact the separation is artificial. The book of Deuteronomy, which originally served as the introduction to the Former Prophets, has been removed from that position to serve as the conclusion of the Tetrateuch (Genesis through Numbers), thereby forming the Pentateuch. The theological significance of this literary surgery is a subject to which we shall return at the end of this study; for now we need only posit the surgery itself.[3]

Those scholars who maintain an originally separate origin and function for the book of Deuteronomy defend their position by a prior claim—that the book derives from a different author than the Tetrateuch. Beginning as early as the sixteenth century it has become increasingly clear that the Pentateuch, traditionally called the Five Books of Moses, is not the work of a single author at all, much less of Moses, but in fact is a composite document containing a number of literary strands, each stemming from a different period of Israel's history. Indeed, it is likely that the gap between the earliest and latest literary strata in the Pentateuch is as much as five hundred years—from about 1000 to 500 B.C.E. The work of distinguishing these strands—usually referred to as literary (or source) criticism—is accomplished by careful attention to differences in language and style, theological emphasis, and logical consistency. The results of many years of research in this area are reflected in a list of code letters: J, E, D, and P. Each of these letters stands for an "author" of the Pentateuch. Thus J stands for the Yahwist (from the German *Jahwist*), and is usually thought to stem from the time of the Davidic-Solomonic empire, c. 1000–922 B.C.E. E stands for the Elohist, usually located in northern Israel around 850 B.C.E. D stands for the Deuteronomist, found almost exclusively in Deuteronomy through 2 Kings and referred to above. The Deuteronomist is located between about 620 B.C.E., a century after the fall of the Northern Kingdom of Israel, and the period of exile that began with the destruction of the Southern Kingdom of Judah in 587 B.C.E. The final strand is designated P, which stands for Priestly. Considerable debate continues about the temporal location of this strand, especially vis-à-vis D; some think that P is earlier than D, some that D and P are basically contemporary, while others maintain that the bulk of P is about seventy-five years later, reflecting the exilic period. Sometimes these literary strands are found in separate blocks, such as P in Genesis 1:1—2:4a and J in 2:4b–25, and at other times they are intricately intertwined, as in the flood story in Genesis 6:1—9:19.[4]

Until recently, at least, there was a general consensus that each of these "authors" wrote with a particular audience in mind and with a particular message for that audience, and that this historical *context* was of primary importance in determining the meaning and significance of the *text*. Walter Brueggemann's synopsis is representative:

> To chasten the pride and prosperity of the united monarchy, J recalled to its notice that "by you the families of the earth will be blessed." To loosen Israel from the quicksand of Canaanite syncretism, E extolled her, "fear God." And to summon her in exile, DtrH [our D] admonished, "return," while P, to encourage, told her to "be fruitful and multiply, fill the land, subdue it and have dominion."[5]

The ambiguity of our dating of P is an indication of the complex development that stands behind all of the four literary strands and is easily obscured by the brevity of the preceding paragraphs. In fact, two other critical disciplines—form and tradition criticism—have shown that the Pentateuch is hardly the product of four individual "authors" whose work was done all at once at four discrete points in Israel's history. Rather, each of the major literary strands, while perhaps located at a particular period of Israel's history, also contains many older traditions. These traditions were originally passed on in oral rather than written form, until they found written expression in one (or more) of the literary strands. The transmission of these traditions from the original oral form (often hypothetical) to the latest written form is called the history of traditions.

Scholars attempt not only to trace the history of traditions but also to establish the "setting in life" (German *Sitz im Leben*) of the original oral form (or one of the later stages). That is, biblical scholars often seek to determine the sociological context of the oral tradition.

An example of the combined use of literary, form, and tradition criticism may be helpful. The custom of Passover is described in at least three major literary strands. The Priestly stratum is found in Exodus 12:1–20, while the Yahwistic stratum picks up in 12:21–39 (perhaps including fragments of E). Another editor (perhaps an early representative of the

Deuteronomic school) has added material about the associated custom of eating unleavened bread in 13:3–10 and, in addition, a significantly different picture of Passover is presented in Deuteronomy 16:1–8. Thus the Passover tradition is crystallized in written form in the three basic literary strata, J, D, and P, and one can trace a development in the tradition chronologically from J to P. Moreover, this history of tradition can be traced *behind* the earliest written record (J) to a likely setting in life out of which the tradition developed in its oral stage, namely a bedouin custom which occurred at the change of pasturage each year. In fact, having traced the tradition backwards, one could then continue to trace it forwards to the practice of Passover among contemporary Jews—a history of tradition stretching for thousands of years.

As already implied, the influence of form and tradition criticism on the results of literary criticism has been enormous. Above all, the first two methods have established that the major literary strata of the Pentateuch are not at all the products of "authors" in the contemporary sense of the word. For example, the so-called Yahwist was not an individual who sat down sometime during the Davidic monarchy and wrote an original history of Israel's beginnings. Instead the Yahwist, and indeed all the Pentateuchal "authors," are more properly understood as editors or redactors. First, they are redactors in that they collected various oral traditions, arranged them in literary formulations, and gave them a particular style and theological emphasis. Secondly, and especially for P, these "authors" were redactors or editors in the more familiar sense—they rearranged written *texts* to conform to their own literary and theological interests.

To return to the Passover tradition as an example, the Priestly "author," who operated at a time much later than J, in all likelihood had the *text* of J available to him (basically Exod. 12:21–23, 29–39). P found this text to be inadequate to his understanding of the Passover, so he added an introduction (Exod. 12:1–20) that provided a framework for the J tradition and thereby changed the way in which the reader would approach the J text. For example, the detailed legal ordinances in the Priestly stratum, given by God to Moses *before* the actual event of the first Passover, prevent the reader from concluding that the customs surrounding Passover arose accidentally during the departure from Egypt itself (e.g., the Israelites baked unleavened bread simply because they had to leave quickly before yeast could be added, 12:39). If we look at the final text, the result of this editorial fusion is highly significant—it means we can speak of a *redactional unit* that is quite different from either J or P taken alone. In fact, the Passover tradition as a whole is contained in a redactional unit that stretches from 11:1 to 13:16, and its inclusion with chapter

11 ties it in with *another* redactional unit, the plague narrative, which runs at least from 7:14 through chapter 11. Indeed, if we extended our literary horizon we could see how the rest of the book of Exodus—and ultimately, the Pentateuch—is a composite of a number of redactional units.

We have now come full circle—from the Pentateuch or Torah as a distinct entity within the canon, to the complex history of traditions which stands behind (or beneath) this entity, and back to the final, redactional form of the whole. In recent years, scholars from widely different perspectives have argued that such a movement toward interpretation of the *present* form of the text is precisely the direction in which biblical research ought to be going. As Robert Polzin has put it,

> Traditional biblical scholarship has spent most of its efforts in disassembling the works of a complicated watch before our amazed eyes without apparently realizing that similar efforts by and large have not succeeded in putting the parts back together again in a significant or meaningful way.[6]

While few, if any, scholars want to abandon completely the fruits of over a hundred years of research, they are raising cogent questions about the methods and goals of that research. Without necessarily disputing the composite nature of the Pentateuch, some scholars wonder about the precision with which we can delineate the classic sources or "authors," about our ability to reconstruct their historical context, and about the extent to which such reconstruction should control our interpretation of the present text. Is "E" really an independent narrative source or, at best, a set of fragmentary editorial glosses? Do we really have a single narrative source which runs throughout the Pentateuch, or a collection of originally self-contained stories (e.g., the Patriarchal stories)? Can we be certain that "J" wrote during the Davidic-Solomonic empire, and even if we can, should we then base our interpretation of the *meaning* of say, his Abraham stories, on that historical context? It should at least give us pause that one can easily make much of the "call" of Abram (Gen. 12:1–3) by a "J" who wrote in the heady days of the tenth century *or* one who wrote to the distraught exiles in the sixth.[7]

Similar questions arise concerning historical events which may (or may not!) lie behind the biblical narratives. Given the nature of the literary materials in the book of Exodus, for example, how successfully can we penetrate to "what actually happened"? Even if such an analysis can yield reliable conclusions, how should we apply those conclusions to the meaning of the text as it now stands? Were we to conclude (as some scholars do) that the events of the escape from Egypt and the encounter with God at Mt. Sinai derive from originally independent traditions and were experienced by different groups of people, what would we then do with the text which connects these events in a narrative sequence?

Hans Frei, among others, has posed most sharply the problems which beset the traditional literary and historical approaches to the text. Frei complains that in literary approaches the biblical stories have been "identified with a reconstruction of the *process* by which they originated and of their cultural setting," and that in historical approaches "critical reconstruction of the reported events constituted the subject matter of narrative texts."[8] In both cases, "the *meaning* of the stories was finally something different from the stories or depictions themselves"—the meaning lay behind the text, not in the text.[9]

The current focus on the final form of biblical narrative, and especially of the Pentateuch, is shared by representatives of diverse methodological perspectives: "New" critics, structuralists, rhetorical critics, and canonical critics, as well as many for whom there is no particular label.[10] Using the terms of modern, secular literary criticism, these scholars frequently speak of their work as primarily "synchronic" rather than "diachronic"—i.e., emphasizing the text as a whole rather than its individual components.[11] If we think of the text as a body, these scholars want to admire its external anatomy rather than dissect it; if we think of the text as an ancient city, these scholars would rather trace the artistry of its surface structures than excavate it.[12] Similarly, there is an increasing tendency among such scholars to look at the text as a story rather than as history. Instead of looking for historical referents, we are encouraged to look for metaphorical language, literary themes, and overarching structures. Instead of looking *through* the text as a window to the historical world, we are invited to look *at* the text as the representation of its own world.[13]

The preceding paragraph is misleading if it suggests that we are confronted with an either/or situation: either read the text as a composite document reflecting actual historical events and authorial situations, *or* read it as a seamless narrative which renders a completely fictive world. While the emphasis in many recent studies (and in this one) is clearly on the latter, this does not mean that we can ignore the significance of the former. To do so would be both foolish and dishonest. The Pentateuch is both a composite document and a unified narrative. To read it as only one or the other would be to distort its character as a text. The depth dimension of the text is the result of a process of fervent reinterpretation of Israel's traditions in order to meet the theological needs of successive generations. If their voices are completely stifled, we fail to recognize the character of the text as *Scripture* as well as story. As Gunther Plaut says at the outset of a massive commentary on the Pentateuch, "what is important is to both understand its background and at the same time treat the book as an integral unit."[14]

Like many other recent studies of the Pentateuch and biblical narrative in general, this book stems from a revived interest in the nature of narrative itself and especially the paramount role which narrative plays in religious discourse. Although most of us have from childhood an intuitive grasp of what a "story" is, even a cursory survey of recent critical studies concerning the nature of narrative reveals a bewildering complex of interpretive problems.[15] Not only are the various forms of narrative often difficult to distinguish (epic, parable, saga, myth, legend, history, etc.), but the ways in which they render a meaning are also frequently intertwined.

As if unraveling the nature of narrative itself were not complex enough, the problems are compounded when we speak of "the Pentateuchal narrative" primarily because, as we have seen, the text is not the product of a single author but of numerous authors over a very long period of time. When we refer to "the Pentateuchal narrative" in the following chapters, therefore, we shall mean the text as we have it now before us but which we also recognize to be the product of a long history of traditions and editorial activity. While our emphasis will fall on the literary integrity of the present text, we shall also at times refer to the traditional "authors" (e.g., J and P) or at least consider those places where different literary sources appear to be joined together. Our major purpose, however, will be twofold: 1) to delineate the internal literary (i.e., redactional) cohesiveness of larger units (e.g., Gen. 1:1—11:9, or the "Jacob cycle," or Num. 1—10)[16] and 2) to delineate the narrative integrity of the Pentateuch as a whole, i.e., how the larger units constitute "books," and how the sequence of these books makes sense.

The integrity of the Pentateuchal narrative, however, derives not only from the form of "story" but also from literary types which are not inherently narrative, especially "law." Law is an essential element in the plot of the Pentateuch, and without that element the story would be incomplete. Indeed, even the discrimination between "story" and "law," however appropriate in terms of distinguishing literary forms, can suggest that narrative texts "only" recite, whereas legal texts "only" command. To deny an imperative force to "story," however, is to ignore the motivational nature of biblical narrative, that is, its "rhetoric of command."[17] Similarly, to limit the meaning of "law" to its imperative force and its content is to ignore that its meaning and authority are partly dependent on its narrative context. The word *torah* in its widest sense means "guidance, instruction, discipline," and only in its most narrow sense "law." *The* Torah is the definitive "guide-book" of ancient Israel, and it guides in the form of both narrative and law so that the two become inseparable and indispensable. We shall therefore devote considerable attention to Leviticus, Numbers, and Deuteronomy. These books are often neglected or even ignored as part of the Pentateuch due to a truncated concept of narrative which implicitly relegates law to an inferior status.[18]

In its present form, the Pentateuch represents a "story-shaped world," to borrow a phrase from Brian Wicker. One could perhaps argue that any story renders a world. Certainly we can talk about the "world" of Homer, or Dickens, or Faulkner (the latter even provided a map for his readers), but because of its nature as Scripture and because of its "rhetoric of command" the Pentateuch does not simply present a world to the reader; it also attempts to *force* its world *on* the reader. As *the* Torah, the Pentateuch enjoys the preeminent share of what Eric Auerbach has called the "tyrannical" character of biblical literature:

> The world of the Scripture stories is not satisfied with claiming to be a historically true reality—it insists that it is the only real world, [and] is destined for autocracy. . . . The Scripture stories do not, like Homer's, court our favor, they do not flatter us that they may please us and enchant us—they seek to subject us, and if we refuse to be subjected we are rebels.[19]

Our observation that the biblical authors are better understood as redactors may have led to the unfortunate conclusion that these nameless literati were not artists at all but merely pedantic editorial technicians who spliced texts together with little or no imagination. This is far from the case. Not only do the biblical authors display considerable artistry in the composition of individual stories, but even in the larger redactional process they display impressive literary and theological sensitivity. The scope of the present study will not allow us to do a close reading of every passage. It is important, therefore, that the reader have at the outset a grasp of the artistry of biblical narrative to aid his or her reading of the biblical text.[20]

In an introduction to an anthology of biblical literature, the novelist Reynolds Price described his youthful fascination with the biblical characters as portrayed in the pictures of Hurlbut's *Story of the Bible*. In those pictures he found himself confronted not with your average "Sunday-school confections" but with "credible ancient orientals, hairy and aromatic."[21] Because the biblical authors persistently refuse to moralize, their characters are adamantly earthy creatures. Far from being cardboard stereotypes of moral virtue—or vice—they are "credible" men and women of great and ultimately impenetrable complexity. As Alter has put it,

> We are compelled to get at [their] character and motive . . . through a process of inference from fragmentary data, often with crucial pieces of narrative exposition strategically withheld, and this leads to multiple or sometimes even

wavering perspectives on the characters. There is, in other words, an abiding
mystery in character as the biblical writers conceive it, which they embody
in their typical methods of presentation.[22]

Whereas in our re-telling of the biblical stories (especially for children)
we tend to convert the characters into types of "good" and "bad," the
text itself refuses to make such neat distinctions. Even the Pharaoh of
Exodus, who comes as close as one can to being an outright villain in the
Pentateuch, remains in the end a character of intricate and inscrutable
motivations. In short, it is precisely the mystery of biblical characters
which makes them so realistic.

This "abiding mystery" of human characterization is a result not
simply of a sophisticated literary aesthetic, or even a probing anthropol-
ogy, but also of the "monotheistic revolution" in ancient Israelite thought.[23]
Even when God is not directly involved in a particular story, the way in
which the story represents reality is profoundly theological. The reticence
of the biblical authors which produces a pervasive ambiguity in their
human characters extends even to the divine. This ambiguity in turn
results from the authors' perception that the world of human experience
is a mixture of what Flannery O'Connor called "mystery and manners,"
by which she meant the way in which the divine will works in and through
the most ordinary (indeed, for her, "grotesque") human motivations and
aspirations.[24] The world of the Pentateuchal narrative is a world of constant tension between the divine will and human will: the biblical characters are free to act on their own, yet they are subject to the sovereign
designs of God.[25] As Auerbach has put it: "The sublime influence of God
here reaches so deeply into the everyday that the two realms of the sublime
and the everyday [O'Connor's mystery and manners] are not only actually
unseparated but basically inseparable."[26] The biblical characters "are
bearers of the divine will, and yet they are fallible, subject to misfortune
and humiliation—and in the midst of misfortune and in their humiliation
their acts and words reveal the transcendent majesty of God."[27]

I
GENESIS—
The Book of Generations

THE PRIMEVAL CYCLE (1:1—11:26)

Introduction

Genesis 1—11 is composed of individual stories which, at least in their original form, must be understood critically as myths.[1] These stories do not have historical persons or events as referents, but describe the origin of aspects of the world which are timeless, e.g., the pain of work and childbirth, the hostility between shepherds and farmers, the rise of cities, and the multiplicity of languages. Moreover, for a long time scholars have recognized that many of these stories are not unique, but are related to earlier traditions recorded in ancient Near Eastern literature: in the story of Adapa one man's offense brings ill to humankind, as does Adam's; a story about the conflict between a shepherd and a farmer resembles the story of Cain and Abel; and traditions concerning antediluvian figures resemble the generations leading up to Noah (Gen. 5). In the story of Atra-Hasis, a tremendous flood covers the earth, though one man is saved through the help of one of the gods—a story obviously very similar to the flood story in Genesis. There are also connections between the account of creation in Genesis 1 and the Mesopotamian story of creation called *Enuma elish* ("When on high").[2]

Despite the similarities to these ancient Mesopotamian texts, we can show that the biblical versions of these stories are radically different, not only individually, but also and especially when each story is read in the context of the *series* which runs to the end of Genesis 11, on into the rest of Genesis, and beyond. A collection of such stories within one text of such magnitude is unknown elsewhere in the ancient Near East.[3] Thus the story at the opening of chapter 6 about the sexual union between the "sons of God" and human women has a blatant mythological background, but its original purpose (to explain the existence of giants on the earth) has been dramatically changed to fit the new purpose of introducing the flood story. The context of the story gives it a moral and theological significance far greater than what the story itself could bear.[4]

The linking of originally independent stories into a progressive series means that a fundamental change has taken place. Each story is not simply an incident that "occurred" in primordial timelessness, and the meaning of each story is no longer limited to a description of "the way we are." The meaning of the individual stories is now significantly augmented in that they have become the prologue to the rest of the Pentateuch. Although we still cannot say that these myths have been converted into history, we can say that they have been transformed into a kind of "history-like" narrative. In other words, they are no longer self-contained "short stories"; they are now the opening chapters of an "historical novel" and as such they provide the dominant themes which will guide our reading of that "novel."

There are two ways in which the individual stories are tied together. First, they share a number of themes and motifs, the repetition and transformation of which constitute a major dimension of the plot of the extended narrative. As we shall soon see, the most important and overarching themes are introduced in Genesis 1.

Second, the individual stories are connected by the familial sequence imposed on them, that is, by a genealogical structure.[5] Thus from Adam and Eve we move to their sons, Cain and Abel, after which the extensive genealogy in chapter 5 brings us down to Noah, the chief character in the flood narrative. Subsequent genealogies bring us to Abraham and thus connect Genesis 1—11 with chapters 12—50. Without some such connection between the characters there would be no continuing narrative at all, only a juxtaposition of self-contained stories, each with its own internal plot, a plot which had no bearing on the story which followed. We can, of course, imagine such a collection of isolated stories (contemporary collections of short stories offer a rough analogy), and can even imagine how such a collection could have thematic unity, providing a picture of the "primeval world," a world which contained alienation, murder, violence, and ethnic diversity. But such a world would have no story; it would simply be the sum of incidents only accidentally related to each other, and perhaps not related at all.

The genealogical structure of the Pentateuchal narrative, on the other hand, portrays a "story-shaped world,"[6] a world shaped by the causal relationships between characters who represent successive generations of a single family line. Consequences resulting from the actions of both divine and human characters determine the development of a plot extending beyond the limits of each individual story. Thus the story of Cain and Abel is not simply an illustration of the animosity between shepherds and farmers, or even of religious hatred; it is also an illustration of how the alienation between God and humankind, and within the human community—introduced by Cain's parents—has spread to the second generation.

The genealogical connections between the characters not only provide the foundation on which the Pentateuchal narrative is constructed, but also mark the points of major transitions in the narrative. Thus chapter 5, which lists the generations from Adam to Noah, marks the transition from the antediluvian world to the flood story; chapter 10 marks the transition from the flood story to the international political picture portrayed by the tower of Babel story (11:1–9); and 11:10–26 follows one line of the family of Noah down to Abraham, marking the transition to the "patriarchal" stories. Moreover, a member of the Priestly school adapted a genealogical formula ("these are the generations of X") and used it to mark divisions throughout the narrative, not only for Genesis 1—11, but also for chapters 12—50 (2:4; 5:1; 6:9; 10:1; 11:10, 27; 25:12, 19; 36:1, 9; 37:2).[7]

Careful examination of the function of this formula in each context reveals two purposes. When the formula is followed primarily by genealogical material, it serves to conclude a preceding narrative segment (5:1; 10:1; 11:10; 25:12; 36:1, 9), whereas when it is followed primarily by narrative material it serves as an introduction to that story (2:4; 6:9; 11:27; 25:19; 37:2). In fact, in several of the latter cases the word "generations" is best translated as "story" (2:4; 25:19; 37:2). Although the formula is not employed with exacting consistency, it seems that the Pentateuchal narrative of Genesis is divided into at least five, and perhaps six parts: a prologue (1:1—2:3), the "story of heaven and earth" (2:4—11:26, perhaps with the "story of Noah" as a separate part beginning at 6:9), the line of Terah (11:27—25:18), the line of Isaac (25:19—36:43), and the line of Jacob (37:1—end).[8] Thus I have provided Genesis as a whole the descriptive title "The Book of Generations," taken from 5:1.

It should be clear by now that the traditional separation of Genesis 1—11 from chapters 12—50 is at best imprecise, for the redactors signal a transition not at 12:1 (the "call" of Abraham) but at 11:27.[9] Moreover, at neither point do the redactors indicate a major break in the narrative that warrants a division of Genesis into two independent units. The redactors have marked off 11:27—25:18 (the story of Abraham and Sarah) only as "Part 3 (or 4)"; they have not marked off chapters 12—50 as "Part Two."[10] This observation has theological implications. However important the call of Abraham may be (12:1–3), it does not represent a radical disjunction within the Pentateuchal narrative. Yahweh has spoken before to humankind and will speak again. Human beings have responded to Yahweh before—sometimes with integrity, usually not—and this too will happen again. In short, the call to Abraham is simply one more step in Yahweh's attempt to come to terms with the world which he has created. The biblical redactors did not choose to present us with two separate collections of stories, one in which the problem is raised, and another in which the problem is answered. In truly realistic narrative things can never be that neat and tidy. If we approach the text from such a simplistic perspective, we shall fail to appreciate the rich complexity of the Pentateuchal narrative, in which the problems of human existence before God and the possibilities for some solutions to those problems are always fraught with ambiguity and uncertainty. With perplexing frequency, a new step in the right direction will be followed by two steps in retreat; Abraham was not the first, and certainly not the last, to be a master at both the one-step and the two-step routines.

As we turn to a contextual analysis of the Primeval Cycle, a schematic outline of the material will help to focus our discussion:

1:1—2:3	2:4—4:26	5	6:1—9:19[11]
Creation	Family failure	Descendants of Adam	World failure Chaos New beginning Covenant
	9:20–27	10	11:1–9
	Family failure	Descendants of Noah	World failure
			11:10–26 Descendants of Shem

1. "In the beginning" (1:1—2:4a)

The world and the Torah begin with a command. The first words reported of God are an executive order, hurled into the unfathomable darkness of space: "And God said, 'Let there be light.' " The world and the Torah also begin with a response to the command totally in conformance to God's will: "and there was light." The terseness of the initial command/execution sequence (only four words in the Hebrew)—"be light, light was"—is without parallel in the following verses, but the message is the same throughout. "God said . . . and it was so." The Priestly author here introduces us to his view of God and the world, and the *way* the world ought to be. Everything fits and works the way it ought to because everything follows what God says. All of this the text says, again with dignified brevity, in verse 31: "And God saw everything that he had made, and behold, it was very good."[12]

The orderliness and harmony of the world are evident not only in the process by which creation takes place, but also in its structural design. The parallelism of the days of creation provides the literary structure of Genesis 1. Thus the origin of light on the first day parallels the appearance of the heavenly lights on the fourth; the separation of the cosmic waters on the second day (forming sea and sky) parallels the creation of sea and air creatures on the fifth; and the formation of earth and vegetation on the third day mirrors the origin of animals and humanity on the sixth. Finally, the Sabbath day (not explicitly mentioned by name) constitutes the capstone of the created order. Readers who search for a connection between the sequence of creative acts reported here and a scientific description of the origin of the universe will search in vain. The author is interested in the artistry of the created order, not in paleontology. The orderly structure of *his* work reflects the orderly design of the cosmos: every part of the world appears before us in perfect balance and symmetry, majestic and wondrous.

"Order" is thus the main theme of the Priestly author's account of creation. This emphasis on harmony with the will and commands of God extends far beyond Genesis 1, forming a nucleus of themes and motifs which continue throughout the Pentateuchal narrative and into the rest of the Hebrew Bible. From beginning to end, the Pentateuch will be preoccupied with a world in which order derives from responsibility to the divine will, and disorder from irresponsibility. Our observations about Genesis 1, therefore, not only delineate local literary features, but also a fundamental theological presumption that governs the rest of the Torah. As Robert Alter writes,

> All this reflects, of course, not only simply a bundle of stylistic predilections but a particular vision of God, man, and the world. Coherence is the keynote of creation . . . . Law, manifested in the symmetrical dividings that are the process of creation and in the divine speech that initiates each stage of creation, is the underlying characteristic of the world as God makes it.[13]

Alongside the harmony resulting from responsibility to the divine will, Genesis 1 announces a second theme that will preoccupy the Pentateuchal narrative—the role of human beings in relation to the earth they inhabit. The distinction of humankind is expressed by the divine soliloquy in Genesis 1:26: "Then God said, 'Let us make humankind in our image, after our likeness; and let them have dominion over the fish of the sea, and over the birds of the air, and over the cattle, and over all the earth, and over every creeping thing that creeps upon the earth.' " Unlike any other part of creation, human beings reflect something of the divine nature, namely, God's sovereignty. Humanity is, as it were, the vice-regent of

God on earth, the little lord of the universe. Of course, this in no way questions the ultimate sovereignty of God. The very fact that human beings are "creatures"—i.e., created by God—enforces their utter dependence. Nevertheless, next to God (and perhaps the angels) humankind enjoys the status of the highest link in what Medieval philosophy called the "chain of being." Humankind's power and control over the earth is unquestioned and—it would seem—unbreakable.

Like the theme of order and responsibility, the theme of humankind's relationship to the earth is not limited to Genesis 1. The cosmic perspective of this chapter will pervade the Primeval Cycle, where the interest is in the whole planet, just as the anthropological focus is on human beings in general. Yet, by the time we reach the end of the Cycle, we will have seen a steady narrowing of the focus, so that "earth" (Hebrew *erets*) points more and more to particular *lands*, just as the characters will increasingly represent not Everyman and Everywoman (as Adam and Eve), but particular nations and ethnic groups. Beginning with Genesis 12, the primary interest will be the "promised land," the land of Canaan. This land will be the sacred space standing at the heart of the Torah. Nevertheless, it would be a grave mistake to conclude that what happens on the "earth" of the Primeval Cycle is only background for what will happen in the "land" of Canaan, for the Pentateuchal narrative makes the radical claim that what will take place in the land *over* the Jordan will be of crucial significance for all of the lands *beyond* the Jordan.[14]

Finally, Genesis 1 introduces a third theme and associated motifs which will continue throughout the Pentateuchal narrative. Following the report of the creation of humankind in verses 26–27, God pronounces a blessing that, in part, repeats the declaration of humankind's dominion over all other creatures. In addition, God pronounces the following words: "Be fertile and increase, and fill the earth and subdue it" (cf. vs. 22). For the ancient world, the basic meaning of blessing had to do with fertility—fertility of crops and herds, as well as human fertility. In the middle of winter an ancient Israelite could not go to the local supermarket and buy canned tomatoes, not to mention fresh tomatoes. The failure of a fall crop could mean starvation. Infertility therefore could be virtually synonymous with death, and was consequently associated with the antonym of blessing, "curse." By extension, blessing also connotes material security, health, and peace: adequate shelter and food, the absence of disease, freedom from violence and war. The meaning of blessing is irreducibly concrete, even materialistic, stubbornly refusing to be converted into a purely "spiritual"category. For this reason the Pentateuchal narrative will often point with ingenuous delight to the great possessions of its characters—numerous children, large herds of sheep and cattle, ample gold and silver—for these *things* are seen not so much as the rewards of hard work as the gifts of a beneficent (if also inscrutable) God. Blessing is a mark of divine grace.[15]

Genesis 1:28 informs us that blessing does not *exclude* human work; indeed it clearly requires some human effort. The pronouncement of blessing is phrased in the imperative mood: be fertile, increase, fill, subdue, rule. Here is one of the most peculiar and interesting features of the blessing. On the one hand, by blessing humankind God empowers them to fulfil the content of the pronouncement of blessing. On the other hand, the pronouncement of blessing itself is couched as a command, implying that human beings are to a significant degree responsible for effecting the blessing. The divine blessing, in other words, is a kind of "charge," in both senses of the word. In the first sense, the blessing "charges" the recipient with a special kind of energy or force; in the second sense, the blessing "charges" the recipient with a task and a responsibility. Both senses must be kept in mind, for to exclude one or the other would be to distort the meaning of blessing. To exclude the first sense would be to make blessing a merely human achievement; to exclude the second sense would be to make blessing a magic power, a type of *mana*.

Given the two senses of blessing as "charge," the theme of blessing clearly overlaps with the themes of order and responsibility we have discussed above. Blessing is rooted in the creative power of God and, at the same time, is expressed as a command. This overlap is only one among many, as we shall see throughout our analysis of the Pentateuch. The various themes and motifs that we shall trace are not rigid categories, easily separated from each other, much less independent of each other. It is precisely the inextricable intertwining of these themes which makes the Pentateuchal narrative so fascinating.

The Pentateuch is one people's understanding of its corporate identity, wrought from the struggle to comprehend its relationship to the rest of the world, to grasp the meaning of divine blessing and curse, and to come to terms with the agony of human failure. The themes announced or at least intimated "in the beginning"—divine command and human responsibility, people and land, blessing and curse—continue to the end, where Israel stands "beyond the Jordan," listening to the last words of Moses, which are also the words of God: "If you obey the commandments of Yahweh your God . . . then you shall live and increase, and Yahweh your God will bless you in the land which you are entering to take possession of it" (Deut. 30:16).[16]

2. East of Eden (2:4b—3:24)

With the Priestly author's majestic exordium behind us, we can turn to the Yahwistic narrative of creation in Genesis 2:4b—3:24. Julius Wellhausen once drew a graphic distinction between the literary style in Genesis 1 and Genesis 2—3. When we move from the one to the other, he said, we cannot help but notice "the fresh early smell of earth [that] meets us on the breeze."[17] By this he meant that the second account of creation is a much more "earthy" story than that of the Priestly author in Genesis 1. Wellhausen's observation was perceptive, because "earthiness" plays a central role in Genesis 2—3. Whereas chapter 1 is interested in the earth (*erets*) as "planet," as well as the sea and sky, chapters 2—3 focus only on earth (*adamah*) as "ground" or "soil." In fact, the relationship between humanity and the "ground" dominates 2:4b—4:16, and the term *erets* does not reappear until near the end of this unit. In 2:7 the author moves immediately to the creation of "the man," Hebrew *ha-adam*.[18] Unlike the majestic sovereign of Genesis 1, here the Lord God (Yahweh Elohim) is pictured as a potter who *forms* the man out of the ground and blows into him the breath of life. The intimate relationship between the man and the ground is even more obvious in the Hebrew, for the author uses the word *adamah* as a counterpart to *adam*, humankind (compare Latin *humus* and *humanus*, or English "earth" and "earthling").

After the man and the woman have tasted of the tree of knowledge, the relationship between the man and the ground is radically distorted. We learn of this in 3:17–19:

> And to Adam he [Yahweh Elohim] said,
> "Because you have listened to the voice of your wife,
>   and have eaten of the tree
> of which I commanded you,
>   'You shall not eat of it,'
> cursed is the ground (*adamah*) because of you;
>   in pain you shall eat of it all the days of your life;
> thorns and thistles it shall bring forth to you;
>   and you shall eat the plants of the field.
> In the sweat of your face
>   you shall eat bread
> Until you return to the ground (*adamah*),
>   for out of it you were taken;
> you are dust,
>   and to dust you shall return."

In other words, the man is alienated from the ground, and his agricultural work—which had been his natural task (2:15)—will now be painful and unproductive.

Despite the many ambiguities in this story, one thing at least is clear: alienation sets in when the man and woman break the commandment of God (vss. 1–7). As in chapter 1, the first words spoken by God to humankind are a command, in this case a prohibition: "of the tree of the knowledge of good and evil you shall not eat" (2:16–17). Among the various motivations for breaking the command (see vs. 6), the determinative one appears to be the possibility of becoming like God.[19] But—the reader may quickly object—according to Genesis 1 humankind already *is* like God, created in God's image and likeness (vs. 26). Why is this likeness affirmed in chapter 1 and then repudiated in chapters 2—3 (cf. esp. 3:22–24)?

The relationship between God and humankind is properly that between one who commands and one who obeys. The maintenance of this relationship—and of all its benefits symbolized by life in the garden—requires that human beings not step beyond the limits imposed on them by the command. Yet the man and woman are clearly free to do precisely that. They are not puppets manipulated by a divine puppeteer. To be human is to be capable of rebellion against God, yet to submit to the divine will. But the woman and the man, prompted by the serpent, do not want to be human in these terms; they want to be superhuman, to be like God. Thus the alienation we have already observed between the man and the ground reflects his willful repudiation of his natural being as a "creature" in an attempt to become like the creator. We shall see this attempt on the part of human beings to become like God again as we move through the Primeval cycle. Reaching a crescendo in the story of the Tower of Babel (11:1–9), the attempt to step beyond the limits of human nature provides a framework for "the story of heaven and earth" (2:4), and how the original goodness of the created order disintegrated into chaos.

We have penetrated into only three chapters of the Primeval cycle, yet already an enormous shift has taken place. Despite the fact that Genesis 1 and 2—3 derive from different authors, in their present juxtaposition these chapters are united by a common concern for the central themes we have delineated. The Pentateuchal narrative is certainly not J *or* P, nor is it even J *and* P, for the combination of these two units has created a "new narrative" that includes but also transcends both units.[20]

In chapter 1 the pattern of command/execution portrayed the perfect order of creation according to the divine will; in chapters 2—3 the irresponsibility of the serpent, woman, and man to the divine command propels the world into disorder and alienation. The dominion which humanity has been given over the earth and all its creatures is threatened and qualified. Humankind (and especially the man) is alienated from the ground, the source of sustenance, and the man's attempt to "subdue" it will be frustrated. Moreover, a permanent enmity has now arisen between one of the creatures (the accursed serpent) and humankind as a result of the woman's implicit denial of her role as co-vice-regent. Finally, the blessing that was placed on humanity seems to withdraw into the darkness of the curse that falls on the ground because of the man, and the fertility accompanying the blessing is thrown into ambiguity by the rupture of the male-female relationship, resulting in the woman's increased pain in child-birth and her subservience to the man. In short, responsibility is replaced by infidelity; community (with God, in nature, within the family) is shattered; blessing seems overwhelmed by curse.

The position of humankind within the world is now fraught with uncertainty and anxiety. With the expulsion of the man and woman from the garden (3:23–24), that alienation is complete, and the Pentateuchal narrative is thrown into suspense. Human beings are permanent exiles from the pristine space and time of Eden. There is no way back and the way ahead is uncertain. The plot of the Pentateuchal narrative, to its very end, will be concerned with the attempt to find *another* way human beings can live with integrity before God, at home on the earth, and within the security of divine blessing. For much of Western culture, at least, this adventure sets in motion what will become the quintessential quest story.

3. Two Murderers (chap. 4)

The story of Cain and Abel in verses 1–16 is permeated with references to the ground. Cain is the first-born of Adam and Eve, and, like his father, is a tiller of the ground. When Cain's offering from the ground is not accepted, he murders his herdsman brother Abel while in the fields (Cain's "home turf"). Yahweh learns of the murder because the ground has soaked up Abel's blood, and his voice cries from the ground. Alongside the theme of ground the author introduces the theme of the curse. Cain is cursed *from* the ground. This is a dramatic shift from chapter 3, where the *ground* was cursed because of the man. Any attempt to till the ground at all will fail—it will not simply yield thorns and thistles as with Adam. Adam and Eve were "banished" from Eden, and from intimate communion with God; Cain is "banished" from the ground and hidden from God's presence (vs. 14). Cain is forced to become a vagabond, a wanderer on the earth (now the word *erets*).

The reason for Cain's punishment is obvious; he is the first fratricide. What is not so obvious is why God acknowledges Abel's sacrifice and not Cain's. It is unlikely that Abel's was more worthy; indeed, both are probably "first-fruits" sacrifices intended to secure divine blessing on crops and herds.[21] God does not explain why the younger brother will, in effect, be blessed, and the elder not (introducing an element of the blessing theme which we shall see many times in Genesis). The divine will is inscrutable, but nonetheless clear. Cain's task is to submit to the divine will rather than to the power of sin (vs. 7). Emphasizing Cain's freedom and capacity to master sin ("you must rule over it"), the text affirms his responsibility as a human being. Yet Cain refuses to be human. The murder of his brother represents not only a failure to heed God's instruction, but also an attempt to wrest the control of blessing from God. In this sense, Cain's sin suggests a continuation of his parents' desire "to become like God."

Thus the story of Cain and Abel presents an augmentation of the estrangement and disorder which began in chapter 3. The separation between man and ground now goes so far that Cain is exiled from the ground entirely; the irresponsibility that was evident in chapter 3 is now explicitly labeled as submission to sin with its resulting guilt (vss. 7, 13). Finally, the curse that in chapter 3 afflicted only the serpent and indirectly the ground now afflicts Cain. The theological alienation that began in chapter 3 and infected the relationship between husband and wife is now compounded by the radical alienation between brothers. Moreover, since Cain and Abel are not only brothers, but also representatives of traditionally conflicting occupations (farmer and herdsman), alienation has spread not only within the family—the basic form of human community—but also within the socio-economic realm. Yet, ironically, Cain is the originator of urban culture (4:17).

It is significant that the curse on Cain did not follow as a result of God's rejection of his sacrifice. Instead, the curse was a result of Cain's negative response to the blessing of another. This situation foreshadows what will become a major issue in the rest of the Pentateuchal narrative beginning with Genesis 12: the attitude of those who stand initially outside the blessing will determine, in part, whether they themselves will eventually participate in that blessing or not. Moreover, explicit references to divine blessing are far more frequent than references to cursing, and in the latter the authors appear to avoid active formulations with Yahweh as subject. For example, Yahweh blesses Adam and Eve directly (1:28), but seems more to state the result of Cain's own behavior when announcing his curse (4:11; cf. 3:14, 17). It is as if Yahweh is always willing to bless, but some people bring on themselves a curse.

Although Cain is exiled and must leave God's presence, God spares his life and does not leave him helpless. Since Cain now has no kinfolk to protect him, God provides him with a protective mark, accompanied by a law: "If anyone murders Cain, it will be avenged sevenfold" (vs. 15).[22] The commandment regarding vengeance plays a key role in the brief and rather enigmatic passage which follows (4:17–24). In its present context this passage traces the family line of Cain through six generations,[23] and describes the growth of civilization—the first city, cattle herdsmen, musicians, and smiths. But the focus of this unit falls on Lamech and the link drawn with his great-grandfather several times removed, by means of the reference to Cain being avenged sevenfold (vs. 24). Lamech's poetic recitation reveals a bombastic bully, rippling his muscles before his wives and bragging about the youth he has killed simply for striking him. For all his heroic posturing, however, what Lamech really represents is an increase in unrestrained violence and an extension of revenge "seventy-seven fold." Lamech supplants God's law with his own, and thus stands in the line of his ancestors who also wanted to be "like God," providing a kind of climax to the literary unit 2:4—4:26. The movement in the narrative is described succinctly by von Rad: "First the Fall, then fratricide, and now the execution of vengeance (which God has reserved for himself!) is claimed by man."[24]

4. "The book of generations" (chap. 5)

Whatever function the genealogy in chapter 5 may have served originally,[25] its juxtaposition with the preceding material is itself dramatic. The lineage of humankind which ran from Adam through Cain and down to Lamech saw a number of cultural advancements, but ended with a figure of reckless irresponsibility and homicidal violence. In contrast, the Sethite line of Adam represents a new beginning, already anticipated by J in 4:25–26.[26] The effect of 5:1–5 in light of the preceding chapters is to reiterate the positive themes announced in chapter 1: the creation of humankind in the image of God and the blessing placed on man and woman. In addition, the corollary motif of fertility is dramatically affirmed by the ensuing list of generations—the man and woman indeed have been fertile and increased! The redactional position of this chapter thus serves an intriguing theological function in the ongoing narrative. Despite the radical disorder which has grown since chapter 2, the author reminds us of the unique position of humankind within the world, thereby injecting a note of hope. The author implies that, despite human failure, humankind's original status "in the image of God" is transmitted to successive generations, for Adam's son is born "in his own likeness, after his image." A similar note of hope also sounds near the close of the chapter when the Yahwist looks ahead to the one who will be the agent of a new beginning after the ravages of the flood (vs. 29; cf. 3:17). Since the Sethite line begins with Enosh ("humankind") and ends with the only family to survive the flood, chapter 5 moves in effect from one "new Adam" to another. Such a transition is highly appropriate since the flood story (6:1—9:19) marks the central turning point of the Primeval cycle.

5. The Flood (6:1—9:19)

The flood story is almost certainly a combination of the two sources J and P, each having a different literary and theological agenda. The

Yahwistic version focuses on the motifs of the human heart and the cursed ground, whereas the Priestly stratum focuses on the role of blessing in the context of a movement from creation to chaos to re-creation. Their fusion has resulted in a narrative of increased depth and richness.

Preceding the flood story we have the tale in which the sons of God had sexual intercourse with human women. Retrospectively, this tale now represents the most serious—indeed, metaphysical—possibility of human beings becoming "like God." Instead, God decrees a further limitation on human longevity (cf. 3:22). In addition, by juxtaposing this tale with the beginning of the flood story, the redactor has directed its etiological function away from the origin of giants (the Nephilim) toward the motivation for the coming divine judgment.

The prologue to the flood story (6:5–8) is linked to the preceding tale by catchwords eliciting familiar themes. Humanity has indeed "begun to increase (*rabab*) on the face of the ground" (vs. 1), yet this is accompanied by divine-human procreation and a corresponding increase (*rabab*) of human wickedness on the earth (vs. 5). Thus Yahweh declares that he will wipe humanity *off* the face of the ground (vs. 7). In describing Yahweh's decision, the author suggests that the evil of the human heart has inflicted pain in the heart of God, thereby drawing a connection to the Eden story (the verb at the end of verse 6 [translated "grieved"by RSV] is derived from the same root as the word for "pain" in 3:16 and 17). Such an authorial observation of the inner thoughts and feelings of God is as bold as it is poignant. Only rarely do biblical writers allow themselves such freedom.[27] Here the depiction renders a character whose pathos matches his indignation—indeed, a God who is vulnerable to human unrighteousness, who can be hurt by human sin. Consequently, we cannot construe the flood as the heartless and brutal act of an uncaring deity. Here there is a tragic element even in the inner life of God, for in order to restore his creation to its original goodness he must all but destroy it.[28]

The motif of "pain" in God's heart makes the flood story intensely personal. The next passage (vss. 9–22) adds a formal, diplomatic dimension by introducing the word "covenant." While the previous passage ends with Yahweh "taking a personal liking" to Noah (vs. 8), in this passage Yahweh promises to establish his covenant with Noah (vs. 18). A covenant—or better, "treaty"—is a formal agreement or contract between two parties. The resolution of the flood story will entail both a movement within the heart of God and the completion of a diplomatic process initiated by Yahweh's pledge. In fact, by the artful arrangement of the J and P sources, the redactor probably intends us to see *one* movement taking place, rather than two separate occurrences. The granting of a unilateral peace treaty by God is rooted in the divine heartache over creation.

The anticipations of divine mercy in 6:5–22 do not lessen the severity of the judgment that follows. The waters that God had separated from the earth in creation, God now unleashes, drowning all land animals and returning the entire earth to watery chaos (cf. 6:17; 1:7). Solitary and silent, the ark floats on the surface of the dark deep, bearing the remnants of all animal life (7:18; cf. 1:2).

The turning point in the story comes when God "remembers" Noah and all the animals with him in the ark (8:1). The movement from creation to chaos is now reversed, and a re-creation takes place: the drying up of the waters, the landing of the ark, and ultimately the restoration of peace among God, humankind, and the world. God's remembering is the manifestation of his character as one who is faithful to his word, in this case, the pledge of a covenant previously made to Noah.

Cleansed by the flood, the earth now appears pristine, as it did "in the beginning," and Noah emerges from the ark as a new Adam. Just as the flood story has revealed new depths to the character of Yahweh, so it renders an equally complex character in Noah. On the one hand God seems to befriend Noah completely out of grace, unrelated to any merit (6:8); on the other, Noah is described as a "righteous man" (*tsaddiq*), the only one in his violent generation who lives with "integrity" (6:9). At this point in the story, the differences could be explained by recourse to J and P, but the story as a whole is more subtle.

To say that Noah is righteous is to say that he lives responsibly, in accordance with the divine will, and it is worth remembering that he is the first character we have met in the Primeval cycle of whom this is said. Noah is the first character who *has* character.[29] His righteousness is rendered by the *way* the story is told. Since Hebrew narrative usually prefers dialogue to develop character and plot, it is striking that Noah never utters a word throughout the entire story. The narration consists only in the speech of God and the words of the narrator. Of Noah, we are only told that he "did all that God commanded him" (6:22; 7:5, 9, 16). In a wider context, Noah is the only character so far in the Primeval cycle who remains completely speechless, and it is not coincidental that he is the only character so far who *listens* to what God says.

If God's selection of Noah is initially prevenient, it is also true that Noah rises to the occasion. His first act upon leaving the ark is to offer a sacrifice as an act of reverent gratitude. At the same time, as an expiatory sacrifice it represents the first and only expressed desire within the Primeval cycle for reconciliation with God.[30] In fact, Noah's gesture is the immediate motivation for resolution within the heart of God, for it is in response to the sacrifice that God resolves "in his heart, 'I will never again curse the ground because of humankind' " (8:21; cf. 6:5–6). The coincidence of human righteousness and divine grace has diminished the alienation which began in Eden—but only in part, for, as God adds, "the devices of the human heart are evil from childhood on."

In a sense, the flood has been a failure in that it has not eradicated the "evil inclination" which was its cause (cf. 6:5). The epilogue (9:1– 17) reflects a similar resignation. The opening section is framed by the repetition of the blessing at creation—"be fertile and increase" (vss. 1 and 7). Here, for the first time, the blessing includes specific laws governing humanity's dominion over the animals and the relationship between people (the prohibition of homicide). Law necessarily accompanies blessing in the "new creation" because of the human tendency toward evil.[31] Corresponding to law as the concrete form for human responsibility under the blessing, Yahweh now fulfils his pledge of a peace treaty with Noah and all living creatures. It is a unilateral, "everlasting treaty" (vs. 16), advertised, as it were, in the "sign" of the rainbow. At the end of the rain, God hangs his weapon in the sky to show that it will never again be used for cosmic destruction.

The plot of the Pentateuch will be marked by a succession of covenants between God and human beings—first with Noah and all creatures, then with Abraham and Sarah (chaps. 15 and 17), and finally with Israel (Exod. 19—24), demonstrating again that the story of Israel is part of a larger "world-story" which involves God and humankind.

The world now stands at the threshold of a new beginning, yet the text has recognized an aspect of the human will which is resistant to a life of integrity before God. The realism of that pessimistic note will soon be confirmed. Rather than a fresh start on the new way of blessing that God has opened, we see a reversion to the old way that leads to a curse. In fact the rest of the Primeval cycle suggests a cyclical repetition of what happened in between creation and the renewal of blessing. We can see this correspondence most clearly in an outline:

Family Failure	Genealogy	World Failure	New Beginning
chaps. 2— 4	chap. 5	6:6–13	9:1–17
9:20–27 (Noah)	chap. 10	11:1–9 (Babel)	

6. From Noah to Babel (9:20—11:9)

Despite numerous problems of interpretation raised by 9:20–27,[32] the contextual significance of this story about "Noah the vineyard owner" is fairly clear. Because of a scandalous incident of sexual impropriety, Noah places a curse on one of his grandsons, while two of the other characters, in effect, receive a blessing. While Noah commits no grave offense, his drunkenness hardly befits his role as the potential new Adam.

When we add this story to those in chapters 3 and 4:1–16 we thus have a complete disruption of the family (again, the basic structure of human community): between husband and wife, between siblings, and now between parents and children (and, for that matter, grandchildren).[33]

At the same time, however, this story introduces a change in characterization. From here on individual characters in Genesis often will represent political entities as well as family members (e.g., Canaan and the Canaanites), and the themes we shall be tracing will rarely, if ever, occur without some political connotation. Already in our present story about Canaan it is at least implied that the political subjection of a particular people within its own land is a result of a curse pronounced on its founding father as a punishment for moral turpitude.

The political configurations introduced by the story of the curse on Canaan are also reflected in the "Table of Nations" in chapter 10. This material, of course, picks up where the genealogy of chapter 5 left off, now tracing Noah's offspring to the line of Shem, which will later produce Abraham. Although many of these names remain obscure, it is clear that they represent geopolitical entities: Egypt, Canaan, Assyria, Aram, etc. By giving us these names, and by specifying geographical borders (e.g., vss. 5a, 10–11, 19, 30), the text presents us with a verbal map of the ancient world, categorized by the repeated refrain "These are the children of X by their clans, their languages, their lands, and their nations" (vs. 31; cf. 5b, 20). As the summary notice in verse 32 puts it, this is the way "the nations spread abroad on the earth after the flood." In the context of the Pentateuchal narrative, therefore, the Table of Nations represents a fulfilment of the renewed blessing on humankind—they have been fertile, increased, and filled the earth. However, chapter 10 must be seen not only as a fulfilment of what precedes, but also as an anticipation of what follows—the story of the tower of Babel. Chapter 10 tells us *that* human beings spread over the earth; 11:1–9 tells us why.

The story of the tower of Babel will make little sense unless we first understand what is wrong about the actions of the builders. On the surface there would seem to be nothing wrong in building a city or a skyscraper. Surely such a massive project would grow out of and continue to nourish a desirable sense of community. Yahweh's frustration of the building project thus appears whimsical and even childish, a result of divine jealousy and resentment at what human beings are capable of doing on their own.[34]

It is not surprising, therefore, that differing interpretations abound.[35] Nevertheless, there are several factors suggesting that the fault lies in an attempt to become independent of God. The context of the story leads us to expect such an attempt, for most of the other protagonists in some way or other have attempted to achieve superhuman status (Adam and Eve, Cain, Lamech, and the divine-human marriage partners). What they all have in common is the desire for *autonomy*—literally rule by "self-law"—which is, in effect, a desire to be like God. In the Babel story, this desire for self-government occurs for the first time on a corporate, political level, for the subject of this story is not an individual or even a family, but a city-state.

What the builders of the skyscraper want, and why they want it, is described most clearly in verse 4. They want a city and a tower "with its top (literally "head") in the heavens." They want to construct, on their own initiative and authorization, "a physical link between the divine and human realms."[36] The city-state will have a transcendent dimension, but only as a facade. Thus the tower represents an attempt to escape the limitations of the human condition. At the same time, by constructing the skyscraper the people express a need to "make a name for ourselves." In other words, the tower signifies a sense of communal identity founded exclusively on human will and effort.

The clearest expression of the *purpose* of the tower occurs at the end of verse 4: "lest we be scattered abroad upon the face of the whole earth." The word "scatter" occurs three times within the nine verses of the story (4, 8, 9), each time with "over the face of the whole earth." The emphasis on this motif suggests that the primary motivation for building the tower is not outright rebellion against God (who is never mentioned in the speech), nor an assault against heaven, nor even arrogance. The real reason for the project is fear. The builders are insecure.

But whence this fear of being scattered? Within the confines of the Babel story, it appears inexplicable and irrational, a manifestation of group paranoia. The people perceive a threat when none is there, yet their insecurity leads to precisely the situation they had hoped to prevent— scattering. The significance of this chain of events is heightened when we realize the connotations of the word "scatter." Elsewhere in the Hebrew Bible the word almost always has a negative connotation, and most frequently it refers to banishment or exile of a people from its land.[37]

Still, we cannot fully appreciate the significance of this story apart from its context. The geopolitical and linguistic diversity of the world that seemed quite natural in chapter 10 now appears to be the result of human failure and divine punishment—or perhaps divine coercion. For we must now ask, what is it that human beings have failed to do? The answer can only be that they have failed to populate the whole earth in conformance to the divine will (1:28; 9:1). To be sure, the story of Babel makes no explicit reference to the divine command to "fill the earth," but the juxtaposition with chapter 10 and the various expressions for filling the earth there, and the way in which chapter 10 itself follows upon the renewed charge to Noah (9:1), point to such a connection.[38] Unsatisfied with the earth as the field of their dominion, human beings refuse to "know their place," and aspire to something higher.[39] To them, filling the earth meant being "scattered." Rather than spread out, they would build up.

Finally, our understanding of the Babel story is enhanced in light of the cultural world of ancient Mesopotamia to which the story itself refers. When we consider that one of the major texts of the Mesopotamian world (*Enuma elish*) begins with creation and ends with the construction of the temple complex of Babylon, it is quite possible that the Primeval cycle, which begins with creation and ends with the construction of the tower of Babel, is in part a polemic directed against that world.

7. The New Way (11:10—12:3)

The narrative of the Primeval cycle takes us from human beings as the "image of God" to human beings as alienated from God, from humankind's dominion over the earth to its "scattering" over the earth, from the garden of Eden and the communal unity of the family to the fragmentation of the nations, from blessing to curse.

The pessimism with which the Primeval cycle ends is all the more striking when we observe that up to this point there were signs that Yahweh's gracious care for his creatures would override the growing disorder: clothing for Adam and Eve, a protective mark for Cain, and for Noah, the rainbow in the sky.[40] After the tower of Babel, however, there is no immediate sign of Yahweh's grace. The genealogical material in 11:10–30 opens "section six," the Ancestral Saga, which brings us down to Abram and Sarai (whose names are later changed to Abraham and Sarah). Yet even this section includes a depressing note: "Now Sarai was barren; she had no child." The creation and blessing of humankind in Genesis 1, with its accompanying motif of fertility, has come to sterility. At the close of the narrative (vss. 31–32) there is merely the added report that Abram has been taken away from southern Mesopotamia (Ur of the Chaldees), has migrated toward the land of Canaan (and the people cursed in 9:25), but has settled in the place called Haran, in northwestern Mesopotamia. Abraham is on a journey with a goal (Canaan), but with no stated purpose.

It is in this context—the context of a world without God—that God again speaks directly to one man, as he once spoke to Noah (12:1–3):

1) Now Yahweh said to Abram, "Go from your land, and from your kinfolk, and from your paternal family, to the land which I shall show you, 2) so that I may make of you a great nation, bless you, and make your name great. So

be a blessing, 3) so that I may bless those who bless you, and the one who curses you I may curse, and by means of you all the families of the earth may be blessed."

While this passage represents a radical shift from the Primeval cycle, it is also a bridge joining the Primeval stories with the Ancestral Saga that follows. In fact, unless we see how the story of Abram and Sarai is also a *continuation* of the Primeval cycle, we shall fail to understand the full significance of their story as a new departure. In other words, while the speech to Abram produces a critical turn in the Pentateuchal narrative, it is only a turn, not a new plot. The pivotal function of the speech is evident in its content, forged out of the thematic elements that run throughout the Primeval cycle: a journey from an old land to a new land, a movement from curse to blessing, and a new divine charge that both empowers and commands.

With Abram comes the promise of a new land, indeed, a new *world*. He will not find this land as a banished fugitive, wandering aimlessly (Cain), nor as a result of forced exile ("scattering"), nor even as a result of ordinary migration (chap. 10; 11:29–32). Rather, Yahweh will *show* him this land. From now on, one specific geographical space will be fraught with divine purpose. The tie between Abram and this particular land also implies the creation of a new community (vs. 2). In contrast to the city-state named Babel (=babble, see 11:4, 9), the community named Israel will be made by God and, at the same time, represent the continuing relation of all of humankind to God. This is the bedrock of the biblical understanding of election.

Verse 2 has already introduced our second theme, that of blessing and curse. The life of humankind in the world began with a divine blessing, a blessing repeated in 5:2 and 9:1, but by the end of the Primeval cycle curse appears to predominate. At this point Abram is singled out as the object—and medium—of blessing: "So be a blessing, so that I may bless those who bless you, and the one who curses you I may curse, and by means of you all the families of the earth (*adamah*) may be blessed."[41] The end of this verse may be translated "will be blessed" or "shall bless themselves." We shall settle for a rather broad generalization: the blessing on Abram and his people involves other peoples as well. The blessing on Abram "also concerns those on the outside who adopt a definite attitude toward this blessing. . . . man's judgment and salvation will be determined by the attitude he adopts toward this work which God intends to do in history."[42]

Will Abram, in fact, live so as to *be* a blessing? This is the central question that will hang over all of the Abraham cycle (chaps. 12—24). The Primeval cycle is marked by a cyclical failure of human will in relation to divine will. What human beings consistently lack (with the partial exception of Noah) is integrity and character—in a word, righteousness. To be righteous is to be genuinely human; to be unrighteous is to be inhuman. One may become subhuman, reverting to a status and behavior beneath the dignity of the "image of God," or one may attempt to become superhuman, trying to "become like God." For the Primeval cycle (and the Hebrew Bible in general), the latter is usually the problem. In various ways throughout these stories human beings attempt "to blur the distinction between the human and the divine,"[43] and they remain human only by divine coercion which necessarily entails tragic and "painful" consequences (e.g., 3:16–17).

The theme of human responsibility is also prominent in the so-called "promise" to Abram. This promise, after all, is initially expressed in the form of a command: "Go from your land . . . to the land which I shall show you." Moreover, the syntax of the second verse indicates that the consecution of the promise of nationhood and blessing is predicated on Abram's response to this command: "*So that* I may make of you a great nation."[44] In other words, the successful fulfilment of the promise to Abram is intrinsically linked to the response of the human will; Abram must, after all, respond to the divine command if the promise of nationhood and blessing is to see fruition. In short, the promise involves human obedience to the divine command. We can therefore refer to Genesis 12:1–3 as a "charge"—a word connoting command and responsibility as well as promise. The charge is reminiscent of the divine blessing in Genesis 1, expressed as both promise and command: "Be fertile and increase." Thus at the beginning of the Ancestral Saga, there is the clear implication that obedience to the divine command is the way out of human failure, and that this way—implicitly for all humankind—is the way of Abram.

Abram and Sarai now depart on a magnificent new adventure. Here is the sign of Yahweh's grace that was lacking after the tower of Babel. Suddenly the whole *world*—and indeed, we the readers—direct our attention to this man and woman. The future of this one couple holds the only hope for the life—the blessing—of the whole world. "Yahweh said . . . Abram went." Yahweh commands, Abram obeys. *This is the way the world, and the Torah, began,* and now we begin to see the new way of faith which will become the *way* of Torah.

THE ABRAHAM CYCLE (11:27—25:18)

Introduction

"A wandering Aramean was my father; and he went down into Egypt and sojourned there, few in number." The Israelite confession of faith contained in Deuteronomy 26:5–10 begins with this cryptic summary of the "patriarchal" stories of Genesis. Although the confession appears to refer specifically to Jacob, it is an appropriate formulation for all the stories, for they are framed on either end by a descent into Egypt (12:10; chap. 46). The frame suggests that Genesis 12—50 forms an interim within the Pentateuchal narrative: on the one hand these chapters provide a retrospective and somewhat ironic link to the Primeval cycle; on the other, they furnish a prospective and "prophetic" connection to the section which follows. In relation to the Primeval cycle these stories represent the new reality God intends for the world; at the same time, the stories point beyond themselves to the central event of the Torah—the redemption from Egyptian bondage and the formation of the covenant community. In the end, the great-great-grandchildren of Abraham and Sarah, who were summoned from the "old world" of Mesopotamia to the "new world" of Canaan, find themselves as resident aliens (albeit highly favored) in the strange land of Egypt, and *their* decendants (highly unfavored) will have to be "brought out" of Egypt "with an outstretched arm and with great acts of judgment" (Exod. 6:6).

For convenience, I shall refer to all of Genesis 11:27 to the end as the "Ancestral Saga," "saga" meaning a long story that follows the life of a particular family as it unfolds over numerous generations.[1] Whereas the Primeval cycle often leaps over several generations and ultimately includes all nations in its scope (4:17—5:32; 10:1–32; 11:10–26), the Ancestral Saga concerns only five generations, from Abraham and Sarah to the children of Joseph. Although we can trace the genealogical connections from Adam and Eve to the children of Joseph, Israel later saw itself as peculiarly "related" to the ancestors of chapters 12—50, and especially to Jacob, whose name *is* "Israel."

As we have seen in our analysis of the charge to Abraham in Genesis 12:1–3, the themes announced at the outset of the Ancestral Saga are continuations of those that run throughout the Primeval cycle: the relationships between divine will and human responsibility, humanity and the earth, and blessing and curse. The repetition of this thematic charge in formal divine speeches throughout chapters 12—50 serves as a structural pillar undergirding the entire narrative edifice.[2] The promises are adumbrated no fewer than five times to Abraham alone (e.g., 13:14–17; 15:1–7, 18; chap. 17; 18:9–19; 22:17–18), but they also form the connection to the Isaac and Jacob cycles. Thus the brief Isaac cycle (chaps. 26—27) is introduced by a repetition of the promises, now made directly to Isaac:

> Then Yahweh appeared to him and said . . . , "Sojourn in this land, and I will be with you, and will bless you; for to you and to your descendants I will give all these lands, and I will fulfill the oath which I swore to Abraham your father. I will multiply your descendants as the stars of heaven, and will give to your

descendants all these lands; and by your descendants all the nations of the earth shall bless themselves'' (26:2–4).

Similarly, the promises are continued with Abraham's grandson Jacob:

"I am Yahweh, the God of Abraham your father and the God of Isaac; the land on which you lie I will give to you and to your descendants; and your descendants shall be like the dust of the earth . . . and by you and your descendants shall the families of the earth seek blessing" (28:13–14; cf. 28:3–4; 35:9–12).

The divine promises are never given directly by God to Joseph, an omission that demonstrates remarkable reserve on the part of the redactors, who apparently refused to violate the distinctive narrative configuration of this cycle in such a manner. Instead the promises are repeated once again to Jacob, now at the moment of his "descent into Egypt" (46:1–4). Later, on his deathbed Jacob invokes the blessing of the God of his ancestors on the sons of Joseph (48:15–16).

We now narrow our focus to the Abraham cycle. Throughout the centuries many Jews, Christians, and Muslims would have agreed with Sören Kierkegaard: " . . . though Abraham arouses my admiration, he at the same time appals me. . . . He who has explained this riddle has explained my life."[3] The one who attracts us because of his singular obedience is also the one who—for the same reason—shocks and repulses us. The man of faith is also the man who would slaughter his own son (chap. 22). We cannot "explain" the story of Abraham in the sense of solving Kierkegaard's riddle; we can only open the story so that we may see more clearly the mystery it holds.

On the surface the central issue of the cycle concerns the birth of a son and legitimate heir to Abraham and Sarah, yet the remarkably brief account of Isaac's birth (21:1–7) immediately suggests that the issue involves far more than the completion of a biological process. The real issue has to do with the son *as gift of God*, how the benefactors live in anticipation and receipt of it, and how they die looking beyond their own lives to the future of the one who embodies the gift. The signification of the son—anticipated, embraced, released, and endowed—transcends the biological plane, becoming something much more than the boy Isaac. The son has become the "seed" of the promise to Abraham, especially the promise that he will become a great nation, and thus by extension the son has become the bearer of the possibility of blessing for the entire alienated world of the Primeval cycle. Of course, this will be true for Jacob as well, and then for *his* twelve sons, and we could even trace the underlying concern back to the treatment of Seth (4:24—5:3). But only in the Abraham cycle is the issue of the son "stretched out," as it were, to become the focal point of an entire redactional unit.

1. "Go from your country" (11:27—14:24)

The preface to the Abraham cycle in 11:27–32 gives us three items of information to prepare us for what follows. First, in connection with the customary "generations" formula, it specifies in exacting detail the family relationships of Abram and Sarai. Second, we learn that Sarai is infertile (vs. 30); and third, the story of Abram and Sarai begins with an uncompleted journey to Canaan, initiated by Abram's father for reasons unknown.

These few verses (not to mention the entire Primeval cycle) provide a rich and ambiguous prelude for the story which follows. When Abram accepts the charge, his journey to Canaan becomes a *mission* to the "promised land." Yet to gain this land and be the founder of a "great nation" he must abandon the land of his birth and leave his brother behind. He must become an alien, without the protection of kinfolk or the rights of a permanent citizen (not altogether unlike Cain!). Moreover, he who would be the "father of a multitude" is the husband of a barren woman.

Following the charge to Abram, Genesis 12:4–9 opens with Abram's unquestioning obedience to the divine charge, followed by a geographical survey of places that figure prominently in the ensuing stories. When Abram arrives at Shechem Yahweh appears to him and says, "To your descendants I will give this land." The "land that I will show you" (12:1) is now utterly concrete: "the place at Shechem, at the oak of Moreh." Moreover, the reaffirmation and specification of this promise is presented as the content of the first formal self-revelation of Yahweh in the Hebrew Bible ("appearance"). Yahweh is "seen" only in what he says and does, which is to say that Yahweh's identity is expressed only in terms of the story in which he is the chief character. The reaffirmation of the promise is also significant in that the recipient is specified as Abram's *descendants*. Thus Abram's obedience to the original charge is not so much for his own sake as for the sake of future generations, and his renewed acceptance of the charge is represented by his constructing an altar to Yahweh "who appeared to him" (vs. 7; cf. vs. 8).[4]

No sooner has Abram toured the land of promise than he is driven from it by famine, and forced to "sojourn" in Egypt (vss. 10–20). Fearful of the ostensible jealousy of the Egyptians over Sarai, he lies about their relationship and hands her over to the Pharaoh's harem and apparent adultery (vs. 18). Abram's abandonment of Canaan was unavoidable, an external threat to the promise that, while unexplained, is nonetheless real. His abandonment of Sarai, on the other hand, is a cowardly act constituting an internal threat to the promise. Although there is a damsel in distress here, Abram is no knight in shining armor. The situation is rectified only by Yahweh's imposition of a plague on Pharaoh's household, with the consequent expulsion of Abram and Sarai from Egypt.

The opening chapter of the Abraham cycle thus portrays a remarkably intricate web of circumstances and characterization. Precisely because of the way in which the story takes us from the high point of the divine charge and its acceptance, and plunges us into the utterly ambiguous situations in which the charge begins to be worked out, chapter 12 functions as a kind of prologue to the entire Saga that follows. Abram is at once the one who responds to the divine charge with trust and obedience, and the one who immediately loses his integrity in the face of difficulties, both real and imagined. One can, of course, sympathize with his predicament. He has been promised a land, yet he learns that it will truly belong only to his descendants. As for Abram himself, he arrives in the land "only to walk, so to speak, straight through it and out the other side."[5] The altars he establishes are marks, as it were, of his claim, but Abram remains essentially an alien.

If the themes of responsibility and land appear fraught with ambiguity, so does that of blessing. When the land of promise proves to be a land of famine, there is little evidence of divine blessing. Still, Abram (or more properly, Sarai) enjoys the special protection of Yahweh, and even Abram's mendacity pays off in considerable wealth (vs. 16)! Also, rather than serving as a source of blessing for others, Abram's actions have led, in effect, to a curse, however temporary (vs. 17). Nor does Yahweh's involvement in the plot escape ambiguity. In order to preserve Sarai, Yahweh must scourge the hapless Pharaoh, who, in fact, is the only one who comes away from this story morally untarnished.

In chapters 13—14 the focus of the narrative turns to the relationship between Lot and Abram, with explicit foreshadowing of the Sodom and Gomorrah episode which will conclude the story of Lot (18:16—19:38). Abram has returned to the altar at Bethel, where he again invokes the name of Yahweh. Both he and Lot possess such great herds of livestock that they must separate in order to resolve contention over grazing lands. In effect, bountiful blessing requires further division of the family of Abram. At first one wonders if Lot has not gained the upper hand, for he takes advantage of Abram's magnanimous offer and chooses the fertile Jordan valley as his territory. Yet the fact that this land is described as similar to the "garden of Yahweh" and the well-watered land of Egypt does not augur well (cf. 3:22–24), nor is the necessity to "journey East" auspicious, judging from the Primeval cycle. Lot is a man headed in the wrong direction, as the adumbration of chapter 19 warns.

In contrast, chapter 13 ends with another divine speech in which the promises to Abram are renewed and again expanded. Now Yahweh promises to Abram and his descendants "all the land" which he can see in every direction, and it is a gift "forever." The expanded geographical scope almost appears a consolation in the face of Lot's immediate gratification. In addition, the motif of "descendants" (literally "seed") is amplified by the metaphor of the "dust of the earth." The vastness of the land will be matched by the multitude of Abram's offspring, again a mark of divine blessing.

In chapter 14 the error in Lot's choice of land already begins to show. Following the defeat of Sodom in a regional war, Lot is taken away as a captive and must be rescued by his uncle (vs. 1–16). Yet the redemption of Lot is hardly the primary thrust of the chapter, for Abram achieves a greater victory on a sacerdotal level (vss. 17–24). As a returning victor, Abram receives a divine blessing mediated by the Canaanite priest Melchizedek and pronounced in the name of his god, El Elyon ("God Most High"). When Abram is approached by the king of Sodom regarding the spoils of war, he refuses any of the booty, declaring that he has sworn an oath to that effect to "*Yahweh*, God Most High, Creator of heaven and earth." In one stroke Abram has accepted the blessing, exalted Yahweh to the status of God Most High, and rejected any deals with the king of Sodom. Thus the "point of the story according to the closing discourse is to teach the virtues of courage, loyalty, and piety by Abraham's example."[6] If Abram lost his integrity at the end of chapter 12, he has regained it by the end of chapter 14.

2. Righteousness and Subterfuge (chaps. 15—16)

The juxtaposition of chapters 14 and 15 suggests a loose connection between the Abram who refuses a reward from the king of Sodom and the Abram who is now promised a reward from Yahweh.[7] The text immediately turns to the question of a son (vss. 1–6), and subsequently to the question of possession of the land (vss. 7–20). Commentators have often observed the apparent contradictions in chronological sequence in the chapter (cf. vss. 5, 12, 17). In fact, in its present form all of the action and dialogue takes place in a dream-like state, for verses 1–11 occur in a "vision" and verses 12–21 take place in a "deep sleep" (cf. 2:21). From this we should not infer that what transpires is unreal; on the contrary, the language of vision and dream conveys "a feeling of awe and mystery" before the disclosure of *ultimate* reality.[8] What happens in this chapter is an unprecedented meeting of the divine and the human—Yahweh and Abram—a moment in which the divine will and the human response stand in full accord. In a word, this is a moment of "righteousness."

There has been no previous dialogue between God and Abram; now for the first time Abram speaks directly to God twice, each time in the form of a question which, though deferential, is nonetheless bold and even skeptical. Yahweh promises Abram a great reward, to which Abram responds, "What good is your reward, as long as I remain childless, with a household servant as my only heir?"⁹ Indeed, vs. 3a sounds like an accusation: "you have given me no offspring." Yahweh replies with the first definitive promise of a son and heir. He then takes Abram outside and tells him to look up at the stars in the sky, for his offspring will be just as innumerable. And then Abram "trusted Yahweh, and he accounted it to him as righteousness."

The transition from Abram's strident questioning to inner trust, unexpressed by word or gesture, is remarkable, all the more so because there seems to be little new evidence of *Yahweh*'s trustworthiness (cf. 13:16). Again, it is only that "the word of Yahweh" comes to him in a vision that heightens the cogency of the promise, even if it does not guarantee its certainty.¹⁰

The primary movement in the chapter so far has been that of Abram's commitment to Yahweh. In vss. 7–11 the focus is on Yahweh's commitment to Abram. The section opens with Yahweh's self-introduction as the one who brought Abram from Ur to Canaan. Mention of the land as gift prompts Abram to pose another question: "Lord Yahweh, how am I to *know* that I shall possess it?" Both the bizarre ritual which follows, and the divine speech which appears to interrupt the ritual (vss. 13–16) provide a response to Abram's request for assurance.

The arrangement of the sacrificial elements now functions as a preparation for the speech. Abram falls into a "deep sleep," and the language emphasizes the awe and mystery of the moment: "a great dark dread descended upon him" (JPS). Yahweh now tells Abram the future that stretches not only to his own death but far beyond, a future that includes the exodus of Israel from Egypt ("a land which is not theirs") and the return to Canaan. This prediction is offered as the assurance Abram seeks that he will possess the land (note "know of a surety" in vs. 13), even though he will *not* possess the land in any ordinary sense of the word.

Thus, with some irony, Yahweh confirms his commitment to Abram by showing that that promise is only part of a larger purpose in which Yahweh, as it were, has invested his own future. The importance of that investment transcends any personal fulfilment within the life of Abram. What is at stake is Yahweh's purpose for the whole world, which must be worked out through the descendants of Abram. At the same time,

Yahweh's prediction provides the greatest possible certainty to Abram that his relationship to Yahweh is trustworthy, for this is a moment of "apocalypse," that is, an "unveiling" of a future reality, disclosing the validity and trustworthiness of a present hope.

The narrative now proceeds to the completion of the sacrificial ritual that will also provide a seal of Yahweh's righteousness. Customarily, the one who passes in between the animal parts invokes upon himself the grisly fate of the animal, should he fail to keep the terms of the agreement. Here it is Yahweh who performs this action, represented by the "fire pot and flaming torch," and who then makes a covenant, including the most geographically extended promise of land in the Pentateuch. By his participation in the ritual Yahweh binds himself to the words already spoken (vss. 13–16) and to the specific promise of land which follows, at the risk of . . . of what? Dismemberment and death? We cannot press such a symbolic story beyond its semantic limits, but it is clear that Yahweh has made himself vulnerable, opening himself to an element of risk, in order to demonstrate his commitment to the fulfilment of his purpose for the world. The movement of the chapter as a whole, therefore, establishes a reciprocal relationship between Yahweh and Abram marked by both mutual risk and mutual commitment.

"And Sarai, Abram's wife, bore him no child." The economy of Hebrew narrative style is especially jolting in this opening line to chapter 16. By sheer juxtaposition we are transported from the visionary to the utterly mundane, from an instance of unparalleled righteousness to an incident replete with the ambiguities of human desperation, pride, jealousy, and cruelty. Now for the first time Sarai appears as a character in her own right rather than a passive victim of circumstances, and she is anything but passive. An admirably determined and resourceful woman, she is willing to face the reality of her situation head-on with whatever methods are at her disposal, and in this regard she resembles a number of remarkable women who follow her, not the least of whom will be her daughter-in-law Rebekah.

Note the objectivity and forcefulness of her opening speech: "Look, Yahweh has prevented me from bearing children; go in to my maid; it may be that I shall obtain children by her." Sarai does not mince words. We have known about her infertility since 11:30, but never has the problem been seen from her perspective nor bluntly attributed to Yahweh's doing. She is more interested in overcoming the problem than ascribing blame, and quickly moves to her solution: she will obtain children by Abram's having intercourse with her maid, Hagar—a suggestion with which Abram willingly complies. Lest we be shocked for the wrong reasons, let us recognize immediately that Sarai's ascription of her infertility to Yahweh is compatible with ancient Israelite theology,[11] and the arrangement with

Hagar was accepted custom (and law) at certain periods in the ancient Near East, however immoral it may seem to us. In what sense, if any, therefore, are the characters culpable?

If we look at the story by itself, it is clear that none of the characters is flawless. Sarai's treatment of the pregnant Hagar is hardly charitable, and Abram's reticence is equally irresponsible. Even Hagar's contempt for Sarai, though understandable, is unnecessarily abrasive and certainly foolhardy. Yet the possibility of a deeper significance to the characters' motivations and actions arises when we look at the wider context of the story. Although no reference is made in the chapter to Yahweh's promises to Abram, we cannot read the story without those promises in the background. Yet even here caution is in order. We might assume that Sarai knows of the promises, but we have not been told that explicitly. Moreover, the promise of a son—which is obviously central here—has never specified that Sarai will be the mother. Of course there appeared to be no other candidate, but now one appears. Will Hagar's child, who, if a male, could legally be Abram's heir, really be the "child of the promise"? Are Abram and Sarai culpable for attempting to circumvent Sarai's condition, which Sarai explicitly identifies with Yahweh's will, and so produce the promised child by their own efforts? In the end, the context of the story leaves us with serious questions about the integrity of the characters—especially Abram—but offers no definitive answers.

The text does clearly suggest two things. First, Ishmael will not be the child of the promise. The description of him as a contentious "wild ass of a man" (vs. 12) seems to exclude his candidacy as Abram's true heir, and this will become explicit in chapter 17. Second, though Ishmael is excluded from the divine promise, he and his mother are not excluded from the *blessing* that accrues to the line of Abram. The promise of numerous offspring to Hagar (vs. 10) is the same promise granted to Abram (13:16; 15:5). The very name of the child—"Ishmael," "God hears"—is an expression of Yahweh's gracious response to Hagar's suffering. Even though the child is destined to live in continual conflict with his kinfolk, he will remain stubbornly independent. Here again, Ishmael is more than an individual character; he is also the eponymous ancestor of the Ishmaelites, a people directly related to the Abrahamic line, but not sharing in the full privileges of the promises to Abram. What is remarkable about this story and its sequel in 17:18–21; 21:8–21 is that it is not a triumphant celebration of Ishmael's exclusion, but an attempt to wrestle with the painful and tragic circumstances in which the divine purpose had to be worked out. While the text represents Ishmael as an example of how the blessing of Abraham will benefit "all the families of the earth" (12:3), it does not flinch from the ambiguities that make it a blessing well disguised.

3. "The sign of the covenant" (chap. 17)

Abram's advanced age, the delay in the fulfilment of the promises, and the maturation of Ishmael provide the setting for a fresh clarification of the relationship between Yahweh and the Abrahamic line. This chapter is by far the longest and most important Priestly contribution to the entire Ancestral Saga.[12] What happens here is a new and definitive disclosure of the identity of God, as well as that of Abram and Sarai, and an indication that the nature of the relationship between God and these characters (and their descendants) defines the constitutive content of the covenant. Accordingly, in the opening scene Yahweh "reveals himself" to Abram by his name, El Shaddai. The name is understood by the Priestly school to be that portion, as it were, of Yahweh's identity associated with the Ancestral Saga as a distinct epoch (cf. Exod. 6:2–3). Who is El Shaddai? He is, of course, the one who makes the familiar promises of numerous progeny, land, and nationhood. But what stands out in the Priestly formulation of the promises, and therefore in the identity of El Shaddai, is the pledge to become the God of Abram and his descendants (vss. 7b, 8b).[13] The identity of Yahweh as El Shaddai is wrapped up in the covenant relationship with the descendants of Abram. As an epithet "El Shaddai" may mean "God of the Mountain" or "God Almighty"; in the context of Genesis 17 it has a demonstrative meaning—El Shaddai is "*their* God." In other words, the identity of God can be grasped only in terms of this relationship to Abram and his descendants. Just as the personal identity of husband and wife is very much determined by their relationship, and even seems to require a change of name (now frequently for *both* partners), so the identity of Yahweh is very much determined—"for better or for worse"—by his relationship with the ancestors and their descendants, namely Israel. The emphasis on mutual identity formation in Genesis 17 requires the introduction of a new name for God and, correspondingly, new names for Abram and Sarai.

The opening address in verses 1b–2 suggests a correlation between Abram's righteousness and Yahweh's granting of the covenant: "I am El Shaddai: follow my ways and be blameless,[14] so that I may grant a covenant between me and you, and multiply you exceedingly." In the second unit (vss. 9–14) Abram's responsibility to "keep" the covenant—that is, to watch over, guard, and maintain it—is delineated. Quite literally, the mark of this new covenant identity is expressed by the rite of circumcision. While the literal applicability of this custom has obvious limitations (particularly for women), symbolically it suggests that covenant identity involves the "whole person" and, moreover, that the recipients of the covenant are responsible for its transmission from one generation to another. Even more remarkable, circumcision, and thus membership in the covenant community, is not restricted to kinfolk, for even a "foreigner who is not of your offspring" must be circumcised. Here the Priestly formulation of the way in which the blessing pronounced on Abraham can include non-Israelites achieves an "ecumenical spirit."[15]

It is difficult, if not impossible, to reconcile the ecumenical implications of the second unit with what transpires in the third (vss. 15–22). Here for the first time the promise of a son to Abraham specifies Sarah as the mother. Now we know why her role, whether passive (12:10–20) or active (16:1–6), has been so important, and will be again (18:1–15; chap. 20; 21:1–7; chap. 23). When the ancestress is in danger, the promises are in danger. Abram's response is bewilderment, if not mockery. In fact, he falls on his face laughing! What a contrast to verse 3a, where the same gesture expresses the conventional act of humility. Abraham cannot help but snicker at the suggestion that he and Sarah, at the ages of one hundred and ninety respectively, will have a child. So certain is he of the impossibility of such a miracle that he immediately suggests an alternative—let Ishmael be the son of the promise. What was apparently an attempt to circumvent Yahweh's will in chapter 16 is now explicitly so. Yahweh rejects this alternative, reiterates that Sarah will be the mother, and now dictates the name of the son: Isaac, "he laughs."

What now of Ishmael? The oracular saying in 16:11–12 has already implied that Ishmael will not be the son of the promise, and now that implication is confirmed. But, as before, that is not the last word for Ishmael. The divine blessing, expressed by the motif of progeny, is also confirmed and extended to include a regal destiny. Ishmael will become the "father of twelve princes," and a "great nation." Even so, the covenant will be established with Isaac, the son of Sarah, and not with Ishmael, the son of Hagar. The text does not confront the apparent contradiction that Ishmael is circumcised, and thus bears the sign of the covenant (vss. 25–26), yet is excluded from the covenant. Perhaps this avoidance is due to the distinctive Priestly understanding of the nature and content of the covenant which pervades the entire chapter. If, like Abraham himself, Ishmael receives a divine blessing, will father innumerable descendants, and will be the founder of a great nation, yet will not be the bearer of the covenant, what is the content of the covenant? The answer can only be possession of the land of Canaan and the promise "to become your God, and the God of your descendants after you" (vs. 7b, and together in vs. 8).

4. Divine Visitors (chaps. 18—19)

The precedence of the annunciation in chapter 17 cannot rob the story in 18:1–15 of its charm. While the Priestly author was interested in the "eternal" *significance* of Isaac's birth (e.g., 17:19), the present story functions more on the level of plot, heightening our expectation of an imminent resolution ("in the spring") and thus pointing towards a climax.

Part of the charm comes from the way we see the elderly couple scrambling "in the heat of the day" to welcome the three passersby. The reader knows from the outset that this is a visitation from Yahweh (vs. 1), but the characters do not begin to intuit this until midway through (vs. 9). There may be something to the proverb derived from this story about those who "entertain angels unawares" (Heb. 13:2), that is, in some sense Abraham and Sarah are rewarded for their generous hospitality to strangers, although the repeated promises to Abram which now precede the story tend to dull such an effect. Still, hospitality to the stranger represents the most elemental form of human righteousness. Since hospitality is here rendered unwittingly to God in disguise, perhaps we should see this story of divine visitation as part of that "testing" of Abraham which pervades the entire cycle. And perhaps we should infer more than a coincidental connection with the scene immediately following, in which God takes Abraham into his confidence. Moreover, the ancestors' hospitality will soon be repeated by Lot, and together their friendly reception of the divine visitors will cast into stark relief the hostility of the citizens of Sodom (19:1–11).

The prologue and epilogue to the Sodom story (18:16–33; 19:27–29) make *Abraham* the protagonist instead of Lot, even though Abraham never appears in the action of chapter 19. This framework forces us to look at the story from Abraham's point of view (both literally and figuratively), the point of view of one "looking down on" Sodom as an informed witness. Further, while we might conclude from 19:1–15 alone that Lot saved himself by also "entertaining angels unawares," verse 29 insists that Lot's salvation is really due to Abraham's favor with God.[16] Thus the prologue and epilogue convert the Sodom story into a piece which connects with the *thematic* unity of the Abraham cycle: Abraham's role as witness derives from the charge that he has received from Yahweh (18:17–19); Lot's salvation ultimately derives from the blessing placed on Abraham, on the basis of which God's mercy overrides God's justice (18:23–33).[17] Moreover, as the sequel to the story suggests (19:29–38), the blessing of Abraham does indeed extend to other peoples (the Moabites and Ammonites), even if their origin is not one of which to be proud!

We may now look at Abraham's role in more detail. The reason for selecting Abraham as the informed witness is given in terms not only of the promises of nationhood and blessing, but also of a specific responsibility to "charge" (*tsivah*) his descendants in the way of "righteousness and justice." The explicit purpose clauses in verse 19 are the clearest indication so far of the responsibility which comes with the promises. Indeed, the logical order of the verse ("that he may charge . . . so that Yahweh may bring . . . ") suggests that the realization of the promises in the future will depend in part on Abraham's attention to his responsibilities.

Abraham's unique role is emphasized in the opening of verse 19 by an unusually direct expression of his election: Yahweh has "recognized" him, which is to say "singled him out" (JPS) as one with authority and a special purpose.[18] Whether or not Abraham hears the words of verses 17–19, the reason for his appointment as a witness is all the more crucial when we realize that there is, in fact, one other informed witness to what happens, namely Lot. He too knows who is destroying the cities and why, because the angels tell him (19:13) in words which may have provided the basis for 18:20. Lot survives the disaster, and presumably he too could relate its theological "lesson." But in the sequel to the disaster story, Lot is discredited—how can a man who allows himself to become so drunk that he unconsciously commits incest with his daughters be a worthy representative of "the way of Yahweh"? Thus Abraham remains the only witness who is not only informed and divinely appointed, but also whose integrity corresponds to his selection. Appropriately, the story concludes with Abraham returning to the spot of his conversation with Yahweh, and looking down on the eery, smoking ruins of Sodom and Gomorrah (19:27–28).

So far Yahweh has allowed Abraham to be a witness because he is the trustee of the promises, responsible for inculcating the "lesson" of Sodom as part of his teaching the way of righteousness and justice. For this reason, Yahweh has drawn Abraham into his confidence and entrusted him with the knowledge and significance of his actions. Still, at this point, Yahweh's decision to include Abraham in his plans is based completely on Abraham's *ex officio* status and not on his personal integrity. The rest of the prologue (vss. 22–33) functions to demonstrate that Yahweh has made the correct decision in the latter regard as well.

In a sense, Yahweh gets more than he bargains for. Apparently Yahweh had intended merely to *inform* Abraham of what was to happen, because of his status as the trustee of Yahweh's "way." Now Abraham demonstrates his acceptance of responsibility not only by receiving the information, but by questioning Yahweh about *his* righteousness and justice: "Shall not the Judge of all the earth do right?" (vs. 25). Yahweh's designated witness now also assumes the role of his counselor. With considerable courage, Abraham lives up to the confidence Yahweh has already placed in him. Indeed, by his willingness to question Yahweh's righteousness on behalf of the *un*righteous, Abraham confirms his own righteousness with respect to Yahweh. Correspondingly, in Yahweh's agreement to Abraham's questions an important principle is established: Yahweh's righteousness transcends a mechanical system of reward and punishment. That this principle may stand in some tension with the ensuing story in which Yahweh annihilates entire cities does not lessen the significance of what is here revealed about Yahweh's character.[19] Moreover, the potential for mercy within Yahweh's righteousness must be balanced against the depravity of an entire citizenry who *assaulted* angels unawares (19:4).

5. Resolutions: Ishmael, Abimelech, and Isaac (chaps. 20—21)

In chapter 20 we find Sarah in trouble yet again.[20] With Sarah in a pagan king's harem, the possibility of offspring through Abraham is jeopardized, a problem more troublesome than before, because now we know that Sarah is to be the "mother" of Israel (chap. 17) Similarly, Abraham again finds himself an "alien" in a land which is not his, and unlike Egypt, this is the *promised* land. Yet these problems are resolved as well as they can be: Sarah is released (untouched) from Abimelech's harem, and Abraham is given permission to dwell[21] in Gerar.

What is not so easily resolved is Abraham's behavior. While the present account in some ways attempts to exonerate Abraham, in the wider context of the story his actions remain irresponsible, and within the story his culpability appears all the more striking in contrast to the probity of Abimelech. When God appears to Abimelech in a dream and warns him of imminent danger, Abimelech proclaims his innocence: "Lord, wilt thou slay a righteous people? . . . In the integrity of my heart and the innocence of my hands I have done this" (vss. 4, 5b). What an ironic contrast this scene makes in comparison to that of Abraham's prior discourse with Yahweh, when he defended the righteous and *un*righteous in the face of Yahweh's judgment (18:22–33). Here it is not the patriarch but a Philistine king who appears to be the paragon of virtue. In his confrontation with Abraham, Abimelech presses his case even further. It is not he but Abraham who is the cause of sin. In short, Abraham has committed the elemental act of unrighteousness—he has "done that which ought not to be done" to another (vs. 9).

In response, Abraham explains the truth behind his apparent lie: Sarah is, in fact, his half-sister. Even if we grant the veracity of this claim, surely it will not excuse Abraham's action, which has again put not only Sarah and Abimelech, but also the promises of God in grave danger.[22] Further, in the face of the "fear of God" which Abimelech and the Philistines have shown (vs. 8), Abraham's attempt to justify his action by portraying the Philistines as *not* fearing God is both hypocritical and self-righteous (vs. 11). Abraham even seems to intimate that the whole affair is God's fault for having "led him astray" in the first place (vs. 13).[23]

Abraham hasn't made things easy for God either. Once again God has to scramble to preserve the bearers of his purpose for the world. At the same time, God acts with deliberate restraint, in recognition of the integrity of Abimelech (vs. 6). Even so, we learn in the end that God had made the Philistine women temporarily infertile—in effect, accursed (vss. 17–18). The one who ought to have been the channel of blessing to the world (as indeed he has been before) has instead been the agent of sterility and potential death. Nevertheless it is through the intercession of Abraham (the prophet!) that fertility and life are restored. In short, Abraham's righteousness is again fraught with inconsistency, and the cycle resumes the tension with which it began (12:10–20).

In the space of only seven verses the text now reports the long-awaited arrival of the son of Abraham and Sarah (21:1–7). Only in the last two verses is this momentous event celebrated, and even here the focus is on the word play on laughter (and is it the laughter of joy or ridicule?), connecting this unit with the following story about Ishmael (vs. 9, where "playing" also derives from *tsahaq*). Repeating numerous phrases from chapter 17 and 18:1–15,[24] verses 1–4 emphasize two points: first, Yahweh has done what he had said he would do (vss. 1–2), and second, Abraham has done as he was told to do (vss. 3–4, naming and circumcision). Thus, in a laconic way, the author represents the birth of Isaac as a divine promise fulfilled and a covenant responsibility maintained.

In context, the following story about Hagar and Ishmael (vss. 8–21) is the logical conclusion to chapter 16 and especially to 17:20–21. Yahweh's purposes are worked out within the harsh reality of human rivalry and jealousy. Indeed, God even overrides Abraham's objection to the "banishment" (*garash*) of Ishmael. Yet, as before, God cares for Ishmael because he too is the "seed" of Abraham (vs. 13). Thus the angel of God comes to Hagar and Ishmael as they wander in the wilderness, opens Hagar's eyes to the source of sustenance, and sets mother and son on the road to becoming a "great nation." Almost as if to embrace a new and separate destiny, Hagar chooses a wife for Ishmael from her own country, from Egypt (vs. 21; cf. 16:1).

With the problem of Ishmael finally resolved, the text turns to Abraham's relations with the native inhabitants, in this case Abimelech. The passage highlights two themes: blessing and land. Abimelech approaches Abraham with the observation, "God is with you in all that you do." Abraham's success and affluence are a sign of blessing, and Abraham quickly learns the truth of the proverb, "wealth brings many new friends"

(Prov. 19:3). Abimelech proposes a formal agreement affirming mutual honesty and integrity, and Abraham agrees. The arrangement is beneficial to both—a potential share of Abraham's blessing for Abimelech, and for Abraham, the chance to improve his status as an alien by gaining legal recognition from a native. In fact, in verses 25–34 the actual ratification of the treaty appears as the means for resolving a dispute over well rights, and Abraham seems to gain legal title to his first piece of Canaanite soil, the well at Beersheba.

In short, a lot has happened in this little unit. The Philistine king, who had every right to *eject* Abraham from the land (chap. 20), has instead treated this alien with honesty and magnanimity, however self-serving his motivation. Thus he stands to benefit from Abraham's charge: "those who bless you, I will bless" (12:3). And Abraham, although still an alien, at least has legal recognition and a piece of the promised land. As if to mark his claim, Abraham plants a tree in Beersheba and invokes the name of Yahweh—El Olam, God Everlasting—reminding us of the altars he built earlier (12:7, 8; 13:18).

6. The Test (chap. 22)

You would think that a man of well over a hundred years would deserve a little rest from the trials of life, but such is not the case with Abraham. Indeed, as chapter 22 tells us, he faced the greatest trial of all at just such a ripe old age. This is a test of unimaginable horror, and it makes for a story which is one of the most inscrutable—and most beautifully told—in the entire Hebrew Bible.[25] For some interpreters, the text represents literary art at its most sublime, and an ideal vision of the nature of God and humankind. For others, the writer is a sadist whose God is the Devil and whose human protagonist is a madman.

The test is set apart from its immediate context by the phrase "after these things" (vss. 1, 20). The entire story is about a journey that begins and ends at Beersheba, but something about this journey transcends spatial and even temporal definition. This is a journey whose beginning reaches back to the initial charge to Abraham, and whose destination leads into the future of Israel. The journey to Moriah is the consummation of a larger pilgrimage that is Abraham's life, and it is only because he makes this journey that there will be an Israel to continue in his way.

Together with the opening words of the original charge to Abraham in 12:1, the command to sacrifice his son forms the framework for the cycle: "Go (*lek-leka*) from your land and your kinfolk and your paternal household to the land that I will show you." "Take your son, your only son Isaac, whom you love, and go to (*lek-leka*) the land of Moriah, and offer him there as a burnt offering upon one of the mountains of which I shall tell you." The one command is full of promise and hope; the other, full of doom and despair. Obedience to the first command led to the birth of a son; obedience to the second would lead to the death of the son.

Both commands are issued by the same God, but they do not come to the same man. The Abraham who answered the first command is not the one who hears the second, for the Abram of 12:1–3 was little more than a name (a name soon to be changed, at that), while the Abraham of chapter 22 is the complex character rendered by the narrative of chapters 12—21. The latter is an altogether human character, capable of that complete conformity to the divine will for which the text reserves the word "righteousness" (chap. 15; 18:17–33; cf. 6:9), yet alternately misdirected by fear and diffidence, and capable of such irresponsibility that even pagan kings find him repugnant (12:10–20; chaps. 16; 20). This is the man who demonstrated the deepest trust in God, yet who could fall all over himself laughing at the preposterousness of God's promise. If there is any answer to the question of why God tested Abraham, it must take into account the context of the entire cycle. God tested Abraham because he wanted to know, once and for all, whether or not Abraham trusted in him completely. "It is not a game with God. God genuinely does not know."[26] And the means of the test—the sacrifice of Isaac—is dictated by the fact that Abraham's most questionable behavior has occurred precisely in situations in which he irresponsibly jeopardized, circumvented, or distrusted the promise of a son.

Along with the reason and means for the test, we must also determine its meaning and significance within the context of the cycle as a whole, and not simply within chapter 22. In chapter 22, God demands that Abraham kill his only son; within the context of the cycle, God demands that Abraham kill the promises God has made, and thus return the world to its state at the end of the Primeval cycle. Of course, son and promises cannot be separated, but the weight of meaning lies in the fact that Isaac is a gift who embodies God's promise of blessing, land, and nationhood. The test is one of obedience and trust. In essence, it is a test of Abraham's relationship with Yahweh. It asks whether Abraham's trust is really in *God*, and not simply in what God has promised. Abraham has built altars before and sacrificed to this God, when God renewed the promises (12:7–8; 13:18). Is he willing now to build an altar and sacrifice the promises themselves, embodied in his son, in order to demonstrate his unswerving trust in the God who stands behind the promises? In chapter 15 a sacrifice was the means by which Yahweh demonstrated his adamant commitment to Abraham. Now the demand that Abraham kill his son *as a sacrifice* is the most radical reinforcement of the fact that the son is a gift from God, a gift which, in his sovereignty and freedom, God can call back to himself. Abraham's corresponding willingness to relinquish the son he has waited so long to embrace signifies his utter dependence on the one who has given the son. Abraham cannot *possess* the promises; they are his by privilege and not by right. They are most truly his only when he "offers them up."

Abraham's obedient response to the divine command in vs. 2 is all the more remarkable because he does not know that this is a test. Only we, the readers, know this, and the difference is crucial. The most effective test is one in which those who are being tested are not aware of their situation. Imagine how much more telling a test of our civil defense network would be if those occasional radio announcements did not include the words "this is only a test," and went on to describe some imminent disaster. Abraham does not know that he is being tested, and must take the command with utmost seriousness; we do know that he is being tested. The author has winked at us, as it were, inviting us to identify more with the author than with his protagonist. Although our collusion with the author does not mean we know in advance the outcome of the tale, it means we can observe the action with a detachment unavailable to Abraham.

The skill of the narrator is again evident in the staccato succession of verbs used to describe Abraham's obedient responses on hearing the command (vs. 3) and on arriving at the designated spot (vss. 9–10). Without melodramatic flourishes the text leads up to the moment when we see the ritual knife poised over the neck of Isaac. This is the turning point of the story, marked by the reentry of God in the form of the angelic voice that repeats the initial summons: " 'Abraham! Abraham!' And he said, 'Here I am' " (vs.11; cf. vs. 1). The silence that has pervaded the story between God's command and this call has been broken only by the brief and ironic conversation between father and son. There has been no subsequent word from God explaining his macabre order, nor has there been any utterance from Abraham about his agony—indeed, the author does not even tell us if it *is* agony. Apart from its context, it would be entirely possible to read the story and conclude that Abraham followed the order with a joyful heart and a radiant smile. Avoiding any description of motivation or thoughts or feelings, the story focuses on *one* question: Will Abraham do what God has told him to do? When he raises the knife over Isaac, we know that the answer is yes. In retrospect we can see that it has been so from the very beginning when Abraham responded to the initial summons by saying "Ready."[27]

Abraham has done what God told him to do and, both in terms of the content and context of this story, his action represents the supreme moment of righteousness in the Pentateuchal narrative up to this point. If the first step on the way out of the primeval world of alienation was taken in chapter 12, the final step (for Abraham) is taken here. Abraham has demonstrated that he "fears God" (vs. 12), which refers not so much to fright as it does to awe and resultant obedience. In one sense, therefore, the story could end with the etiology in verse 14. That it does not end here, but is followed by a renewal of the promises, is of great significance. First, the addition of the promises indicates a crucial aspect of the purpose behind the test. The test was posed not only to evaluate Abraham's personal trust in Yahweh, but also to establish the *trustworthiness* of the one through whom Yahweh's promises are mediated to the world. The story's greatest significance lies not in the fact that Abraham is the father of Isaac, but that he is the "father of a multitude"— the father of Israel—and thus the father of the promises. Yahweh's main purpose in the test was to establish that the trustee of the promises was worthy of his office.

The second point is implicit in the first. Yahweh's promises now come to Abraham as a reward for his righteousness. The author makes this explicit at the beginning and end of the divine speech: ". . . because you have done this . ... because you have obeyed my voice." Never before in the cycle has there been such a clear causal connection between obedience and promise. A hierarchy among the major themes we have traced is apparent here: the theme of responsibility is primary. The significance of this development for the meaning of the Pentateuchal narrative is eloquently expressed by Mordecai Kaplan:

> These words place the Abrahamic promise in a totally different light. For, while hitherto the promise given to Abraham is mainly an expression of divine favor, it now comes for the first time as an acknowledgment of Abraham's worth. *This is the point where divine effort meets with full response in the human being.* It is toward this goal, first in Israel and then in all of mankind, that all divine efforts from the viewpoint of the Torah tend.[28]

The formulation of the promises here thus stands in permanent balance—and tension—with the formulation at the beginning of the cycle (12:1–3): on the one hand the promises of nationhood, land, and blessing are a gift of God prevenient to any worth on the part of the recipient; on the other hand, the continuation and fulfilment of those promises is contingent on the responsibility of the recipient. This is a tension which will pervade the Torah from now to the end, but will not achieve its fullest expression until Israel as a people arrives at the mountain of Sinai (Exod. 19).

Finally, the significance of the renewed promises is indicated by the fact that Yahweh's speech takes the form of an "oath" (vs. 16a). The

use of the formula adds a solemnity to the promises similar to that evoked
by the covenant ceremony in chapter 15. But an even greater significance
of the oath here in chapter 22 is that it becomes one of those few redactional threads highlighting the continuity of the Pentateuchal narrative *in
its entirety*. At a number of critical points a retrospective reference to
Yahweh's oath will serve to indicate Yahweh's faithfulness to the promises
made to the ancestors.[29] Thus Abraham's exemplary obedience and Yahweh's corresponding oath represent not only the climax of the Abraham
cycle, but also one of the literary pillars of the Torah.

7. Epilogue (chaps. 23—24)

The brief verses at the end of chapter 22 provide a transition to
the epilogue by referring to Abraham's family in Haran and especially to
Rebekah, who, of course, will become the wife of Isaac in chapter 24.
The position of these verses demonstrates the role of the preceding story
as part of the framework to the Abraham cycle, for these verses have
their counterpart in the prologue preceding Abraham's charge (11:27–30).
The text then immediately turns to the subject of Sarah's death and burial.
Chapter 23 makes no reference to God and seems devoid of any theological
implications. That, however, is far from the case. The point of the story
in its context is that now Abraham holds legal title to a piece of the land
of Canaan. Indeed, the purchase of the burial plot is narrated as the report
of a legal transaction, as if we had before us a court stenographer's notes
and the accompanying deed. The action takes place in the city gate (vss.
10, 18), which served as the courtroom in ancient Israel (cf. Ruth 4), and
includes repeated references to the presence of formal witnesses ("in the
sight/hearing of," vss. 11, 13, 16, 18). In the lively bartering between
Abraham and Ephron, Abraham insists on *buying* the land. As if the point
were not yet clear, the author concludes the chapter with a deliberately
redundant summary reemphasizing the legality of Abraham's title.[30] Now
Abraham—"a stranger and alien"—has a "possession" (literally a "hold")
on the land of the promise (vs. 4), minimal though it may be. By the end
of the Ancestral Saga, all of the patriarchs and matriarchs will be buried
in the cave at Machpelah (except Rachel): " . . .in death they were heirs
and no longer 'strangers.' "[31]

The remainder of the epilogue is dominated by a concern comparable to that of securing a portion of the land, namely, finding a wife
for Isaac and thus insuring that Abraham will become the "father of a
multitude." Things would not work well if the son of the promise remained
a bachelor.

The story of Abraham began with a journey from Haran to Canaan, and it ends with a journey from Canaan to Haran and back again. When this journey is over, Abraham's life will be complete, even though he will then take another wife and have six more sons through her (25:1–4). Like Ishmael (and Eliezer), these are not the sons of the promise. Abraham will give these sons "gifts," but he will give "all that he has" to Isaac (vss. 5–6a; cf. 24:36). Abraham will send them away "eastward to the east country" (25:6), but he will bring the wife for Isaac *from* the east country. This is not a journey Abraham himself will make, but it is a final movement in that spiritual journey that is the story of his life.

The initial scene suggests that Abraham is nearing the point of death, a scene which will recur with Isaac, Jacob, and, more briefly, with Joseph.[32] From the outset, the search for Isaac's wife takes place without any divine initiative. Abraham's commissioning of the servant is not in obedience to a divine command rejecting a Canaanite wife or demanding a wife from kinfolk. Abraham is acting on his own. However, the opening scene is the *only* place in the cycle where Abraham quotes the divine charge:[33] "Yahweh, the God of heaven, who took me from my father's house and from the land of my birth, and who spoke to me and swore to me, 'To your descendants I will give this land,' he will send his angel before you, and you shall take a wife for my son from there" (vs. 7). Thus Abraham understands what he is doing to be in conformity with his status as trustee of the promises. That status is the core of his narrative identity, and what he does now is an expression of that identity, or in other words, consistent with his character.

When Abraham refers to Yahweh's "oath," he limits the content to the promise of land. This emphasis is all the more striking since the promise of land was the *weakest* part of the divine oath in 22:15–18. The focus on the land promise arises in response to the servant's question— should he take Isaac back to Haran (presumably to stay) if the suitable fiancée will not leave? Abraham vehemently rejects this possibility, for if Isaac were to return to Haran it would represent a complete reversal of Abraham's life, a repudiation of the promise of land. Indeed, it would amount to a renunciation of the charge Abraham had first obeyed. While Abraham cannot prevent Isaac's own repudiation of the promises, he can at least arrange his marriage in such a way that repudiation will be less likely. This he does by forbidding the servant to take Isaac back to Haran.

Of course if Isaac could marry a Canaanite there would be no threat to the promise of land. In fact, his status as an alien might even improve (cf. chap. 34). A long history of revulsion against Canaanite culture and religion stands behind the prohibition of this solution. Throughout Israel's history, marriage with Canaanites was understood to be the cause of disloyalty to Yahweh, and thus ultimately of *loss* of the land.[34] The primary concern is not ethnic but theological purity.[35] If, as seems likely, Genesis 24 fits within this tradition, then Abraham's refusal to allow a Canaanite marriage is intended to protect not only the son of the promise, but also the promise itself.

Abraham's strictures are twofold: no Canaanite wife, no wife even from kinfolk unless she will come to Canaan. When we combine these two, an interesting result appears. The wife who may not be a Canaanite must come to Canaan. Consequently the new matriarch will in a way share Abraham's story even more than Isaac does, for she too will be told to "go from your land and your kinfolk and your father's household, to the land that I will show you" (12:1). The future matriarch is marrying the son of an alien, and must therefore become an alien herself. Moreover, at the very moment that she says, "I will go," she receives the traditional family blessing, "be the mother of thousands . . . and may your descendants possess the gate of those who hate them" (24:58, 60). The latter part of that blessing is almost identical to part of Yahweh's "oath" in 22:17b.

While Rebekah's declaration, "I will go," is not in response to a direct command from God, it *is* portrayed as a response to the divine guidance of events which has led to this moment. As her father and brother proclaim after hearing the servant's story, "The thing comes from Yahweh" (vs. 50). From the moment the servant takes his hand out from under Abraham's thigh, the entire story moves according to incredible "coincidences" of the divine will, making it unlike any other story in Genesis.[36] But the fantastic quality of the narrative should not detract from its function, which is to demonstrate that God has confirmed Abraham's actions. In a sense this story is about *human* initiative and a divine response, human conviction and divine confirmation, human responsibility and divine faithfulness. What Abraham does here is not only consistent with his own character, it is also consistent with Yahweh's character, as Abraham himself predicts at the outset (vs. 7).

"Go from your land and from your kinfolk and from your father's household, to the land that I shall show you" . . . "Go to my land and to my kinfolk and take a wife for my son Isaac." The climax of the Abraham cycle may come with the binding of Isaac, but its consummation comes with Abraham's charge to his servant. In this charge, Abraham's identity is now complete—he knows who he is not only in terms of the past and the present, but also in terms of that future which extends beyond his life.

THE JACOB CYCLE (25:19—36:43)

1. Prologue: "The elder shall serve the younger" (25:19–34)

We might call Isaac "the shadow," for he appears as an independent character only in chapters 26 and 27. In the former he is little more than a reflection of Abraham, and in the latter he is already an old man on his deathbed. Jacob is really the protagonist of "the story of Isaac," which runs from 25:19 to the end of chapter 36; thus we call this unit "the Jacob cycle."

Already in the prologue we can see the distinctive thematic focus of the Jacob cycle in contrast to the Abraham stories. Like Sarah, Rebekah is barren, but this problem, which persists for twenty years, disappears within the space of one verse (25:21; cf. vss. 20, 26)! Similarly, the problem of who will be Isaac's legitimate heir, a problem which begins *in utero*, reminds us of the young Isaac and Ishmael, but in the Jacob cycle the problem is one of overt rivalry, which was never the case before. Here the two boys are not only full brothers but twins, and much of the tension in the plot derives from the fact that the younger "supplants" the older, who presumably deserves privilege. Indeed, this problem continues to the end of the Saga.

If before we thought that Yahweh had to work out his purposes through human agents whose integrity was often questionable, we quickly find that with Jacob, we have to reckon with an even more unscrupulous character. Moreover, from the outset the cycle resists any attempt at discerning whether the corresponding inscrutability in the character of *Yahweh* comes as a result of having to deal with such shady people or, on the contrary, it is Yahweh's incomprehensible will that invisibly directs the human characters. In the prologue, the first words from God are an oracle delivered to Rebekah: "Two nations are in your womb . . . ; the elder shall serve the younger." Standing at the outset of the cycle the oracle appears to determine the fate of Esau and Jacob, much like the Delphic oracle in Greek drama.

On the other hand, the oracle comes as an *interpretation* of Rebekah's suffering caused by the two fetuses "crashing together" in her womb.[1] The struggle between the elder and younger brothers has already begun before the oracle is spoken. The Jacob cycle is a story of constant wrangling and wrestling, an extended and sometimes violent family feud that spills over into the Joseph cycle, and even there is not fully resolved. The characters seem the victims of their own cussedness rather than the helpless pawns of fate. When Jacob emerges from the womb gripping

Esau's heel he may be fulfilling a divine destiny, but he is also acting out of his own nature. While the newborn Esau seems to be an innocent victim of his brother's jealousy, if not of fate, in the following episode he succumbs as much to his own boorish stupidity as to Jacob's wily ploys. Jacob has a sharp mind and no conscience, but Esau is all belly and no brain.

In short, when Esau and Jacob "crash together" in Rebekah's womb, they set in motion the predominant tension in the Jacob cycle. But already the oracle suggests that this struggle involves more than human characters. It is not by coincidence that the people Israel identifies itself with Jacob. His original name means "he supplants," and approaches both in etymology and connotation a contemporary pejorative epithet—Jacob is a "heel." But his new name "Israel" has several meanings. Literally it can mean "God (El) struggles" or "rules," although one text makes God the object—Jacob is "he who struggles with God" (32:28). The ambiguity may be deliberate. If the Jacob cycle is the story of a family feud, it is also the story of Jacob's struggle to come to terms with the God who befriends him despite his perversity, then fights with him despite his friendship. The Jacob who grabs the heel of Esau is also the Israel whom God wounds in the thigh.

While the structure of the cycle is not completely concentric, there are corresponding sections which an outline reveals:

25:19–34 Prologue
  26 *Isaac and Canaanites: Conflict and covenant*
    27 JACOB AND ESAU: DECEPTION
      28:10–22 Bethel: Departure
        29—31 Jacob and Laban: Deception and reconciliation
        32:1–2 Mahanaim
    32—33 JACOB AND ESAU: RECONCILIATION
  34 *Jacob and Canaanites: Deception and enmity*
    35 Bethel: Return
36 The Edomites

2. The Isaac Stories (chap. 26)

The story begins almost where Abraham's began, with a famine in the land (cf. 12:10–20). Isaac moves to Gerar, the city of Abimelech, king of the Philistines.[2] Immediately Yahweh appears to Isaac and admonishes him not to go down to Egypt, but to "dwell in the land of which I shall tell you" (cf. 12:1). Then follows a repetition of the blessing and promises of Abraham (vss. 3–5) with explicit references to the climax of the Abraham cycle (chap. 22), for the promises descend to Isaac as a fulfilment of Yahweh's "oath" to Abraham, and "because Abraham obeyed my voice and kept my charge, my commandments, my statutes, and my laws.'' The continuation of Yahweh's blessing and promises for the world is a gift only Yahweh can grant, but which now also comes as a divine response to the righteousness of Abraham.

The next incident reveals the truth in the proverb "like father like son." No sooner has Isaac received the promises than he fears for his life and repeats the "sister/wife" ruse (vss. 6–11). As a result he wins the scorn but also the protection of Abimelech. Once again a sojourner has irresponsibly brought the natives to near catastrophe, yet enjoys undeserved welfare. In fact, in the next passage, Yahweh blesses Isaac so abundantly that the Philistines are intimidated by his affluence and send him away, apparently to the outskirts of Gerar (12–17). Although verse 15 seems clumsy, it suggests that the Philistines had already tried to protect themselves from Isaac's expansion by filling up the wells that had belonged to Abraham (21:22–34). In effect, therefore, they have broken the treaty between Abraham and Abimelech.

The rest of the chapter describes the process through which the characters are reconciled and the treaty is restored. The names of the wells Isaac's servants dig trace this development: from Contention and Enmity to Room and Oath. But the determinative factor in the reconciliation is the second pronouncement of divine blessing on Isaac (vs.24). By juxtaposition, the pronouncement effects a dramatic reversal in the Philistines' attitude; they can now see that Isaac's good fortune is not a threat to them but a potential boon. "We see that Yahweh is with you . . . ; you are now the blessed of Yahweh" (vss. 29–30). The result is a renewal of the treaty and the restoration of "peace" (vss. 29, 31).

Perhaps more than any other part of the Ancestral Saga, the brief story of Isaac gains its greatest significance from its context. Retrospectively, it affirms Yahweh's faithfulness to his promises—and to Abraham. Prospectively, it holds up an example of blessing and peace for those who recognize the "blessed of Yahweh"—"those who bless you I will bless" (12:3). We now know Isaac as the one who bears *Yahweh*'s blessing, as well as one who can bequeath his own blessing. Thus, in the next story, when Jacob steals his father's blessing, we will wonder if he has stolen Yahweh's as well.

3. Deception (27:1—28:9)

"But Jacob said to Rebekah, his mother, 'Look, my brother is a hairy man, and I am a smooth man. Perhaps my father will feel me, and I shall seem to be mocking him, and bring a curse upon myself and not a blessing' '' (27:11–12). Jacob's words are almost as oracular as those of Yahweh in the prologue. They reveal a central trait in Jacob's character, and also foreshadow the rest of the cycle and the Saga as a whole. Like his mother, Jacob possesses that rare and dangerous combination of deceitfulness and cunning, a combination that both serves him well and is the source of unending anxiety. Jacob is a "slick" character. In collusion with Rebekah, his deception of Isaac and theft of the patriarchal blessing introduce a tension that is maintained until near the end of the cycle (chap. 33). From now until his old age, Jacob will be both the deceiver and the deceived, and it will seldom be clear whether his reward is one of blessing or of curse.

The themes of nationhood and land appear in verses 27b –29a, 39–40. The language about the earth concerns agricultural fertility more than political geography, but the line about nations bowing down to Jacob clearly echoes the oracle of the prologue and refers to Israel as a people. The most obvious of the Pentateuchal themes here, though, is that of blessing and curse. At first sight, the story is about a human blessing belonging to the patriarch and at his disposal. The setting is similar to that of chapter 24 and identical to that of chapters 48—49 (*Jacob*'s deathbed blessing). Thus the patriarchal blessing is distinct from the divine blessing, which only Yahweh can grant. Or is it? Suspicion is aroused by Isaac's invoking God as the source of Jacob's blessing (vss. 27b, 28a). In addition, the last half of verse 29 sounds very much like 12:3: "Cursed be every one who curses you, and blessed be every one who blesses you!" Thus we are again left to wonder whether what has happened in this story is merely a result of human actions, or also an outcome of the divine oracle of the prologue. Finally, when we consider that the story is about blessing gained by deceit—a deceit which really *does* "mock" the patriarch and tear apart his family—we realize that the theme of responsibility is also involved. Thus the theological ambiguity of the story increases. A scoundrel has made himself heir to "the blessed of the Lord."

Unlike the gullible fool of the prologue, the Esau in chapter 27 is an innocent victim, and he reacts first with unconsolable despair and then with a consuming hatred for Jacob. Rebekah, who seems to be listening outside everyone's door, hears of Esau's plan to kill Jacob, and she urges Jacob to flee to her brother Laban until Esau's wrath subsides. Her tactic with Isaac is more devious. How dreadful it would be, she says, if Jacob were to marry one of those Hittite women, referring to Esau's wives (26:34–35). As if on cue, Isaac summons Jacob and dispatches him to Laban, admonishing him not to marry one of the Canaanite women (cf. chap. 24).

The dismissal scene has an ironic effect on Esau, who has done a little eavesdropping of his own. Realizing his father's disapproval of Canaanite wives, he marries a daughter of Ishmael! He who has sold his birthright and lost his father's blessing and, apparently, the special divine blessing as well, marries a daughter of the one who would share Abraham's blessing but not Yahweh's covenant. Esau never seems to make the right move, at least not yet, and there he is with his Ishmaelite wife, waiting for Jacob to return.

4. Departure (28:10–22)

This passage is the linchpin in the cycle and provides the most explicit connection to the wider literary context. Jacob is on his way to Haran (vs. 10), and has come to "a certain place" where he decides to spend the night (vs. 11). He has a dream in which Yahweh addresses him for the first time (vss. 12–15), though not as we might expect. Yahweh says nothing of Jacob's deception of Isaac, much less does he reprimand him. Instead, he introduces himself as the "God of Abraham your father and the God of Isaac," and immediately offers him the promises of land, offspring, and blessing, emphasizing again that the blessing will be one from which "all the families of the earth" will benefit. In addition, Yahweh promises something peculiarly fitting to Jacob's situation: "Behold, I am with you and will keep you wherever you go, and will bring you back to this land; for I will not leave you until I have done that of which I have spoken to you."

The Bethel story is to the Jacob cycle what the charge to Abram was to the Abraham cycle (12:1–3); it provides the foundation for the redactional unity of the narrative. In both passages the patriarchs stand at the threshold of a journey, but their points of origin and destination are reversed—Abram is leaving Mesopotamia for Canaan; Jacob is leaving Canaan for Mesopotamia. Jacob is going where Abraham forbade Isaac to go (24:6, 8), and is the only patriarch to court disaster by going East. Thus the threshold on which Jacob stands is fraught with danger, both behind and ahead. But the place on which he stands, or lies, is a threshold of a different order; it is "the gate of heaven" (vs. 17). Yahweh is here in this "awesome place." Bethel is both literally and figuratively an intersection of divine and human paths. Jacob is standing at a strange door which opens in three directions: behind is his past of failure and alienation; ahead is his future of both hope and uncertainty; and over above, coming down to meet him, is the presence of God.

The explicit *pledge* of divine presence and protection is distinctive to the Jacob cycle and indicates a concerted redactional effort. The cycle revolves around Jacob's journey from Bethel to Haran and back.[3] At crucial points the text will either reiterate the pledge of divine presence or refer back to 28:10–22. Thus the thresholds which shape Jacob's identity coincide with moments in which Yahweh discloses his own identity.

How shall we interpret the fact that a cheater has become Yahweh's beneficiary and the agent of Yahweh's purpose in the world? First we should remember that Yahweh's previous agents, Abraham and Sarah, Isaac and Rebekah, were hardly above reproach. For that matter, the portrait of Esau in the prologue did not display a very worthy candidate either. We would hardly want the promises in the hands of one who might give them up for a bowl of mush. At least, as Robert Alter has put it, Jacob is a character to whom destiny does not just happen—he knows how to make it happen.[4]

At the same time, the selection of Jacob represents the freedom of Yahweh, which has a revolutionary and creative dimension. As Northrop Frye suggests, "the deliberate choice of a younger son represents a divine intervention in human affairs, a vertical descent into the continuity [of normal succession] that breaks its pattern, but gives human life a new dimension by doing so."[5] The text, of course, does not speculate on these questions. As the rest of the cycle unfolds, it is interested only in how the two characters respond to their respective destinies. It is not interested so much in a doctrine of rewards and punishments as it is in a process of conversion that takes place over the course of Jacob's life. "Conversion" here does not connote an instantaneous and powerful emotional experience. It refers to a gradual development towards righteousness, a growth marked by setbacks as well as advances. The scoundrel will never become a saint, but he will become a character who has struggled with God.

Jacob's vow at Bethel is the beginning of his conversion. Already in response to Yahweh's appearance and promises, Jacob erects a commemorative monument, a tangible reference point for the future that lies ahead of him, and he pledges that it will be devoted to God. In response to the divine blessing, he vows a tithe.[6] Of course there is still something of the old bargainer in this vow, but Jacob is no longer simply the one who grasps blessing on his own; he is now also the one who receives blessing, promises, and protection as an undeserved gift. Thus "the central thought of the story" is this: God starts a dialogue with Jacob and Jacob succeeds in giving the absolutely adequate response . . . ."[7]

Those who remain impatient for Jacob to receive his just desserts will soon find themselves more than satisfied. Indeed, already Jacob's future lies before him with the hope for a new family, but he leaves behind a shattered family and a brother who waits for the day of reckoning. The one who bears the divine blessing also bears the scars of alienation. The country to which he is headed is the "old world," and the place he leaves behind is the "promised land."

5. Jacob and Laban (chaps. 29—31)

Jacob's arrival in Haran is described in terms of the convention of a meeting at a well, and his fortuitous introduction to Rachel reminds us of the servant's good fortune in finding Rebekah in chapter 24. The story portrays Jacob as someone who will make a good foreman, as he issues orders to the shepherds and gallantly uncovers the well for Rachel. Along with Jacob's natural abilities, the author also emphasizes his kinship ties with Rachel and Laban, for it is primarily on this basis that Laban welcomes Jacob into his household as "my bone and my flesh" (29:1–14). Jacob has found a new home and a new family.

After Jacob has worked six years for the hand of Rachel, the oracle of the prologue assumes an ironic twist. Jacob the trickster has met his match in Laban, a "selfish, greedy, exploiting, suspicious man of wealth, who never fails to observe good manners."[8] By exploiting a wedding custom, Laban substitutes the elder daughter for the younger, and thus "deceives" Jacob.[9] By the time that Jacob wins the hand of Rachel, fourteen years have passed (29:15–30).

The chronic problem of the matriarchs now frustrates Jacob's favoritism for the beautiful Rachel, for Yahweh opens Leah's womb, but Rachel is barren (30:1–24). The rejected older sister triumphs over the younger. But Rachel is not to be outdone. Like Sarah before her she offers Jacob her maid as a concubine, and through Bilhah Jacob fathers two more sons. Rachel's naming of the second son continues one of the central themes of the cycle and shows that she really is the perfect match for Jacob: "with mighty wrestlings I have wrestled with my sister, and have prevailed" (vs. 8).

Eventually the sisters trade Jacob back and forth enough to produce five more children, the last being Rachel's own Joseph: "May Yahweh add (to me another son)!" Jacob, on the other hand, has probably had enough. The point of all this is not to portray Jacob as the world's greatest lover. This frenetic sexual activity is clearly a manifestation of the divine blessing—there is no question that Jacob has been fertile and increased! In addition, Jacob's sons will become the twelve tribes of Israel, and the order of their birth and the identity of their mothers will continue the theme of younger over older to the end of the Saga. "Israel" has emerged out of the intense struggle between Rachel and Leah, just as "Israel" will emerge from the struggle between Jacob and God in chapter 32.

Having gained the family he had sought, Jacob is ready to return to Canaan (30:25–43). But Laban is reluctant to let go of such a prolific worker and son-in-law, and acknowledges that Yahweh has blessed him

because of Jacob. In all good faith (*tsidqati*, vs. 33) Jacob agrees to work
for Laban in exchange for a share in the herds, but Laban again tricks
him out of his earnings. Now it is Jacob's turn at the game of deception.
While his magical breeding methods would make Mendel smile, the results
are not amusing to Laban and his sons. To their dismay, Jacob "grew
exceedingly rich." Laban's greed for the blessing, and his unjust treatment
of the one who bears it, have produced his own financial ruin and alienated
him from Jacob and from his own daughters.

So far Yahweh has not been involved in the story overtly, except
for opening and closing wombs. Now in the midst of the rising tension
between Jacob and Laban, Yahweh intervenes, speaking to Jacob for the
first time since he left Canaan, and ordering him to return home with the
assurance that Yahweh will be with him (31:1–16).

The story of Jacob's flight stretches the tension in the unit to its
greatest degree (31:17–42). Laban is outraged because he has lost his
daughters and grandchildren, but also because Rachel has stolen his
"household gods," which represent legal title to his estate. "Stealing,"
already so prominent in the cycle, becomes a leitmotif in this climactic
section.[10]

Of course, Jacob does not know that Rachel has stolen the household gods, and thus when Laban searches for them in vain (thanks to
another savvy piece of deception by Rachel) Jacob's defense of himself
is ironic (vss. 36–42). Nevertheless, when Jacob credits his successful
escape to the presence of God, his statement is consistent with the divine
pledge at Bethel, and also with Laban's own encounter with God (vs. 24).

The unit now reaches its climax with a treaty ceremony (vss. 43–
55). The pursuit has produced a remarkable change in Laban. It is he who
initiates the treaty, in part, of course, out of desperation, but also out of
an unusual surge of paternal devotion. While he persists in his claim of
ownership of his family and property, he will resist any action which
would bring them harm (vs. 43). The terms of the treaty are intended to
protect the marital rights of his daughters, and Laban even invokes Yahweh as the witness and guarantor of the agreement (vss. 49–50). The unit
ends with a brief and touching scene of benediction, in which the old
rascal kisses his daughters and grandchildren, and leaves them with his
blessing.

The unit has also produced even more remarkable changes in the
character of Jacob. His closing speech to Laban may be ironic, but it is
not self-righteous. His opening words, "What is my offense? What is my
sin . . .?" are entirely appropriate in the context of the preceding story,
where Jacob has resorted to his former trickery only in self-defense (and
on the advice of angels, no less). Moreover, if what he now adds about
his past dealings with Laban is true (and we have no reason to doubt it),

Jacob appears to be a model of integrity. Despite his affluence, he has suffered a great deal, not only from the humiliation of *Laban*'s deceptions, but also from physical deprivations (vs. 40). Here his speech sounds like a psalm of the righteous protesting unjust treatment by enemies.[11] What a different Jacob this is from the one who left Canaan, the victim of his own dishonesty and pride.

Jacob's sojourn in Haran brought him a new family which soon encountered its own problems of deception and jealousy, but from this came a blessing and a renewed affirmation of communal harmony sealed by treaty. Jacob has "struggled with men and prevailed," and in his struggles God has indeed been with him. Now he stands at another threshold, one which will bring him face to face with Esau, and with God.

6. Jacob and Esau (chaps. 32—33)

"Jacob went on his way and the angels of God met him." The little bridge between the Jacob–Laban stories and the sequel to the Jacob–Esau stories is a masterpiece of rhetorical brevity and allusion (32:1–2). Together with the appearance of the angels at Bethel, the encounter forms a frame for the preceding unit. At the same time, the text serves as an introduction to the Jacob–Esau story which follows. The redactor has accomplished his purpose partly by the use of catchwords: here Jacob meets angels (literally "messengers"), and immediately afterwards he will send messengers to Esau (vs. 3); here he names the place Mahanaim (literally "Two Camps"), and soon he will divide his family and possessions into two camps (vs. 7). But the wider context is even more suggestive. The Hebrew for "meet" in verse 1 can have a neutral, positive, or negative connotation, but most frequently it refers to a hostile encounter.[12] The ambiguity is altogether appropriate, for while the preceding context would suggest that the angels are there to serve as Jacob's protective escort, before long Jacob will be wrestling with a divine *opponent*. He has struggled with Laban and now faces the possibility of a struggle with Esau, but first he will have to struggle with God.

Jacob's preparations for his reunion with Esau reveal two sides to his character that approach contradiction. On the one hand there is the old Jacob—shrewd, calculating, and cautious, he still thinks he can cope with his relationships by manipulation and barter. Thus he divides his "camp" and sends "presents" on ahead to Esau. Perhaps the one who sold his birthright for a bowl of pottage will be appeased by Jacob's generosity.

In a passage placed in between the report of these tactics, we see the other side of Jacob's character (vss. 9–12), one which had previously emerged in his impassioned speech to Laban in 31:36–42. In the midst of his frantic precautions, Jacob appeals for help to the one of Bethel who promised his presence and protection (vs. 12), and the one who summoned him home, promising to "do him good" (vs. 9). Jacob finally confesses what we have known all along: "I am not worthy of the least of all the loyalty and all the faithfulness which thou hast shown thy servant" (vs. 10). If there is a moment of righteousness in Jacob's life, it is surely here, where he acknowledges that the blessing he enjoys is not one he has earned, but the gift of a gracious God.

We do not have two Jacobs here; we have only the one man, at once calculating and contrite, an inextricable combination expressed by the position of Jacob's prayer in between his two precautionary maneuvers. First he plans, then he prays, then he plans again. Even in his planning there is irony, for the customarily courteous language in his messages to Esau ("my lord," "your servant") comes from the younger who will still be the master of the older (25:23).

With his planning and praying done, Jacob is left alone for the night, much as he was on that night so many years ago at Bethel. But there he was fleeing the wrath of his brother; now he is about to come face to face with him. "Face to face" is the appropriate phrase, for the author has sewn together the central sections of this unit with the catch-word "face" (*panim*). Especially when it refers to God, the word is often translated "presence," and thus suggests a major theme of the cycle—"I will be with you wherever you go." The "face" motif begins in verse 16, where Jacob instructs his servants to "pass on before me," that is, "to my face." Then come verses 20b–21 where the motif abounds: "For he thought, 'I may cover his face with the gift which is going to my face, and afterwards I shall see his face—perhaps he will lift up my face.' So the gift passed on to his face." While these verses obviously look ahead to Jacob's confrontation with Esau, they also tie that confrontation to the one that immediately follows. Before Jacob can face Esau, he must first face the mysterious "man" who wrestles with him in the night, and when that match is over Jacob names the place Penuel, "The face of God," and says, "For I have seen God face to face, and yet my life is preserved."

The interlacing of these passages prevents us from reading each of Jacob's encounters separately. It is as if the redactors were saying, "You may not interpret Jacob's wrestling with the divine being apart from his confrontation with Esau, and vice versa." The result is the same when we come to the latter (33:1–11), and we come to it as did Jacob—instantly. Although the effect is slightly weakened by the etiology in 32:32, Jacob has scarcely left Penuel when he looks up and sees Esau and his four hundred men. Reeling from "The Face of God" he turns toward the face of Esau. The connection is pursued when the two actually meet, and

Jacob says to Esau, "for truly to see your face is like seeing the face of God, with such favor have you received me" (33:10).

Seeing the face of his brother is like seeing the face of God. Jacob's simile also applies to the preceding story, only in reverse; seeing the face of God is like seeing the face of Esau. Whereas Jacob had every reason to expect his confrontation with Esau to be hostile, Esau came running to meet him with an embrace and a kiss (the very actions which Jacob had used to seal his deception of Isaac, 27:26). Esau acts like God. Whereas Jacob had every reason to expect that any new encounter with divine presence would be friendly, as it always had been, here God appears as an unrecognizable "man" who attacks Jacob like a nocturnal demon. God acts like Esau.

Part of the richness of the story is that it tells us absolutely nothing about the motivations of the characters. We do not know why God attacks Jacob, nor why Esau welcomes him. Such questions lead us only into a dark mystery. Indeed, the previous paragraph has already oversimplified things, for Jacob's painful struggle with the demonic opponent ends with a divine blessing, and the simile he applies to Esau is equally ambivalent; seeing the face of God is usually terrifying, or even fatal.[13] Yet for all of this ambiguity the heart of the story lies in the revelation of the identities of the characters, identities rendered in terms of their attitude toward blessing.

The most obvious change in identity occurs with Jacob, for he emerges from his nocturnal struggle with a new name, given by God; now he is "Israel," he who struggles with humans and God and prevails. Yet immediately the interpretation of the meaning of the name suggests that this is still "Jacob" as well, and the story bears this out, for Jacob *does* prevail over his opponent (vs. 25a). He is still one who grasps for blessing, who will literally pin the source of blessing to the ground until it releases its benefits to him—and he succeeds. But while he receives the blessing which he demands, it is a Pyrrhic victory, exacted at the cost of a permanent and disabling injury. He leaves "The Face of God," "limping because of his thigh."

The reverse of "grasping" takes place when Jacob meets Esau. Jacob tries to protect those dearest to him by placing Rachel and Joseph at the end of his entourage, while he goes in front. Now the younger brother bows down seven times to the ground before the elder. But all this posturing proves to be unnecessary, for before he can even explain it Esau has embraced the brother whom he had sworn to kill. The context suggests that Jacob now offers the gift he had sent before him, and when Esau refuses the gift, Jacob responds with the simile about the face of God. Then he presses the gift on Esau with an equally significant expression: "Accept, I beg you, my *blessing* (*birkati*) that is brought to you, because God has dealt graciously with me (*hannani*), and because I have enough" (vs. 11). Jacob does not simply offer a "present" (*minhah*, 32:13), he offers his blessing. This does not mean that he is now returning all that he had taken from Esau, for that blessing cannot be returned (27:33f.). But it does mean that Jacob here acknowledges the operation of divine grace in his life, and is willing to release his grip on the blessing he had so often grasped. Like Abraham, Jacob has been tested by God, and now acknowledges the divine blessing as an unmerited gift.

Jacob's release of his blessing marks the most dramatic conversion of his character up to this point, a process which we have traced from his initial vow at Bethel to his final speech to Laban and his prayer to Yahweh. But his conversion is not complete (true conversion rarely, if ever, is). Even as he releases the blessing he presses a gift on Esau, as if he cannot quite trust the sincerity of Esau's welcome. Similarly, in the sequel (vss. 12–17) Jacob's reluctance to travel with Esau or to accept an escort suggests his fear that his "favor" with Esau may run out, and in fact Jacob does not continue to Seir as he promises, but makes a permanent detour to Succoth.

Jacob is not the only one whose identity changes before our eyes in this story. There is also Esau, whom we last saw as an outraged victim, bent on murder, but who now appears as a loving brother. Even here we cannot be too sure of the extent of Esau's transformation, or, again, the motivations behind it. Why *does* he arrive with four hundred men? Is his welcome of Jacob a result of Jacob's gift and subservient attitude, or does it reveal an intrinsic spirit of forgiveness, or simply a case of time healing all wounds? Is his offer of an escort to Seir really an insidious form of "protective custody"? We do not know. All we do know is that he appears to Jacob like the face of God, and that in his hospitality to his brother— the one who bears the blessing of Abraham—he too receives a blessing (cf. chap. 36 below). Thus in the end the movement of the Jacob cycle is in a direction we could not have anticipated at the beginning; it is perhaps the most dramatic instance in the Pentateuch of the divine promise, "those who bless you, I will bless."

Finally, one more character appears in altered guise, the one who stands behind, as it were, "The Face of God." Who is this mysterious being who wrestles with Jacob in the night? All along we have treated this character as if he (or it) were transparently Yahweh, but is that the case? Is it really a "man," and not God (vs. 24)? Or is it a Hebrew troll who lurks by this river, waiting to devour passersby? In terms of the history of traditions, the character who appears here is probably a little of each of these. But Jacob's declaration at the end appears definitive—

he has seen God face to face. Unless we take this identification to be Jacob's alone, and not that of the author, the text affirms that Jacob's encounter at this threshold of his life is an encounter with God—the God of "Israel." Jacob has struggled with humans all along (Esau, Laban), but all along he has been heading for this struggle with God.

The text is nevertheless concerned to maintain the obscurity of this deity. With Jacob a new identity emerges from the struggle, which is at least revealed in a new name. But his antagonist refuses to reveal his name. At Bethel, Yahweh appeared to Jacob, introducing himself as the "God of Abraham your father and the God of Isaac." The God who now wrestles with Jacob remains nameless. Even as he appears face to face, he effaces himself. The character of God reveals a new dimension here, one deriving from the context of this story within the overall cycle; all along, God has appeared as Jacob's friend, even (and especially) when he did not deserve it. Now God appears as Jacob's enemy. Before he protected Jacob on his way; now Yahweh stands *in* his way. No doubt we would have expected it to be otherwise, for God to be an antagonist to the cheat and a protector to the penitent. But the fact that God is otherwise is precisely what is revealed about his identity.

Jacob has become Israel, he who struggles with God. Yahweh has become an ineffable power who struggles with Israel. The cycle which began with two brothers "crashing together" reaches its climax with Jacob and Yahweh fighting together. Here even God is one who struggles. Yahweh is now not only the one who tests those whom he blesses, but also the one who will fight with them and, if necessary, *wound* them in order to maintain his sovereign freedom. This is the same freedom out of which Yahweh granted his promises to Jacob at Bethel. If "Israel" means that Jacob "has struggled with God and with humans and prevailed", it also means "God rules."

7. Jacob in Shechem (chap. 34)

Along with the stories about Isaac and Abimelech, those about Jacob's relationships with Laban and Esau portray a movement from contention and hostility to reconciliation, and with Abimelech and Laban the resolution is sealed by a covenant. The story about Jacob and the city of Shechem represents an antitype to that pattern, especially in contrast to its structural counterpart in the Isaac stories, where the subject is also that of relationships with the native inhabitants rather than kinfolk.

Jacob's sons make their first appearance here as full-fledged characters, and they do not get off to a very good start. In the end they are more guilty of "folly" than the young man Shechem, and they make

Jacob odious to the Canaanites. At the same time, the significance of the story transcends the relationships between the characters as individuals, extending to the social and political relations between Israel as a people and Shechem as a city representing Canaanites in general. The text itself moves in this direction when the potential union of Shechem and Dinah becomes a precedent for further intermarriage (vss. 9–10, 20–24). From the perspective of the Shechemites, the motivation for intermarriage goes beyond Shechem's love for Dinah to include the possibility of benefitting from the wealth of the family of Jacob (vs. 23a). At the same time the arrangement would benefit Jacob by extending his privilege of residing in the land and obtaining property, thereby improving his status as a resident alien (vs. 10). Indeed, both parties agree that intermarriage would lead to the formation of "one people" (vss. 16, 22).

In the context of the Pentateuchal narrative the story takes on far greater significance, therefore, than it would if we read it by itself or even within the confines of the Jacob cycle. In the wider context, the story involves the central themes of the Pentateuchal narrative: blessing, nationhood, progeny, and land. Will Israel become a great nation by becoming "one people" with the Canaanite population? Will they gain possession of the land by intermarriage (vs. 10)?[14] Throughout the Pentateuchal narrative the answer to such questions is always a resounding no.

The irony, of course, is that Jacob's sons rightly reject the Canaanite offer of marriage, but for the wrong reasons, and with irresponsible tactics. For Jacob's sons only the family name is at stake, even at the expense of what might be Dinah's best interests. Their goal is not reconciliation or even just retribution but cold-blooded revenge, and their method is one that reverberates throughout the cycle: "deception" (vs. 13). Rather than resolving their differences with the Shechemites by means of covenant, or simply withdrawing from the scene, Jacob's sons exploit the *sign* of the covenant between God and Israel (circumcision) as a device for trickery and bloodshed.[15] Rather than coming to peaceful terms (cf. 26:29–31) they pretend to be peaceful (34:21) in order to wage war. If this is the way of Jacob's sons, it does not augur well for the way of Israel.

8. The Return to Bethel (35:1–15)

Although Jacob never lived in Bethel, when he returns to this place he comes home, and the Jacob cycle comes to its end. The material which follows the story of his return to Bethel is not, however, insignificant (35:16—36:43). It reports the birth of Benjamin, Jacob's second son by Rachel, and Rachel's death. It reports Reuben's sexual misconduct with

Bilhah, Jacob's concubine, followed immediately by a complete list of Jacob's sons. With the juxtaposition of the birth of Jacob's last son and the explicit reference to Reuben as Jacob's firstborn, this section repeats the continuing theme of younger over older brothers and foreshadows the Joseph narrative.[16] Finally, the material reports the death of Isaac, his burial by Jacob and Esau, and "the descendants of Esau, that is Edom" (chap. 36). The latter has its structural counterpart in the Ishmaelite notice in 25:12–18. In its present context it emphasizes the Canaanite origin of Esau's wives, Esau's withdrawal from Canaan to Seir (because the land cannot bear both his and Jacob's possessions, cf. 13:2–12), and his numerous descendants. Though he lives apart from the line of Jacob, his younger brother, and away from the land of Canaan, Esau too has been blessed. He becomes the father of a multitude of peoples, and kings come forth from him (cf. 17:20).

As we have seen, Jacob's departure from and return to Bethel provide the main structural pillars of the cycle. Appropriately, his return takes the form of a pilgrimage, including an initial ritual of purification (vs. 2), a summons to "go up" to Bethel (vs. 3a), and a vow to construct an altar in gratitude for God's continual presence with him (vs. 3b).[17] Although there is no reference to the formal vow that Jacob swore previously (28:20–22), his return clearly functions as the consummation of his original encounter at Bethel. In fact the unusual number of allusions to previous stories in the cycle suggests that the author constructed this passage as a conclusion.[18]

In the immediate context Jacob makes his pilgrimage to Bethel in response to a divine command (cf. vss. 1, 7), and as a result he receives the reward for which all pilgrims fervently hope—a new appearance of God at the shrine, and a blessing (vss. 9–15).[19] But the primary function of the passage in its wider context is not simply to reiterate the divine blessing and promises, but to have them pronounced on *Israel*, that is, on the character who has changed so dramatically since the original encounter at Bethel. The significant *position* of the text thus resembles that of chapter 22 (the testing of Abraham). The one who receives the blessing and promises now is not the scoundrel and cheater, fleeing from the wrath of his brother, but the penitential pilgrim, responding to the call of God.

The Jacob cycle represents a journey with numerous dimensions: geographical, psychological, and religious; individual and communal; human and divine. It is a journey during which Jacob spent a major portion of his life "beyond the Jordan," away from the land of promise, just as he will spend the end of his days in the land of Egypt. The essential movement of the story, however, has gone from the "House of God" to exile and back to the "House of God," and at each of the major turning points of this journey from Bethel to Bethel, God has fulfilled his promise to be with Jacob. Now Jacob has fulfilled *his* vow. The pilgrim has come home to consecrate that place that represents the center of his life. As with Abraham, God has said, "Go to the land that I will show you," and Israel has obeyed.

THE JOSEPH CYCLE (37:1—50:26)

1. The Dreamer (chap. 37)

Much of what happens in this story will remind us of the bitter proverb coined in the situation of Israel's later exile: "The fathers have eaten sour grapes, and the children's teeth are set on edge" (Ezek. 18:2). Like his father, Jacob favors one son above all. At first it is Joseph, and later his younger brother Benjamin—Jacob's two youngest, and the only sons of his beloved Rachel. Jacob's special love for Joseph produces a deep jealousy among his brothers, and they seize on the first opportunity to get rid of this favorite son. But while they can rid themselves of Joseph, they cannot dispel Jacob's love for him, and the opening story concludes with Jacob's insistence that he will spend the rest of his days in mourning.

Jacob's obsession for the sons of Rachel thus sets the plot in motion, but it is not the only factor involved. While it is not Joseph's fault that he is the object of his father's exclusive devotion, he does little to ingratiate himself to his brothers. In fact, even before the author tells us of Jacob's dotage we learn that Joseph has "brought a bad report" about his brothers' work (vs. 2). Joseph is a tattletale. He is also a prolific dreamer who doesn't realize that some dreams are best kept to himself. Instead he taunts his brothers with the prospect of their bowing down before him, and it is not until his father appears as one of his subjects that Jacob at last rebukes him. In adaptations of the Joseph narrative for children, interpreters often portray the adolescent protagonist as a model of virtue when, in fact, he is a Mr. Goody-Two-Shoes whom almost anyone would want to throw into a pit.

The central theme of family tension that runs throughout the cycle is associated with a cluster of words and motifs introduced in the opening chapter. Many of these had already become central to the larger story of Jacob when he "crashed against" Esau in his mother's womb (25:22–23): rivalry between siblings, subservience of the older to the younger, hatred and jealousy, and, above all, deception. Just as Jacob had used clothing to deceive Isaac, so his sons use clothing to deceive him (Joseph's bloody coat). Moreover, the motif of "recognition" which figures in the latter scene will recur in the following story of Judah and Tamar, and again much later when the brothers appear before Joseph in Pharaoh's court.[1] In addition the motif of buying and selling runs through the cycle, beginning with the sale of Joseph to the caravan bound for Egypt.

In many ways, therefore, the Joseph cycle continues the family feud which began with the Jacob cycle. Yet within the context of the Pentateuchal narrative the story also concerns the survival of Yahweh's blessing on this family, and through them, the fate of the world.

2. Judah and Tamar (chap. 38)

The following story about Judah and his daughter-in-law, Tamar (chap. 38), immediately interrupts the plot.[2] The story covers at least fifteen or twenty years in the life of Judah, but does not even mention Joseph. Interpreters have thus often ignored its contextual significance. The story clearly illustrates the problems which arise when a member of Jacob's family marries a Canaanite (contrast chap. 24; 28:1; chap. 34). But there are closer associations as well. Judah has just joined in the selling of his brother as a slave, and now we find him buying his daughter-in-law as a prostitute. Both he and Tamar are masters at the favorite family game of deception. First Judah withholds his third son from Tamar, breaking his ambiguous promise (vss. 11, 14b). Then Tamar deceives Judah by disguising herself so that he cannot recognize her, and by securing his signet, which he can "recognize" (nkr, vss. 25–26, cf. 37:32–33). Decked out in her whore's veil, Tamar could easily have upstaged Jacob in his goatskin sleeves.

It is all a messy affair, but why is it here? First, the story continues the motif of the first-born, so prominent in the larger Jacob story. Judah's first-born son is wicked, and Yahweh kills him. Judah's second son refuses to fulfil his obligation to continue the "seed" of his brother, and Yahweh kills him also. The characterization of Yahweh is hardly attractive, but a fundamental issue is at stake; Onan balks at his proper responsibility in the continuation of the divine blessing, "be fertile and increase," and his refusal is more active but no more effective than Judah's withholding of the third brother. Moreover, while Judah is not Jacob's first-born, he is destined for preeminence over the later twelve tribes, as the "Blessing of Jacob" will make clear in 49:8–12. Indeed, one of the *twin* sons of Tamar—Perez, the *younger*—founds the line which leads to David, himself the founder of the kingdom of Judah (Ruth 4:18–22). Again we hear ironic echoes of the earlier oracle to Rebekah.

But the story has a more immediate significance in connection with chapter 39. In the latter Joseph falls prey to the treachery of a temptress (the wife of his master, Potiphar), not because he accepts her sexual proposition, but because he refuses her. Thus the incontinence of Judah functions as a foil for the integrity of Joseph.[3] At the same time, Judah stands in contrast to Tamar who, he says, "is more righteous than I" (vs. 26). The Canaanite woman who married into the family of Jacob and resorted to prostitution to continue the family line deserves the status of ancestor of "Israel" more than does Israel's son.

3. Joseph's Rise to Power (chaps. 39—41)

So far there has been no reference to divine involvement in the story of Joseph. There will be no dramatic interventions, numinous manifestations, or even direct communications between God and Joseph. But from the moment Joseph arrives as a slave at the house of Potiphar to the day of his death as the viceroy of Egypt, Joseph's life is marked by Yahweh's blessing and guided by Yahweh's invisible presence. In chapter 39 the author tells us of Yahweh's presence at two crucial junctures. First, as an introduction to the initial story of Joseph's experiences in Potiphar's household, we learn that "Yahweh was with Joseph, and he became a successful man." As often elsewhere, "success" or "prosperity" is a manifestation of divine blessing. Everything that Joseph touches turns to gold, including the business of Potiphar. Like others before him (Abimelech, Laban), Potiphar quickly appreciates what a find he has made, and he promotes Joseph to the position of chief of staff. Unfortunately for Joseph, Potiphar's wife has additional duties in mind for the handsome servant. When Joseph rejects her proposition she maliciously accuses him of attempted rape, and Joseph lands in prison. At this critical juncture the author immediately assures us again that "Yahweh was with Joseph," extending him "faithfulness" (*hesed*) and "ingratiating" him to the prison warden (vs. 21). As a result, the warden promotes Joseph to the position of chief of trusties, and again everything that Joseph does "Yahweh prospers" (vs. 23).

In addition to the theme of blessing, chapter 39 concerns the theme of responsibility and raises a question about Joseph's identity. Joseph's rejection of Potiphar's wife (vs. 9) suggests that the blessing of God and the favorable treatment by Potiphar have produced a sense of commitment and loyalty—in a word, a sense of righteousness. But who is this Joseph, an alien and a prisoner, separated from his family and his native land? Will he maintain his identity as one of the "children of Israel," or will he remain in the limbo status of an alien, or will he become an Egyptian? At this point the only answer comes in the form of Potiphar's wife's categorization of Joseph as a "Hebrew," a categorization which here appears derogatory (vss. 14, 17).[4]

In the next two episodes (chaps. 40—41) Joseph moves from the prison to Pharaoh's palace. Here too his success is the result of divine guidance, though not expressed as Yahweh's being "with him." Joseph is no longer the starry-eyed dreamer; he is an *interpreter* of dreams who could rival any Jungian analyst. Indeed, his reading of dreams goes far beyond the psychological meaning. For Joseph, every dream becomes a crystal ball disclosing the future. When the butler and baker lament their lack of an interpreter, Joseph gives a stunning reply: "Do not interpretations belong to God? Tell them to *me*, if you please!" (vs. 8). The apparent presumptuousness in this response is soon dispelled not only by the accuracy of Joseph's predictions, but also by his subsequent acknowledgment that his skill is a divine gift (41:15–16, 25). Even Pharaoh is so impressed with Joseph's interpretation that he extols the divine origin of his skill: "Can we find such a man as this, in whom is the Spirit of God?" (vs. 38).

While the story thus emphasizes Joseph's reliance on God for his success, it also brings out an inherent resourcefulness in his character that complements the divine gift. Having contrived an audience with Pharaoh (40:14), Joseph adds his *own* advice to the interpretation of Pharaoh's dream. If God has revealed the disaster which is about to happen, Joseph will provide the administrative actions which will circumvent the problem (vss. 33–36). The prophet is also a politician. Rarely has the power of suggestion been so potent, and Pharaoh's response seems virtually predetermined: "Since God has shown you all this, there is none so discreet and wise as you are; *you* shall be over my house!" (vss. 39–40a).

But Joseph's remarkable rise to power raises anew the question about his identity. Almost half of his life has been spent in Egypt (41:46), and now he wears the signet ring of Pharaoh himself. Indeed, Pharaoh has also given him a new name—an *Egyptian* name—as unrecognizable as is Joseph himself: Zaphenathpaneah. Does a new identity accompany the new name? Is Joseph now the "favorite son" of Egypt? So it would seem, for Joseph not only marries an Egyptian (and the daughter of an Egyptian priest, nonetheless), but also names his first son Manasseh, meaning "God has made me forget all my hardship, *and all my father's house*" (vs. 51).

4. Joseph and His Brothers (chaps. 42—44)

Almost every section of these chapters contains an ironic allusion or connection to the preceding chapters. At the outset, Joseph has not seen his family for at least twenty-five years. He is now second in command over all of Egypt, and controls the food supply for the entire world. The author has tied chapters 41 and 42 together with the motif of buying and selling. The Hebrew root *sbr* provides the basis for "grain," "buy (grain)," and "sell (grain)" (41:57—42:6). Thus those who sold their brother into slavery come to him (unknowingly) to buy grain. This ironic reversal constitutes the primary level on which the plot will develop until chapter 45. The opening paragraph (42:1–5) also contains a new motif that will become increasingly significant as the narrative progresses. Jacob orders his sons to go to Egypt for grain, "that we may live, and not die" (vs. 2). Here his remark is limited to physical survival, but as the story progresses "live and not die" will come to signify the second level of the plot—the survival of God's purpose for the world.

The rest of chapter 42 portrays Joseph's first meeting with his brothers when they "bowed themselves before him with their faces to the ground." Joseph's adolescent dreams finally have come true—and yet again, they have not. Throughout this unit the brothers will "bow down" to Joseph in one way or another many times, but *they* do not know that this is Joseph. They are bowing down before Zaphenathpaneah.

Joseph's reaction is not what we might expect. He does not tell them who he really is, and thereby fully savor his victory. Joseph recognizes them (*nakar*), but he plays the role of a foreigner (*hitnakker*)— and the author plays with words. Joseph assumes the identity of an Egyptian, speaking to them only through an interpreter (cf. vs. 23). Here arises a puzzle that we can solve only as we move through the entire unit. Why does Joseph not immediately disclose his identity, embrace his brothers, and summon his father and Benjamin to Egypt? That is what he will do in the end (chap. 45), so why prolong the reunion? Why, at the very moment when Joseph remembers his old dreams, does he devise a false accusation that the brothers are spies (vs. 9)? What motivation stands behind this deception of his brothers, a deception he pursues with increasingly relentless cruelty?

The first clue comes when Joseph tells his brothers that he wants to "test" their claim to have a younger brother at home (vs. 16), although he knows full well the truth of their story. Even a confession of guilt, which is precisely what Joseph hears when his brothers say "In truth, we are guilty concerning our brother" (vs. 21), does not satisfy him. Of course, when he hears this (unbeknownst to them) he is overcome with remorse, and must leave the room to weep, a gesture he will repeat (43:30). Apparently his brothers' words have met part of the larger test Joseph has in mind, but not all, for immediately Joseph returns and gives orders to his servants which will bring his brothers even greater dismay.

At this point the most obvious motivation behind Joseph's actions would be revenge: he wants to make his brothers suffer for what they have done to him, and that certainly happens. But when he demands that his brothers bring Benjamin to Egypt, he must surely know what agony this will cause his father as well. Indeed, *we* have known from the outset Jacob's deep fear that something might happen to Benjamin (42:4). Joseph would know this too, for he and Benjamin are the favorite sons, the only children of Rachel. This, in fact, is the essence of the following scene in Canaan (vss. 29–38). When Jacob hears the ultimatum that Benjamin must go to Egypt, or there will be no more grain and Simeon will remain enslaved, his refusal is adamant. Even when Reuben, the most innocent of the brothers, offers the life of his own sons if he does not bring Benjamin back, Jacob refuses to listen.

Thus if Joseph's ruse is a test of his brothers, it is also and even more so a test of Jacob. The deepest significance of this situation derives from the larger story of Jacob and, indeed, the Ancestral Saga as a whole. The old deceiver is deceived again, and by his own son, his favorite son. "He who struggles with God" must struggle again. Like Abraham, Jacob's character is now probed at its most vulnerable spot—his love for Benjamin, who is in effect his son, his only son, whom he loves (42:36; cf. 22:2). In order for the *family* to survive, Jacob must be willing to risk the life of Benjamin. If "Israel" is to "live and not die," Jacob must give up the one whom he holds most dear.

Jacob is in no hurry to take this test. Not until his family is again facing starvation does he raise the question of another trip to Egypt (with poor Simeon, the "other brother," languishing in prison all the while; cf. 43:14). When Judah reminds him of the demand for Benjamin, Jacob upbraids him for disclosing Benjamin's existence. It is only when Judah offers himself as a "pledge," as the one who will "bear the blame forever" if Benjamin were to die, that Jacob rises above his obsession and grudgingly agrees to the ultimatum. His response to Judah is characteristic. If it must be so, he says, then let's send a "present" (*minhah*) to the Egyptian. Jacob is ever the strategist (cf. Esau, 32:13–21). First he plans, then he prays: "May God Almighty grant you mercy before the man" (vss. 11–15).

Judah's brief speech (vss. 8–10) deserves further attention. His words contain a gesture that goes beyond an expression of guilt, for here Judah offers himself as a "pledge" for Benjamin's safety, thus placing himself in jeopardy for the sake of the family, "that we may live and not die, both we and you and also our little ones." What a different Judah this is from the one who suggested selling Joseph to the Ishmaelites. And what a change in character for the one who, out of fear, refused to allow his son to continue the family "seed" (chap. 38).[5]

Judah's offer of himself as security for Benjamin, and Jacob's willingness to release Benjamin represent the turning point in that portion of the narrative set in Canaan. In both these gestures the characters tear off the shackles that have bound this family in jealousy, guilt, and despair for over twenty-five years. The characters themselves are not aware of what has happened, anxious as they are over the outcome of their decisions. But when the one, in effect, embraces Benjamin as a true brother, and the other gives him up as his "only" son, the family of Israel begins a process of healing and reconciliation.

Joseph, of course, knows nothing of what has happened in Canaan, except that Jacob has agreed to send Benjamin. The final episode in this unit (43:16—44:34) thus focuses on the relationship of the brothers. When they return to Joseph's house, the steward abruptly dismisses the issue of the money in their sacks, and announces that the brothers will dine with Joseph (43:32–34). The seating is arranged in three sections: Egyptians, Hebrews, and Joseph, since, for the Egyptians, it is an "abomination" to eat with a Hebrew. No doubt there was a sign on one table saying "EGYPTIANS ONLY." But where does that leave Joseph? In the middle. He is a man without a community. He is Zaphenathpaneah, but not an Egyptian; he is Joseph, but no longer identified as a Hebrew as before (39:14, 17; 41:12). His family does not recognize him, and in fact assumes he is dead, and he has not identified himself with them. In short, Joseph is a man whose identity is wrapped up in two separate narratives, or in what *were* two separate narratives, for the two have now collided. Like his father, Joseph must struggle with the conflicting stories which make up his life. What character will emerge from this collision? At this point we do not know, and Joseph may not know either.[6]

The seating of Joseph's brothers also represents the conflict within the family that has so disrupted their lives. On the one hand, the brothers are seated in strict order of succession, but when the meal is served, Benjamin receives five times as much as his brothers! The banquet thus reflects a critical stage both in Joseph's identity and in the identity of the brothers. They wine and dine merrily in Joseph's house, but on the way home will they throw Benjamin into a pit?

The banquet scene leads to the climactic episode in the unit (chap. 44). No sooner is the banquet over than Joseph orders what will be the final test of his brothers. Again he returns their money to their sacks, and now he has his silver divining cup placed in the sack of Benjamin. The brothers depart for Canaan, no doubt with a great sense of relief that their dangerous mission is over. But Joseph's steward quickly overtakes them and accuses them of stealing the cup. The brothers rightly profess their innocence, backed up by a rash vow: if the cup is found all of them will become slaves and the one who has the cup will die. Both the steward and later Joseph mollify this vow (only the guilty one will become a slave), but this modification hardly lessens the brothers' dismay when the steward opens their sacks—"beginning with the eldest and ending with the youngest"—and finds the cup in Benjamin's sack.

The brothers must now confront Joseph one more time. As in the preceding scene in Canaan, Judah emerges as the spokesman and confesses their culpability: "God has found out the guilt of your servants" (vs. 16). But what guilt is this? Surely it is not the theft of the cup. Rather, Judah seems to express their corporate guilt in the "theft" of Joseph (40:15; cf. 42:21–22), a theft of which Benjamin, of course, is innocent. But Joseph insists that only Benjamin will become his slave, while the others can go home "in peace" to their father.

At this critical moment, Judah delivers a long and impassioned speech that concludes, "Now therefore, let your servant, I beg you, remain instead of the lad as a slave to my lord; and let the lad go back with his brothers." Here Judah has made the definitive gesture that reveals the transformation of his character. He has made good on his pledge to his father. He has offered his own life for the life of his brother, and not just any brother, but Benjamin, the favorite son. At the same time, he has voluntarily (but still unknowingly) offered himself as a slave to Joseph, thus fulfilling Joseph's dreams of long ago. The irony of this transformation is evident when we compare the last words of his speech to that opening scene where Judah and his brothers sent the bloody coat to Jacob: "How can I go back to my father if the lad is not with me? I fear to see the evil that would come upon my father."

5. Reunion (45:1—47:27)

Should we condemn Joseph himself as the perpetrator of unnecessary anguish within his family, or does the end justify the means? Certainly Joseph's tactics are not beyond question, but if his objective was to determine whether or not there had been a change in his brothers—and father—the test he devised was as successful as it was tortuous. All that he has heard and seen from them he has observed as if from behind a see-through mirror. Jacob has given up Benjamin, the brothers have confessed their guilt, and Judah has offered himself as a slave—all to Zaphenathpaneah, the viceroy of Egypt, and not to Joseph. If it had been otherwise, if Joseph had immediately disclosed himself to his brothers and they had professed their guilt and repentance for their wrong to him, would he really know if their repentance was genuine? Or, for that matter, would *we*?

Another significant factor in deciphering Joseph's motivations appears when he reveals himself to his brothers (45:1–15). Once he has told them who he is, Joseph does not demand an apology for their former acts, nor does he insist that they bow down before him *as Joseph*. Instead, he immediately absolves them of their guilt. Apparently he is not interested in personal vindication. From here on he will treat his brothers magnanimously and perhaps condescendingly; and he will continue to favor Benjamin (45:22), but he will not be to the others as a lord to servants. He will be their brother.

Judah's gesture has thus revealed not only his own character, but also that of Joseph. At last Zaphenathpaneah *is* Joseph. The arrangement of the characters on the stage, as it were, already suggests Joseph's confirmation of his "Israelite" identity; he removes all the Egyptians from the room before speaking those definitive words to his brothers (for the first time, in their common language)—"I am Joseph." When Joseph embraces his brothers, he also embraces who he has always been—a Hebrew—in the context of who he is—the Egyptian viceroy. Joseph reaffirms his identity within his family, and thus within the larger story in which this family plays the central role.

At the same time that Joseph reaffirms his identity as one of the children of Israel, he also recognizes that his personal identity is relatively unimportant when compared to his role as an agent within the story of "Israel." For the first time in the cycle, Joseph's words provide an explicit statement of the theological purpose that has been at work throughout the narrative. When the author told us earlier that God was "with" Joseph, he did not tell us why. Now Joseph says God was with him, not simply to make him "a successful man" (39:2) and eventually "lord of all Egypt" (45:9). Much more was at stake than his own rise from rags to riches: "For God sent me before you to preserve life. . . , to preserve for you a remnant in the land, and to hold open for you a great escape" (vss. 5, 7).[7] The key word here is "sent." We knew that Joseph had been bought and sold, thrown into prison, and exalted to power, but we did not know he was on a *mission*, much less a mission of God.

Joseph's statement reminds us of the oracle that began the Jacob cycle. Who are the real "actors" here? Joseph's statement suggests it is God alone: "It was not you who sent me here, but God," (vs. 8). But when we look at the narrative as a whole it is clearly both God and humans, and their actions are inseparable.

> The human figures in the large biblical landscape act as free agents out of the impulses of a memorable and often fiercely assertive individuality, but the actions they perform all ultimately fall into the symmetries and recurrences of God's comprehensive design. Finally, it is the inescapable tension between human freedom and divine historical plan that is brought forth so luminously through the pervasive repetitions of the Bible's narrative art.[8]

At this point we, the readers, have every right to ask the viceroy of Egypt a question he might find embarrassing: How do you know all this?

By what authority do you claim a divine mission, and how can we know if your claim is true? After all, one of the most distinctive features of the Joseph cycle is that God *never* appears to Joseph or talks with him; much less does God inform Joseph of his role in a divine plan. A redactor has provided his own answer in the form of a divine speech to *Jacob,* the first such speech since we left the Jacob cycle (46:1–4). By this time Joseph has sent word to his father that he is alive and that Jacob should bring all his family and possessions to Egypt. Jacob is at the final threshold in his life (45:28). What happens now will determine not only his own limited future, but also the future of his family, "the children of Israel" (46:5). As Jacob leaves the land of Canaan, which he will never see again, he stops at Beersheba to offer a sacrifice. It is significant that he goes there, and not to Bethel, for in doing so Jacob invokes a heritage and a God which transcends his own life—"the God of his father Isaac" (vs. 1). His gesture almost seems a farewell to this God, as well as to the land of his ancestors.

Now at this threshold God speaks to him in another nocturnal vision and assures him that he will not go down to Egypt alone: "I am God, the God of your father. Do not be afraid to go down to Egypt, for I will there make of you a great nation. I will go down with you to Egypt, and I will indeed bring you up, and Joseph's hand shall close your eyes." Though Jacob is not at Bethel, the God of Bethel who went with him to Haran is still with him wherever he goes, even into Egypt. The speech thus serves as a divine confirmation of *Joseph's* theological interpretation of all that has happened to this family. It also explicitly extends the significance of this story to include the entire Ancestral Saga, for as Jacob departs for Egypt God repeats the ancient promise to Abram (12:2), adding a very important little word: "I will *there* make of you a great nation."

What an enormous shift this statement represents. God's promise to Abram was a new initiative, a new way out of the old world of the Primeval cycle. That new way led to Canaan, and now, near the end of the Ancestral Saga, it leads to Egypt. From this point the function of the Joseph narrative as a bridge between the Abraham and Jacob cycles and the book of Exodus becomes increasingly clear. From the beginning, of course, Jacob has been both an individual character and the corporate personality "Israel"; both are present in God's speech. When God says he will go down with Jacob to Egypt, we think of the individual, but when God says he will "indeed bring you up" we think of Israel the nation and the story of the exodus.[9] The following genealogical material points in the same direction. In fact, the opening line ("now these are the names of the descendants of Israel who came into Egypt") has its exact parallel in the opening sentence of the book of Exodus.

Joseph now develops another ingenious ploy whereby his family gains "a possession in the land of Egypt" apart from the Egyptians (47:11).

The plan is another step in Joseph's reaffirmation of his Hebrew identity, as well as a clear manifestation of the blessing that accrues to the family of Jacob, who now enjoys "the fat of the land" (45:18; cf. 27:28). Of course, the blessing extends to the Egyptians, who will also "live and not die" (47:19), an extension beautifully symbolized when Jacob pronounces his blessing on the Pharaoh (47:7, 10). He who first sent his sons to beg now comes to bless.

Nevertheless the blessing, first pronounced at creation, continues to be fraught with irony. The family of the one who came to Egypt as a slave has become an independent community that owns land, while the native Egyptians have become landless slaves (47:13–26). "So Israel dwelt in the land of Egypt, in the land of Goshen, and they gained possessions in it, and were fertile and increased exceedingly" (vs. 27).

6. The Blessing of Jacob (47:28—50:26)

The deathbed scene that governs all of chapters 48—49 reminds us of its counterpart in chapters 24 and 27 (Abraham and Isaac). In particular, the latter again assumes an ironic significance in the life of Jacob. What Jacob had done to his father (reversing the order of blessing), he now does to his grandsons, exalting the younger (Ephraim) over the older (Manasseh). The old favoritism for the children of Rachel again comes to the fore (vs. 7). But here and in the extended blessing of all the sons in chapter 49, the narrative significance of the characters gives way to sociological and historical concerns.

In terms of the plot of the Joseph cycle, the reconciliation within the family is completed in 50:15–21. In a final fulfilment of Joseph's dreams, his brothers fall down before him and exclaim, "we are your servants." Indeed, this is the first time they have bowed down to Joseph *as Joseph*. Joseph meets their humility with his own: "Fear not, for am I in the place of God?" This maturity in his sibling relationships is matched by the theological maturity with which he views all that has happened: "you meant it for evil against me, but God meant it for good, to bring it about that many people should be kept alive" (vs. 20).

This unit, which opened with Jacob on his deathbed, closes with Joseph on his, and with Joseph's death. Perhaps the most significant part of Jacob's deathbed statement was not his last will and testament (his "blessing"), but his testimony to Joseph: "God Almighty appeared to me at Luz [= Bethel] in the land of Canaan and blessed me, and said to me, 'Behold, I will make you fertile, and multiply you, and I will make of you a company of peoples, and will give this land to your descendants after you for an everlasting possession'" (48:3–4).[10] Reciting the definitive experience of his life, Jacob transmits the fundamental religious heritage of the ancestors, much as Isaac transmitted it to him (28:3–4). Since the tradition does not include a scene in which *God* delivers the promises to one of Jacob's sons, Jacob's own testimony is the only way the knowledge of those promises can continue. Within the Ancestral Saga, Jacob is the last "eyewitness" to the direct disclosure of the divine will. As he approaches the ultimate threshold of death, he also approaches the moment of his greatest responsibility, which is precisely to testify to that disclosure for all generations to come.

When Jacob assumes the responsibility of telling this story, the process of conversion transforming his identity is complete: he is now Israel, the father of his people. And Israel *is* this story—past, present, *and* future. Indeed, it is only because of Jacob's testimony that Joseph can transmit the legacy of the ancestors from *his* deathbed: "God will visit you, and bring you up out of this land to the land which he swore to Abraham, Isaac, and Jacob" (50:24; cf. 48:21). This is the first and only time Joseph refers to the divine promises. They are promises he has never heard directly from God. Thus his trust in these promises—and in the God who stands behind them—is perhaps the most exemplary in the entire Ancestral Saga, for in order to trust in God, Joseph must also trust in the "witness" to God.

We can now see in retrospect how crucial Yahweh's "oath" to Abraham in chapter 22 is to the redactional unity of the Ancestral Saga. The oath is repeated at critical moments throughout the narrative, in each case at the transition from one generation to another (24:7; 26:3; 50:24). In the last occurrence Joseph's final words also connect the oath to the exodus tradition, which is soon to unfold (cf. Exod. 3:7–8).[11] The Saga ends with the bones of Joseph resting "in a coffin in Egypt," but the vision of the characters is already directed toward another horizon.

> [Yahweh] established a testimony in Jacob,
>   and appointed *torah* in Israel,
> which he commanded our ancestors
>   to teach their children;
> that the next generation might know them,
>   the children yet unborn,
> and arise and tell them to their children,
>   so that they should set their hope in God. (Ps. 78:5–7a)

II
EXODUS—
Yahweh Reigns Forever

Introduction

The most important factor in our interpretation of Exodus is the way the text itself forces us to read it as a unity. The traditioning process has accomplished this by collecting all the material together within one "book" that renders a narrative without any major divisions. It has also accomplished this unity by a number of critical references both prospective and retrospective. For example, Moses' initial encounter with Yahweh, the God of the ancestors, occurs at "the mountain of God," and in his commission he is told that the most significant confirmation of his selection as Israel's deliverer will be when he and all Israel come back to this mountain to "serve God" (3:1, 12). The goal of chapters 1—15 is not simply escape from Egyptian servitude; it is servitude to Yahweh by the covenant community constituted at Mt. Sinai (chaps. 19—40). Similarly, the opening words of Yahweh's revelation of the *law* at Mt. Sinai are predicated on the preceding *story* and incomprehensible without that predication: "I am Yahweh your God, who brought you out of the land of Egypt, out of the house of bondage" (20:2). Finally, at the end of the book (40:34–38) the tabernacle is erected and at once infused with the theophanic cloud of Yahweh's presence, continuing a theme that began with the "exodus" (13:21–22) and continued at Sinai (19:9; 24:15–18). The conclusion of the Exodus story does not come with the defeat of Pharaoh or with the revelation of the law at Sinai, but with the advent of the glory of Yahweh in the midst of the covenant community.

What type of story is this story called Exodus? Here for the first time the Pentateuchal narrative portrays both a hero and a villain—Moses

---

In Exodus, read all of the book *except* 25:10—31:18 and 35:22—39:31.

and Pharaoh. Moses' heroic stature results not only from his opposition to Pharaoh and victory over him, but also from his role as the leader of Israel. The patriarchs are Israel's eponymous ancestors, each of them, and especially Jacob, a *paterfamilias* writ large. Moses, on the other hand, is the founder of a nation. Just as the Pentateuch from Exodus to Deuteronomy focuses on a people and not a family, so too it focuses on a founder and not a father. Indeed, so central is Moses' role in all that follows that we could easily construe these books as the biography of Moses, or as a "heroic saga" following upon the "Primeval" and "Ancestral" sagas.[1]

While Exodus traces the rise of a hero and a people, it also traces the movement of the deity named Yahweh. That movement is from conflict to victory to the exercise of sovereignty and the enthronement of the sovereign. The movement of the book reaches its midpoint with the defeat of Pharaoh at the sea and the consequent exaltation of Yahweh as victor over Pharaoh and all other gods (chap. 15). It is from this stage in the narrative that I have chosen a title for the whole book: "Yahweh reigns forever" (15:18). The rest of the book focuses on Yahweh and Israel—on the constitution of Yahweh's kingdom (19:6) and the construction of the tabernacle as Yahweh's throne room where he will grant audiences with the people's representatives (25:21–22; 29:43–46). Those representatives are the priests, but especially Moses, for the movement of the book also follows the process through which he becomes the unquestioned leader of Israel (14:31; 19:9; 34:29–35; 39:43).

The movement of the book therefore results in the exaltation of three characters: Yahweh as the supreme deity in heaven and on earth, Moses as the servant of Yahweh, and Israel as the kingdom of Yahweh and his "special possession among all peoples" (19:5). This combination alone would suggest that the most appropriate genre for the book is that of "epic." What the *Aeneid* was to ancient Rome, Exodus is to ancient Israel. But we need not look to the classical literature of Rome as the only analogue. In fact, the movement that takes place in Exodus has a close parallel in a "typology of exaltation" which appears in epic literature of the ancient Near East.[2]

One of the benefits of applying the typology of exaltation to Exodus is that it reflects both the final form of the book and the history of traditions that in all probability stands behind it. Thus Yahweh's rise to prominence is highlighted not only by the redactional structure of the book but also appears specifically in a tradition maintained by the Priestly author, in which Yahweh says that his identity *as Yahweh* is a new revelation to Moses and the people of the exodus generation (6:2–3).[3]

The delineation of Yahweh's identity is not simply an arcane topic for philologists and historians of religion whose search leads them far afield from the biblical text. It may not be so important whether the divine name originally was pronounced "Yahweh" or "Yahwi" or even "Yahoo!". What is important is that the determination of Yahweh's identity and character lies at the heart of the Exodus narrative. This development of divine identity is closely correlated with that of Moses' identity, and with the identity of Israel as a people.

1. "Go down, Moses" (chaps. 1—4)

The narrative opens with a description of the transition from the family of Jacob to the people of Israel, overlapping with Genesis 46:8–27 and the reported death of Joseph at the end of the book (Exod. 1:1–6). This transitional material concludes with the following notice: "The Israelites were fertile and increased greatly; they multiplied and grew exceedingly strong, so that the land was filled with them" (vs. 7). This is not simply a demographic report; rather, it is the author's way of saying that a fundamental step toward the fulfilment of the divine promise to Abraham has been accomplished—"I will multiply you exceedingly" (Gen. 17:2). Moreover, this promise ultimately derives from the blessing pronounced on humankind at the creation: "Be fertile and increase, and fill the earth and subdue it" (1:28). Thus with this one verse (Exod. 1:7) the author has stitched together the Primeval cycle, the Ancestral Saga, and the book of Exodus.[4]

Yet the blessing once again proves to be well disguised. In the opening scene in Pharaoh's court, one wonders if even *he* knows of Genesis 1:28, and especially the command, "fill the earth and subdue it"! The Pharaoh sees the incredible reproduction of the Israelites as a threat to the security of the Egyptian empire. In effect, his reaction to the blessing is to resist and control it, and he therefore subjects those who had come to Egypt as sojourners to the status of forced laborers. Each step in Pharaoh's policy is as ruthless as it is irrational. Indeed the purpose of his initial policy is not simply to control the population nor to provide a labor force but "to *afflict* them with heavy burdens." Yet each of Pharaoh's ploys meets with an uncanny ability of the Israelites to reproduce, leading him to the ultimate solution of genocide.

In the midst of this desperate situation—but with no explanation of its significance—a Hebrew child is born and given the name of Moses (2:1–10). Ironically, he is rescued from Pharaoh's decree by Pharaoh's own daughter, who unknowingly gives him to his real mother to be nursed. The actions of these two women, along with those of Moses' sister and the Hebrew midwives of chapter 1, represent the only resistance to Pharaoh's villainy so far in the story. Of course the reader (both ancient and modern) knows full well what this child will become. In fact, such a birth story is a conventional device for describing the origins of a heroic figure.[5] But the narrator leaves the significance of the birth story undisclosed, and jumps immediately to an incident occurring after Moses has reached maturity (vss. 11–15a).

The young Moses, who apparently has grown up in Pharaoh's court, one day suddenly realizes the plight of "his brothers." In a spontaneous burst of rage, he kills an Egyptian who is beating a Hebrew. The text emphasizes the secretive nature of his actions (vs. 12), but they are no secret to the Hebrew for whom he has intervened. When Moses encounters the same man fighting with a fellow Hebrew, he upbraids him, only to be rebuffed. In the light of what will become of Moses in the rest of Exodus, the irony of the man's words is unmistakable: "Who made you a prince and a judge over us?"

Rejected by his own people and hunted by Pharaoh's henchmen, Moses flees from Egypt to the land of Midian (vss. 15b–22). In a story reminiscent of Jacob's meeting with Rachel, Moses happens upon the daughters of Reuel at a well, and "delivers" them from the bullying of some shepherds. If the would-be hero cannot deliver the Israelites, he can deliver damsels in distress, and Reuel rewards his actions with a wife. She soon bears him a son, whose name signifies Moses' current status: Gershom, which means, "I have become a sojourner in a foreign land." If there was a glimmer of hope at the birth of the hero, that glimmer has now gone out.

The first two chapters have thus moved with startling speed from the oppression of the Hebrews to the birth of Moses, his failure as a liberator, and his exile in the land of Midian. This material has already raised one of the central questions dominating the book of Exodus. Who *is* this Moses? He was born a Hebrew (and a Levite, at that), but raised as an Egyptian and named and adopted by Pharaoh's daughter. The Egyptian meaning of his name is apparently "son of," but whose son is he really? As a young man, he recognizes his identity as a Hebrew, but his violent attempt at leadership results in rejection by his own people as well as his alienation from Pharaoh's court. In the end Moses has started a family and gained a new identity, but it is as "a sojourner in a foreign land." At this point, Moses is no one.

Here the Priestly author has made a deceptively brief insertion (2:24), informing us of what the people in the story have no way of knowing: "God heard their groaning, and God remembered his covenant with Abraham, with Isaac, and with Jacob." The author thus invokes the divine promise to the ancestors just as he invoked the blessing in 1:7. This insertion has a dramatic effect on chapters 1—2 and prepares us for chapter 3. The question "Where is God?" increasingly haunts the reader of chapters 1—2, where the only divine action in the midst of such desperate circumstances is the gift of fertility to the Hebrew midwives (1:21)! Thus the insertion at the end of chapter 2 assures us that the silence of God in the face of evil is only apparent, and what is about to happen is a result of God's "remembering" his people. The text affirms the faithfulness of God despite God's apparent absence. At the same time, it alerts us to a crucial theological understanding of the character of Moses as we approach chapter 3. Moses does not "discover" God as if by some accident having more to do with the intent of sheep than the divine purpose; instead, Moses is discovered *by* God and is drawn into God's purpose for Israel which has been activated by the divine memory.[6]

When Yahweh appears to Moses out of the midst of the burning bush he speaks for the first time in the Exodus narrative. His words break the silence which pervades chapters 1—2 and extends backwards for generations to the last divine speech to Jacob (46:1–4). Indeed, as the dialogue with Moses unfolds it becomes clear that the passing of generations has led to a state in which Yahweh must introduce himself anew both to Moses and to the new generation of the Israelites. No one seems to know who Yahweh is, and thus the loss of Moses' identity is paralleled in the loss of Yahweh's.

First Yahweh introduces himself simply as the God of the ancestors: "I am the God of your father, the God of Abraham, the God of Isaac, and the God of Jacob" (vs. 6). The text then moves immediately to the statement of the divine mission, connecting with 2:23–25. Yahweh has seen the affliction of his people in Egypt, and he "has come down to deliver them" (vss. 7–9). The severity of Israel's oppression has produced a radical movement on the part of God, not seen since the tower of Babel and the destruction of Sodom and Gomorrah (Gen.11:5, 7; 19:20–21). In effect, the exodus from Egypt will occur because of an exodus from heaven and a direct intervention in the world of human affairs. Thus a fundamentally new dimension to the character of Yahweh appears.

The divine speech concludes with a direct address to Moses (vs. 10): "So now, go so that I may send you to Pharaoh—and bring my people the Israelites out of Egypt."[7] God has saved the bad news for last. He has come down to deliver Israel but—as the old Spiritual puts it—Moses must "go down" to Egypt as well. Moses is the human agent of divine salvation. The formulation of the commission thus revives a familiar theme of the Pentateuchal narrative—divine grace and human responsibility. The two cannot be separated, nor can the exodus be reduced to one or the other. Both divine and human action must occur for there to be liberation. To be sure, the divine intervention is prior to the human act, and without it there would be no deliverance. Without this commission, Moses was a failure (2:11–15) and would have spent the rest of his life as an unknown shepherd in Midian. Yet, like Abram before him, Moses' response to the initial command—"Go!"—is an essential part of the divine act. If Moses had said no, God would have had to find another to fill his place.

By the time the dialogue is over, Moses will have come very close to saying no. His initial response is perhaps as close as we will ever get to the original "Who, me?": "Who am I that I should go to Pharaoh, and bring the Israelites out of Egypt?" In response to his "Who am I?" Yahweh answers "I will be with you." Moses' identity is defined only in terms of the "I" of God. As we move through the book each of the crucial manifestations of this divine presence will confirm Moses' identity as Yahweh's agent.

Now it is Moses' turn again and he responds with a request for the name of the deity with whom he is talking (vss. 13–15). We the readers know that this is Yahweh, but Yahweh has introduced himself to Moses only as the "God of the fathers." On the surface Moses' request seems perfectly natural and understandable. After all, if he rallies the Israelites and proclaims himself their divinely appointed leader, yet doesn't even know the name of the God who appointed him, he will not be a very credible figure. On the other hand, the request for the deity's name may be an attempt to gain control of the deity's power, for knowledge of a person's name is a key to his or her essential nature (cf. Gen. 32:29; Judg. 13:17–18).

Deciphering the motivation behind Moses' request is not any easier after we have read Yahweh's immediate response (vs. 14). This verse contains some of the most difficult interpretive problems in the Hebrew Bible.[8] The response, usually translated "I am who I am" and "I am has sent me," seems to be as much an evasion as an answer. Of course, this is followed by verse 15, where "the Lord" (i.e., "Yahweh") is equated with "the God of your fathers." On the one hand, Yahweh is identified as the divine protagonist of the Ancestral Saga; on the other, Yahweh's identity, which remains hidden, is still a mystery.

Whatever the original intention of these verses, in their present position they point away from any revelation of Yahweh's identity in a single and private moment of unveiling, and point instead toward the progressive disclosure of Yahweh's identity as it is rendered by the narrative that follows. Accordingly, another possible translation of God's answer to Moses may be more appropriate: "I will be what I will be," or even "I am what I will be." Yahweh's identity cannot be reduced to a single word—even if that word be his personal name—but can be grasped only in and through the story that relates all of his words and deeds. His identity is rendered by his pledge of blessing and promise in the past ("the God of your fathers"), by the expression of his intention in the present (3:7–10), and by what he will do and say in the future. As one of J.R.R. Tolkien's marvelous characters says, "it would take a long while [to tell my name]: my name is growing all the time, and I've lived a very long, long time; so *my* name is like a story."[9] As the divine protagonist of the Pentateuchal narrative, Yahweh's character develops as does any character rendered by a story. As another author suggests, "The name which was almost totally open and devoid of denotative content at the beginning, gradually acquires a meaning in most narratives, so that at the end the name has been given a definition based on the events which have transpired."[10]

We must not forget that something has already happened to *God* in this story of Exodus; he has been forced (the classical rabbis would say, "as it were") to come down to Egypt, primarily because the enslavement and genocide of Israel threatens to extinguish the blessing he has pronounced on Israel, and through them, for the whole world (1:7). It would be surprising if such a radical gesture were not accompanied by a change in Yahweh's character. Both from the standpoint of the history of traditions and from the perspective of the text in its present form, the story of the exaltation of Yahweh renders a new God. The central aspect of the divine character that the exodus story reveals has already appeared in Yahweh's announcement to Moses in 3:7–10. Yahweh is a God of justice who champions the cause of the oppressed. He is a "deliverer" of the unjustly persecuted, and in order to act as deliverer within the circumstances of the ensuing narrative, he will also have to become a "man of war" (15:3).

Yahweh's answer to Moses' request for his name continues with a preview of the entire plague cycle from the perspective of Yahweh's foreknowledge (vss. 16–21). The passage has two parallels, one in 4:21–23, focusing on the death of the first-born, and another in 7:3–5. These three previews are alike in that they occur in conjunction with Moses' commissioning. From his perspective, they serve as a warning that deliverance will not come easily or quickly. From our perspective as readers, however, these previews at first seem to betray the incompetence of the narrators. They are like people who emerge from a suspenseful movie and tell everyone in the ticket line how the movie ends.

On the other hand, these preview passages provide a corrective to our understanding of the purpose of the overall narrative. The authors are not interested in creating a "thriller." Their concern is to exalt the figure of Yahweh, and perhaps the most important way of doing that is to show that Yahweh is in control of events in the narrative from the outset. These previews are thus reminiscent of the initial oracle in the Jacob cycle (Gen. 25:22–23) and the retrospective interpretation which Joseph gives of the Joseph cycle (45:5–8; 50:20). In fact, the previews in chapters 4 and 7 go even further, for here the coming events are not only foreknown by Yahweh but also predetermined: Yahweh will "harden Pharaoh's heart so that he will not let the people go" (4:21; 7:3). Whatever we may have thought of the young Jacob (who had a hard heart in a different sense), we never thought he was "programmed." Do we have here in the plague cycle a form of divine predestination in which Pharaoh is a mere puppet with whom Yahweh plays? A later text will come close to suggesting that (10:1–2).

The theological implications of the hardening of Pharaoh's heart present one of the most difficult problems in the Exodus narrative.[11] I have introduced it here because the text forces us to recognize it before the plague cycle begins; but in fact we cannot understand the motif adequately until the cycle has run its course—until the first-born Egyptians are dead and Pharaoh's troops are drowned in the sea.

The final unit in the first commissioning of Moses focuses on Moses' increasingly negative reactions to his call (4:1–17). When Moses first asked for some legitimation of his status as Yahweh's agent, Yahweh promised his presence with him (3:12), and subsequently predicted that the representatives of the Israelites ("the elders") would obey him ("hearken to your voice," vs. 18). Moses now raises the possibility that they will *not* "believe" him or obey him, but will question his claim that Yahweh has appeared to him (4:1). Here the author introduces a motif that will figure prominently in the definition of Moses' character, the verb *'aman*.[12] It means "to affirm, to trust or believe in," and is the origin of our English word "amen." The word is used four times in the rest of this passage, accentuating Moses' need for the people's confirmation. Even after Yahweh gives him the miraculous signs to confirm his legitimacy, Moses pleads that someone else be commissioned, and at this point Yahweh angrily provides his brother Aaron, not as a replacement, but as a spokesperson.

The recurrence of the "trust" motif at crucial points later in the narrative (14:31; 19:9) indicates a central tension in the book of Exodus: will the people accept Moses as their divinely appointed leader? Will they trust in him and obey him? Perhaps we are so accustomed to Moses' fame as a "man of God" that we fail to see the seriousness of the issue from the perspective of the characters in the story—especially the Israelites. The issue is not limited to trust in Moses, but includes the people's trust in God. Moses is their only medium for knowledge of the divine purpose. After all, God has not spoken directly to *them,* and will not do so until

they arrive at the mountain where he first appeared to Moses (cf. 3:12).[13]
How would *you* respond to someone who told you God had appeared to
him in a burning bush and appointed him to be your leader? This is the
reason Yahweh gives Moses the miraculous signs to demonstrate his claim.
Even the signs, as we shall see, eventually prove to be less than con-
vincing. At the end of chapter 4 Moses returns to Egypt and performs
his magic tricks before the people. They "believe" him, and bow their
heads in worship to Yahweh, but that trust and worship soon prove
ephemeral.

2. *"Let my people go" (chaps. 5—11)*

In chapter 5 Moses and Aaron have their first encounter with Pharaoh and it is a complete failure. Moses' demand for a religious holiday
results only in a stretch-out. The suggestion that the Israelites want to
"hold a feast" to Yahweh in the wilderness is an obvious attempt at
deception. It is clear from what has already happened that neither Yahweh
nor Moses intends for the Israelites to return. Although Pharaoh is suspicious for the wrong reasons, he will increasingly appear to realize the
real motive behind Moses' request. For his part, Moses will hold to his
excuse to the end, and for an important reason: a sacrificial feast, he
argues, requires that *all* of the Israelites participate (men, women, and
children) and that they take their cattle with them as well (10:24–26).

Those who fret over Moses' telling a lie miss the import of the
motif in the narrative. The pretense of a religious service is a shrewd
bargaining ploy, but it also points to a fundamental theological dimension
of the plot. Repeatedly Moses' demand for release will be the line, "Let
my people go, that they may *serve* me." This demand poses a central
issue: whom will Israel serve, Pharaoh or Yahweh?

The question of Israel's true master is accentuated in chapter 5 by
Pharaoh's refusal to "acknowledge" Yahweh and thus Yahweh's claim
on Israel. Pharaoh's initial response to Moses is, "Who is Yahweh, that
I should heed his voice and let Israel go? I do not acknowledge (literally
"know") Yahweh, and indeed I will not let Israel go." Pharaoh's response
represents the first direct challenge to Yahweh's authority in the Pentateuch. Moreover, his refusal to acknowledge Yahweh combines with the
earlier question about Yahweh's identity ("what is his name?," 4:13). In
fact, along with the question of Moses' identity and authority, Pharaoh's
question poses the central issue in chapters 1—15: "Who is Yahweh?"
The exaltation of Yahweh is a narrative description of Yahweh's identity
in terms of his sovereignty over the world.

By the end of this incident, a second issue emerges, an issue already
raised in chapters 3—4: "Who is Moses?" When Moses fails to win the

release of the Israelites, their foremen denounce him as a trou-
blemaker whose scheme has put them in grave danger (vs. 21). Moses
then directs the complaint against Yahweh himself in a bitter accusation.
He wonders why Yahweh commissioned him, and claims that Yahweh
has not only failed to deliver Israel, but has "done evil to this people"
(vs. 22).

The next major block of material in 6:2—7:13 (perhaps originally
an *alternate* tradition of Moses' call) now functions as a *renewal* of the
call. Yahweh encourages Moses despite the failure of his initial mission.
In 6:2–8 the introduction of Yahweh's personal name as a *new* revelation
is much more explicit than in 3:14–15. Of course, the author knows that
the name is used in the text of Genesis, but he is not bothered by this
apparent contradiction. In context the emphasis on this tradition of a new
name is a forceful way of suggesting what was already implicit in chapter
3; what is about to happen in Egypt will disclose something absolutely
essential to the identity of God, something unprecedented.

The structure of the divine speech points toward the definitive
disclosure. The speech is framed by the stately formula, "I am Yahweh"
(vss. 2, 8). The formula occurs again in the middle of the speech, at the
pivotal point between past and future (vs. 6, note also the "therefore").
Yahweh appeared to the Ancestors as El Shaddai, establishing his covenant with them "to give them the land of Canaan." He has heard their
groaning and remembered his covenant. Yahweh is faithful to the promises
of the past, but what he is about to do in Egypt is the definitive revelation
of his identity: he will "bring out," "deliver," and "redeem" Israel, and
adopt Israel as his people. Then *they* will "acknowledge" ("know") that
he is Yahweh. The conjunction of the three verbs in verse 6 and the
adoption formula in verse 7, concluded by the recognition formula, provides a succinct description of Yahweh's identity—the identity disclosed
by the rest of the book of Exodus, where Yahweh "redeems" his people
(chaps. 7—15) and makes them his own (chaps. 19—40).

We turn now to the plague cycle that begins at 7:8.[14] Three motifs
within the plague cycle highlight the questions "Who is Moses?" and
"Who is Yahweh?" The first is the motif of Pharaoh's magicians, and
belongs to the P source. In the first three incidents with Pharaoh (rod/
serpent, blood, frogs), the "wise men and the sorcerers" of the Pharaoh
are able to duplicate "by their secret arts" the miracles wrought by Moses
and Aaron (7:11, 22; 8:7). That the magicians are confounded in the first
instance by Aaron's rod devouring theirs does not detract from their
impressive skills, nor does the fact that their feats merely compound the
existing problem (an irony the author probably relished). The signs Yahweh gave to Moses to legitimate his position may have worked with the
Israelites (4:30–31), but they have not impressed the Egyptians.

However, in the fourth plague (gnats) the magicians muster their "secret arts" to no avail. Overwhelmed by their defeat, they even suggest to Pharaoh that "this is the finger of God!" (8:18–19). Finally, in the plague of boils the magicians come to an ignominious end: "the magicians could not stand before Moses because of the boils, for the boils were upon the magicians and upon all the Egyptians" (9:11). Thus the motif of the magicians is one way in which the problem of Moses' legitimation is cast in a new light; at first challenged by their occult powers, in the end Moses stands unrivaled in Pharaoh's court. Even the pagan magicians testify to the power of the God of the Hebrews, then exit backstage, scratching themselves.

A second motif derives from the Yahwistic stratum, and concerns the concessions Pharaoh makes to Moses. Here is a progression not only in the stature of Moses, but also in the recognition of Yahweh's power. Up until the invasion of frogs, Pharaoh has remained adamant. Evidently the croaking becomes too much for the royal ears, however, for at this point Pharaoh promises to let the Israelites go if Moses will "entreat Yahweh to take away the frogs" (8:8). Of course, no sooner has Moses complied with the request than Pharaoh stubbornly changes his mind. A similar course is followed in 8:25–32, where Pharaoh first offers a temporary release *in Egypt*, then agrees to a short trip outside the land. Once again, however, and despite Moses' intercession for him (vs. 28), Pharaoh balks.

The vacillations of Pharaoh become more drastic with the plague of hail. Pharaoh suddenly becomes penitent: "I have sinned this time; Yahweh is in the right, and I and my people are in the wrong. Entreat Yahweh . . . ; I will let you go" (9:27–28). Nevertheless, with the cessation of the hail, "he sinned yet again" and refused Moses' request (vs. 34). With the plague of locusts, Pharaoh will allow only the adult males to leave, then with the onslaught of the locusts he confesses his sin again (10:16–17), only to fall back into his pattern of refusal. In response to the plague of darkness, Pharaoh will allow all but the flocks of the Israelites to leave. Moses rejects the offer and he and Pharaoh break off negotiations, ostensibly for the last time (10:21–29). After the death of the first-born, however, Pharaoh "summoned Moses and Aaron by night, and said, 'Rise up, go away from my people, both you and the people of Israel; and go, serve Yahweh, as you have said. Take your flocks and your herds, as you have said, and be gone; and bless me also!' " (12:31–32). At this point—and we are already jumping ahead of the story—the narrative tension involving Moses' abilities as leader, and Yahweh's power over Pharaoh *appears* to be resolved; Pharaoh has yielded, the people are free.

The motif of Pharaoh's concessions and withdrawals is closely tied to a third motif, the "acknowledgment" of Yahweh's sovereignty.[15] This

motif began with the initial encounter between Pharaoh and Moses, when
Pharaoh said "Who is Yahweh? . . . I do not acknowledge him" (5:2).
The motif resumes with the plague of blood, which Moses introduces with
these words: "By this you shall acknowledge that I am Yahweh" (7:17).
In the next plague (frogs), a comparative thrust is introduced. Moses has
not only agreed to "entreat" Yahweh to end the plague, but has allowed
Pharaoh to set the time, "so that you may acknowledge that there is no
one like Yahweh our God" (8:10). Again, in the plague of flies the first
formula is combined with a spatial expression. Yahweh's ability to "set
apart the land of Goshen, where my people dwell," while the land of
Egypt is swarming with flies, is for Pharaoh's instruction, "that you may
acknowledge that I am Yahweh in the midst of the earth" (8:22).

The author has drawn out the theological implications of the motif
in the plague of hail, 9:14–16:

> For this time I will send all my plagues upon your heart, and upon your servants
> and your people, that you may acknowledge that there is none like me in all
> the earth. For by now I could have put forth my hand and struck you and
> your people with pestilence, and you would have been cut off from the earth;
> but for this purpose have I let you live, to show you my power, so that my
> name may be declared throughout all the earth.

The same theology appears more succinctly in the reason given for
the cessation of the hail, "that you may acknowledge that the earth is
Yahweh's" (9:29). By his control of the forces of nature, Yahweh has
demonstrated his lordship over all the world. In the beginning, Pharaoh
questioned Yahweh's identity and sovereignty; in the end, Yahweh's name
will be universally recognized.

While the motif of the magicians was resolved with their humiliating
defeat, no such resolution of the concession and acknowledgment motifs
takes place within the plague cycle. In the announcement of the final
plague, the acknowledgment motif appears again (11:7), and both motifs
play a prominent role in the climactic story of Pharaoh's defeat at the sea
(chap. 14). In short, the plagues—including the death of Pharaoh's own
first-born—fail to secure Pharaoh's final concession or his acknowledgment of Yahweh's sovereignty. Such is the hardness of Pharaoh's heart.

3. "A night of watching" (12:1—13:16)

Between release and redemption comes Passover. There is one
verse in this unit that is remarkable for both its brevity and its profundity:
"It was a night of watching for Yahweh, to bring them out of the land of
Egypt; this same night is for Yahweh a watching for all the Israelites

throughout their generations" (12:42). This is an unusual example of authorial commentary in which the author steps outside the narrative mode
in an overt attempt to instruct his readers. The "for Yahweh" is ambiguous, perhaps deliberately so. It refers to Yahweh's "watching" for Israel,
and Israel's "watching" for Yahweh, in two senses of the term—one a
provision of protection, the other an expectation of arrival. This "night
of watching," the author suggests, is not confined to the past—it is a night
that both "was" and "is."[16]

The redaction turns the original story into a play each subsequent
generation of Israelites can enact. As the French would say, *recit* has
become *rite*; narrative has become ritual. The seriousness of this transformation is indicated in that it is fixed by law, "an eternal ordinance"
(12:14, 24). All future generations are commanded to enact this play once
a year throughout their lives. Law demands repetition of the story, because
this particular story has become the narrative core of what it means to
be an Israelite. Just as the Exodus story represents the definitive identity
of Yahweh and Moses, so it represents the definitive identity of the community called Israel. Those who do not perform this ritual cut themselves
off from the community and, in effect, cease to be Israelites (12:15, 19).
When the celebrants put on their hats and coats and grab their walking
sticks (12:11), they are not just *pretending* to be Israelites in Egypt—they
are those Israelites—because who they are is defined by the story they
are enacting. The Passover service is a "memorial" (12:14; 13:3, 9), but
one reflecting a distinctive understanding of memory. Future generations
cannot "remember" the exodus any more than contemporary Americans
"remember" Washington's crossing of the Delaware, but within the
Passover ritual, the participants identify themselves with the story in such
a way that they transcend the temporal and spatial boundaries separating
them from the original event. Thus in the contemporary Passover ritual,
the celebrants say, "*We* were Pharaoh's slaves in Egypt." What they are
saying is not so much we *were* there as we *are* there.

The consequence of this emphasis on the exodus story as the core
of Israelite identity appears when we note what has happened to the
promise of land. At three places in the text, arrival in the land of promise
serves as the setting in which the Passover ritual is to take place (12:25;
13:5, 11). Remarkably, it is not the fulfilment of the promise of land that
is celebrated, but the exodus from Egypt. When the Israelites arrive in
Canaan, they are not enjoined to tell their children of the promise of the
land to Abraham, but to tell them of their deliverance from the land of
Egypt. While the exodus story has by no means effaced the promises to
the Ancestors, it has removed them from the central position they here-
tofore held.[17] Now one cannot *be* an Israelite—even in the land of Canaan—unless one "remembers" this story.

In terms of the text and later tradition, the Passover ritual has thus become the primary medium for the transmission of the entire exodus story. Passover is so familiar (even to non-Jews) that this function may not seem surprising, but the literary context of the biblical story suggests that it is extraordinary. The Passover text represents the end of the ten plagues and includes Israel's escape from Egypt (12:37, 41, 51). Yet freedom soon proves more apparent than real, for Pharaoh changes his mind and pursues the former slaves. Israel's redemption does not really take place until Pharaoh's forces are defeated at the sea. Thus the Passover ritual celebrates the night *before* redemption, a night haunted with a spirit of fear and excitement. The characters in the story (and therefore the participants in the ritual) are frozen in a moment of incompleteness, in between slavery and freedom, death and life. Only on the other side of this night, "in the morning watch" (14:24), will the tension of the exodus narrative finally be broken, and only then will there emerge a new people, a new leader, and, as it were, a new God.

That the author has explicitly lifted up this sense of incompleteness and legislated it to future generations means that when they identify with this story they too experience this incompleteness. A similar sense of incompleteness pervaded the book of Genesis, where the fulfilment of the promises to the Ancestors was left in suspense, but never in those stories did the author step outside the narrative framework and suggest—indeed, demand—such an attitude for the reader. In fact, as we shall see at the conclusion of this book, the Passover text provides a metaphor for the significance of the "end" of the Pentateuch and thus of the final shape of the Torah as a whole. "A night of watching" is another way of expressing what "beyond the Jordan" will mean in the book of Deuteronomy.

4. *"Yahweh reigns"* (13:17—15:21)

Two sets of characters make up this story: 1) those who have yet to acknowledge definitively either the sovereignty of Yahweh or the leadership of Moses—the people of Israel and the Pharaoh; and 2) those whose legitimation has been in question all along—Moses and Yahweh. The plague cycle repeatedly hammered at Pharaoh concerning his acknowledgment of Yahweh's sovereignty. Chapter 14 brings the issue to a dramatic resolution. In two almost identical phrases (vss. 4 and 17–18) Yahweh declares, "I will get glory over Pharaoh and all his host, and the Egyptians shall acknowledge that I am Yahweh." Characteristically, Pharaoh *never* acknowledges Yahweh's sovereignty. In the end, the text seems more interested in demonstrating Yahweh's "glory" to the reader. The narrative description of Pharaoh's defeat is itself a vindication of the God of Israel. Yahweh has done what he said he would do.

Similarly, the element of narrative tension that began at least with Moses' questioning whether or not the people would "trust" in him (chaps. 3—4) is brought to a final resolution. When the people, who think they are free from Pharaoh's power, look behind them and see with utter horror that the Egyptian chariotry is bearing down on them, they angrily rebuke Moses for his apparently disastrous leadership: "Is not this what we said to you in Egypt, 'Let us alone and *let us serve the Egyptians*?' For it would have been better for us *to serve the Egyptians* than to die in the wilderness" (vs. 12). In this scene, reminiscent of the end of chapter 5, the people reject the leadership of Moses and the divine deliverance that stands behind it. Moses had repeatedly gone to Pharaoh with Yahweh's command, "Let my people go, that they may serve me." Now Israel wants to serve *Pharaoh*—and at the very moment of their salvation! This picture is all the more telling when we realize that the people have scarcely appeared at all as a prominent character before this point in the narrative. Indeed, this is the first time the people have spoken.

To this bitter and despairing cry, Moses responds with a stinging summons: "Fear not, stand firm, and *see* the *salvation* of Yahweh, which he will work for you today; for the Egyptians whom you *see* today, you shall never *see* again. Yahweh will fight for you, and you have only to be still" (vss. 13–14). With these remarks ringing in their ears, and with divine protection both in front and behind, the people enter the path through the sea. Rabbinic legend rightly extols the first person to step between the walls of water! But we need not rehearse the events that follow, for the author's main point is contained in the closing verses: "Thus Yahweh *saved* Israel that day from the hand of the Egyptians; and Israel *saw* the Egyptians dead upon the seashore. And Israel *saw* the great work which Yahweh did against the Egyptians, and the people *feared* Yahweh; and they *trusted* in Yahweh and in his servant Moses." By recapitulating the language of Moses' previous summons ("fear," "see," "salvation"), the author has shown how the act of salvation has brought the people from the fear of Pharaoh to the fear of Yahweh. Even more significantly, by the resumption of the motif of "trust," the entire narrative of Exodus up to this point comes to a magnificent conclusion.

Now we have the first part of the answer to the question "Who is Yahweh?" The answer receives its quintessential formulation in the *narrative* of Exodus 1—14, which is summarized most succinctly in the opening lines of the Decalogue (20:2): "I am Yahweh your God, who brought you out of the land of Egypt, out of the house of bondage." Moreover, the predication following this self-declaration also answers the question raised in Moses' commission—"what is his name?" The answer can never again be limited to "Yahweh, the God of your fathers, the God of Abraham, the God of Isaac, and the God of Jacob'' (3:15–16), but must also, and primarily, be ''Yahweh your God, who brought you out of the land of Egypt.'' God does not simply have a new personal name, although that lies within the history of the exodus traditions; God also has a new identity.

The closing phrase in chapter 14 rightly places a theological statement, strictly construed, in preeminent position—the observation of Yahweh's act of salvation has led to trust in him. But closely correlated with this is a statement about Moses. The identity of the man who at first did not even believe in himself, the man whom the people increasingly had more reason to doubt than to trust, is finally confirmed. He is the servant of Yahweh. The rest of the book—and the rest of the Pentateuch—will define in increasing detail the nature of Moses' identity as Yahweh's servant. Already the text has cast him in the role of a deliverer and a prophetic figure, one who bears the message of Yahweh (''Thus says the Lord'') to a stubborn and haughty king. If Moses is a hero, his role as prophet and servant will redefine the characteristics of heroism. For now, the central focus is on his role as an object of the people's trust (14:31). The correlation of trust in a human being and in God is unprecedented and will remain unequaled (though not unchallenged) in the Pentateuch. From now until the end, Moses will become *the* central model of ''what human life might be like if lived to the full.''[18] In short, Moses will become the one who responds to the divine will with virtually complete integrity, a man of righteousness, the true ''man of God'' (Deut. 33:1).

What could one add to this, the opening act of the exaltation of Yahweh, other than a hymn of praise? That is precisely the function of Exodus 15:1–18, which represents in poetic form what was already implicit in the preceding narrative—the universal significance of Israel's salvation.[19] The theme of the first part is announced in the opening verse: ''I will sing to Yahweh, for he is highly exalted;/horse and rider he has thrown into the sea.'' The defeat of Pharaoh has disclosed a new dimension of Yahweh's identity: ''Yahweh is *a man of war*,/Yahweh is his *name*.''

The battle is between Yahweh and the historical forces of Pharaoh. On the other hand, what happened to Pharaoh was not simply a divine victory over human power. Rather, this event also had ''theo-political'' significance,[20] the fundamental aspect of which is expressed in verse 11: ''Who is like you, Yahweh, among the gods?/Who is like you, terrible among the holy ones?/Awesome in praises, wonder worker.'' No power on earth *or in heaven* could compete with the Holy Warrior of Israel. Thus the liberation of the people has as its corollary the exaltation of their God.

Just as the other gods stand in fear of Yahweh, so the other peoples stand in fear of Israel (vss. 13–18).[21] Thus in the Song of the Sea Israel celebrates the new identity of Yahweh as savior, and at the same time celebrates her own birth as the *people* of Yahweh (cf. 3:7, 10). The poem concludes with an accolade to Yahweh's exaltation as king: "Yahweh reigns for ever and ever." The line is not only an appropriate conclusion to the poem; it is also a fitting doxology to the first act of the exaltation of Yahweh.

The exodus story began with Egypt's leader and its people opposing those who mediated Yahweh's blessing.[22] The oppression in Egypt is the most outrageous example of the mistreatment of the "alien" in the Pentateuch, and it is also the first direct assault against "the blessed of Yahweh." Exodus 1—15 is a grim story that illustrates part of the charge to Abram: "him who curses you, I will curse" (Gen. 12:3).[23] Once the Egyptian people recede into the background of the story, they become the victims of their own ruler's despotic evil. The text explains this tragic situation in terms of Pharaoh's hardened heart.

On the one hand, events take their course because Pharaoh hardens his own heart and refuses to allow the Hebrews to leave.[24] "Pharaoh is a thinking, arguing, *deciding* character,"[25] and he has plenty of opportunities to make the right decision before disaster strikes. But the narrative also attributes the death of the first-born and Pharaoh's troops, and indeed the entire series of plagues, to *Yahweh*'s coercion of Pharaoh—his "hardening" of Pharaoh's heart.[26] Contemporary readers often find the apparent contradiction between the two causes of Pharaoh's downfall not only intellectually baffling but also morally repugnant. How can Pharaoh and his people justifiably be punished for what Yahweh has predetermined?

It seems the more the authors reflected on Pharaoh's resistance, the less they could understand how a human being could defy the God of Israel with such obduracy. How could a human being—even if the king of Egypt—impudently ask "Who is Yahweh?" How could it be that the first plague disproved Yahweh's own words, "By this you shall acknowledge that I am Yahweh" (7:17), and that Pharaoh persisted in his defiance, one plague after another, even after the death of his own first-born child? In short, the authors "found it impossible to regard the causes of something so atrocious, such a plunge into madness and ruin at one's own hands, as lying simply on the human and immanent level: in the last analysis they could only be the inscrutable working of the deity."[27] The divine hardening of Pharaoh's heart is another expression of the central thrust of the story, the exaltation of Yahweh.

Theologically, the authors appear more willing to throw into question the morality of God than to risk undercutting the sovereignty of God. The hardening motif illustrates the Hebrew Bible's adamant refusal to assign evil to some force outside Yahweh's power and control. Pharaoh may be a villain, but he is not the Devil. What is even more remarkable is that the authors accomplished their task without making Pharaoh a mere puppet. If Pharaoh is not the Devil, he is also not a wimp. The result is "a drama of cosmic proportions occurring at the same time in the framework of expectable human behavior."[28]

However unsatisfactory the resolution may seem to the moral sensibilities of the modern reader, the fate of Pharaoh and his people reveals the dirty side of the earthiness of the Pentateuchal narrative. Divine liberation of the oppressed takes place within the ambiguities of human nature, and within an all too realistic world of maniacal persecution that can only result in tragedy. Freedom from such a relentless political system ultimately occurs within grim and violent circumstances; in this case the violence engulfs Egyptian people who are not directly responsible for Pharaoh's actions. "God cannot save the Israelites without killing Egyptians."[29] In his last encounter with Moses, Pharaoh had finally sought the *blessing* that could bring life (12:32), but all of his actions, previous and subsequent, brought upon himself and his people a curse. In Moshe Greenberg's eloquent words:

> In this dramatic evolution of Pharaoh's reactions, there is a consistency of principle—the core of his intransigence—namely, the maintenance of his sovereignty. That is the crux of the matter; that is the offense to the Godhead's kingship; that is what cannot coexist with God's authority. Thus the opposition of Pharaoh is the archetypal opposition of human power, of human authority to the claims of God. Under pressure it will show flexibility and accommodation, even reversing itself—first by crying for help, then by confessing guilt and making concessions. But after all its retreats, it clings to its last redoubt, a core of self-assertiveness and independence, to surrender which would mean the end of its claim to ultimate, self-sufficient power. Here it resists, careless of the cost, unto death.[30]

5. From Egypt to Sinai (15:22—18:27)

Despite the complicated history of traditions that lies behind the rest of the book of Exodus, the present text has a clear structure:

1) 15:22—18:27   The wilderness journey from Egypt to Sinai
2) chaps. 19—20   The charter of the covenant community
3) chaps. 21—23   The laws of the covenant community
4) chap. 24   The covenant ratification ceremony
5) chaps. 25—31   Instructions for the tabernacle
6) chap. 32   The sin of the golden calf
7) chaps. 33—34   Reconciliation and covenant renewal
8) chaps. 35— 40   Construction and sanctification of the tabernacle

We have now come to the heart of the Torah.

From the moment the escaping Israelites crossed the border of Egypt, their story became one of a wilderness journey, one that would take them from the banks of the Nile to the banks of the Jordan. In fact, the Pentateuchal narrative from Exodus 13 to the end of Deuteronomy can be summarized in terms of an itinerary (cf. Num. 33), one the redactors have used periodically throughout the text to mark the "stages" of Israel's journey.[1] But, as in the case of the Ancestral Saga, the resultant narrative is far more than a travelogue. The wilderness journey is also a metaphor for a spiritual journey, a painful process of learning and "testing" in which Israel is constantly offered the grace of divine guidance (*torah*), only to reject that guidance in search of an elusive and disastrous autonomy.

By far the most important "stage" in Israel's wilderness journey is the one that takes place at Sinai, the mountain of God. The preeminent significance of this "stage" is indicated by the sheer bulk of literary material attached to it—all of Exodus 19 through Numbers 10—a period of some fourteen months. This massive literary unit is surrounded by two much smaller ones describing the events "in the wilderness" before and after Israel's stay at the mountain of God: Exodus 15:22—18:27 and Numbers 11—14.

The first three stories concern the people's complaints in the face of thirst and starvation. Although these are legitimate complaints, the people express them in an increasingly hostile and accusatory manner, charging that Moses has led them into the wilderness to kill them (16:3; 17:3) and wondering "whether Yahweh is among us or not?" (17:7). Chapter 16 is the centerpiece of these three stories.[2] Having already provided water, Yahweh now provides food: manna with a side dish of quail. It is not bad fare for wilderness survival. Although we know that manna is a naturally existing substance, the text emphasizes the miraculous circumstances in which it occurs. No matter how much they gather, the people end up with what they need. When they try to keep it overnight (which is against the rules), it rots, but not so on the weekend. No manna appears on the Sabbath. That, after all, is the day when God rests, and when the people should rest, wilderness or no wilderness. So extra manna appears on the day before the Sabbath, and it keeps overnight. Yet some of the people have to have fresh manna, Sabbath or no Sabbath, and again they break the rules.

The manna story thus depicts a God who provides for the people's needs, and a people who are not satisfied with that provision because it is beyond their control. They are too insecure to rely on "daily bread," so they gather more than they need, hoard it even though it is perishable, and work to get more when they already have enough.

In Israel's unruliness—literally construed—the manna story anticipates the necessity of a community ruled by law. Already in the Marah story Yahweh (or Moses) had given Israel laws and posed a test for them:

if they would follow Yahweh's laws they would be exempt from the diseases with which Yahweh had afflicted the Egyptians (15:25b–26). The laws were given *after* the provision of water as a condition of their continuing relationship with Yahweh, the source of blessing, their "healer." Now in the manna story many of the Israelites exhibit their failure to follow Yahweh's commandments. In fact, here the purpose of providing the manna is not only to meet their legitimate physical need, but also "to test them, whether they will walk in my law or not" (vs. 4). Obviously many of the people fail the test because they are unwilling to trust in Yahweh's promise of daily food.

In short, the manna story demonstrates the failure of *ad hoc* laws in maintaining the relationship between Yahweh and the people whom he has redeemed from bondage. Many of the people are incapable of integrity when they are governed by rules that apply only to specific situations. For them righteousness is not possible apart from *the* law—the Torah of the *covenant* community.

When we look at all the stories in chapters 15—18 we can see the fundamental problem: the people do not know who they are with respect to Yahweh, or to Moses. They are the people whom Yahweh has liberated from slavery under the leadership of Moses, and their immediate past is constitutive for their identity. How, though, does that past impinge on the present and the future? Now that they are free, what is their relationship to Yahweh and to Moses?

The problem appears most clearly in terms of Moses, as it did in chapters 1—14. Here, as there, it becomes increasingly apparent that the people need some public definition and confirmation of Moses' role. They see him acting as a miracle worker who can turn bitter water sweet, and even produce water from a rock with his magic wand. Daily they see that his promise of divine sustenance is trustworthy. They observe him as a man of mysterious power who can control the course of a battle by raising or lowering his arms (17:8–16). Yet one thing is missing: they still have never heard God speak to this man and thereby confirm for them that his words truly represent God's words. They came to trust Moses as their liberator because they saw God's act of liberation (chap. 14). What they now need is a public legitimation of Moses' role as their legislator. The situation is strangely reminiscent of a question addressed to Moses long ago: "Who made you a prince and judge over us?" (2:14).

The need for divine confirmation of Moses' role is all the more pressing because Moses *is* already acting as the people's legislator and "judge" (18:13–17). Note the counsel of Jethro (Moses' father-in-law): "You shall represent the people before God, and bring their cases to God; and you shall teach them the statutes and the laws (*torot*), and make them know the way in which they must walk and what they must do" (18:19–20). The point of Jethro's advice, of course, is to designate Moses as the "chief justice" and thus to spare him all of the relatively petty legal cases, which his newly appointed assistant judges will decide. The story also concludes with Moses enacting the recommended policy. However, the context of the story points again to what will happen at Sinai, for only there will Moses' new role as legislator be publicly confirmed by Yahweh and formally accepted by the people.

In short, the stories of Israel's journey through the wilderness from Egypt to Sinai again raise the question that dominated the narrative of chapters 1—15: who are Yahweh, Moses, and Israel now? To borrow an analogy from American history, the situation is something like that in between the defeat of the British in 1783 and the ratification of the Constitution in 1789. The analogy is one of contrast as well as similarity, for at least the American people had the Continental Congress of 1775 as a guiding body. Israel, on the other hand, is a people without a polity, led by a general without political portfolio, marching under the "banner" (17:16) of a God whose sovereignty over them remains formally unaccepted and undefined.

6. "A holy nation" (chaps. 19—31)

With Israel "encamped before the mountain" in the wilderness of Sinai, Moses goes up the mountain to meet with God. Yahweh delivers a brief speech to Moses, which he then relays to the people. The content of the speech (vss. 3b–6a) is a paradigm of covenant theology, and in its present position it insures that the peculiar stamp of that theology governs all that follows. This speech encapsulates the new identities of Yahweh, Moses, and Israel that the subsequent narrative will develop in detail. Yahweh is Israel's covenant lord, Israel is Yahweh's covenant community, and Moses is the mediator of the covenant.

> Thus you shall say to the house of Jacob, and tell to the children of Israel: "You have seen what I did to the Egyptians, how I bore you on eagles' wings, and brought you to me. Now, therefore, if you will indeed obey me and keep my covenant, you shall be my treasured possession among all peoples, for all the earth is mine; so you shall be to me a kingdom of priests, and a holy nation."

The speech opens with a messenger formula,[3] then moves immediately to a recollection of the exodus and Yahweh's careful guidance of Israel up to this point. Everything that follows is based on this recollection, especially of the exodus: "You have seen what I did to the Egyptians." The people have *seen* the action of God that brought about their redemption from slavery (cf. 14:13, 30–31). Before that event, Israel *as a people* had no concrete referent on which to base their trust in Yahweh's claim to be their God. Now that referent—one the whole people witnessed—has occurred. When the people enter into a covenant relationship with Yahweh, they do so on the basis of their corporate experience of salvation. Becoming the covenant community is an expression of gratitude for Yahweh's antecedent grace, and an expression of the desire to continue in that grace now that the act of salvation stands in the past.

The rest of the speech specifies what is required of Israel in order to continue in Yahweh's grace. Yahweh has brought Israel to himself. Freedom was the beginning, not the end, of Yahweh's purpose for this people. Thus the speech takes a dramatic turn in verse 5, beginning with the emphatic "now, therefore." The "therefore" indicates that the act of God is leading to a consequence. The people have seen, now they are summoned to obey—literally to "hear my voice"—and to "keep my covenant." The purpose of this covenant is to provide a formal constitution for the relationship that has already existed between the two parties, the relationship that found its primary expression in Israel's liberation.

"*If* you will obey me and keep my covenant, *then* you shall be my own possession among all peoples." This is surely the most explicit transformation of the theme of peoplehood in the Pentateuchal narrative, especially when we compare this speech with the one at the burning bush. There Yahweh said "I have seen the affliction of my people . . . and I have come down to deliver them" (3:7–8). There were no conditions for this act of liberation, but now there is a condition: for Israel to be "my people" from now on, Israel must accept and obey the covenant.[4]

If keeping the covenant is the condition of Yahweh's summons, the promise of a special relationship is the result. "You shall be my treasured possession among all peoples, for all the earth is mine." This one sentence is the crystallization of a process that reaches back into the Primeval cycle. Out of all the peoples of the world, God chooses Israel to be his "treasured possession."[5] This is the "scandal" of election, already implied with the charge to Abraham. Israel, fresh from the slave camps of Egypt, is God's special people on earth! Yet within the context of the speech, no explanation appears other than what follows in verse 6: "You shall be to me a kingdom of priests and a holy nation." The first expression means that Israel is to be the sacerdotal domain of Yahweh, the people who serve him as priests. The second expression is closely related to the first, and also to the election formula in verse 5, where the Hebrew literally means "*from* all the peoples." To be "holy" (*qadosh*) means to be "set apart," to be "consecrated" for a particular task. Israel is set apart from all the peoples of the earth to render priestly service to

Yahweh, and, in the context of the Pentateuchal narrative, to act as priest to the world. Israel is to be the "great nation" promised to Abraham, the community through whom God's purpose for the world he created may be renewed. In retrospect, the Ancestral Saga was a preparation for the founding of this covenant community. "Israel is to achieve through service to Him what the whole of mankind, even after the Flood, proved incapable of doing."[6] Israel is to be the community of righteousness.

The first act in the exaltation of Yahweh concluded with a song of praise to Yahweh by "the people whom thou hast redeemed" (15:13). The second act is concerned with "a holy nation," a sanctified community. These are not two separate communities, but one and the same, redeemed *and* consecrated to a particular task. A great deal of the rest of the Pentateuch is concerned with the proper correlation of these two aspects of Israel's corporate identity—redemption and holiness, salvation and sanctification. Sanctification here refers to the realization of God's purpose and intentions for Israel, *by* Israel. Of course, such a realization presupposes the redemption that preceded. But sanctification also points to something the people themselves must do, to their response to the redemptive act. Sanctification—becoming the "holy nation"—means living out the implications of Israel's redemption. The narrative of Yahweh's redemptive act is incomplete without the narrative of Yahweh's instruction—his Torah—and that instruction is not mere indicative suggestion, but an imperative command.

From the perspective of the opening speech, therefore, chapters 19—40 represent an attempt to answer a number of fundamental questions: What does it mean to be the people of Yahweh? How are the people to define their relationship to the God who has redeemed them? What are the responsibilities that result from their redemption? How does their redemption by God affect the way in which they live with one another? In short, what is the nature and purpose of this newly created community? How is the redeemed community to become the sanctified community, and what is the Torah, or guidance, that enables this sanctification?

In the next section of chapter 19, Moses reports Yahweh's covenant speech to the people, receives their agreement to enter into the covenant, and returns to Yahweh with their reply (vss. 7–9). Already Moses is performing the role of a diplomatic mediator between the two parties of the treaty. Now, in a second address to Moses, Yahweh declares that his self-manifestation to the people will confirm the office Moses already exercises: "I am coming to you in a thick cloud, that the people may hear when I speak with you, and may trust in you forever." By employing the motif of "trust" (*'aman*) this speech recalls the tension in chapters 4—14, that was resolved when the people saw God's presence at work in the cloud and "trusted" in God and in Moses (14:30–31). But still the people have not *heard* God talking to Moses. The emphasis on hearing rather than seeing is altogether appropriate because in what follows Moses will act primarily as the agent of God's words rather than God's actions.

The motif of "trust" does not recur in the ensuing theophany, but at the height of the divine appearance, accompanied by all sorts of meteorological phenomena, "Moses spoke and God answered him in thunder" (vs. 19b). For the first time, the people have witnessed direct communication between Yahweh and Moses. To be sure, the text does not specify the content of this communication, or even that it was intelligible,[7] but *that* Moses speaks and God answers is enough to produce the intended result. Thus, in the sequel to the theophany (20:18–20), the people recoil in terror and appeal to Moses for help: "You speak to us, and we will hear; but let not God speak to us, lest we die."

Moses' leadership now takes on a new configuration: Moses is not simply the human agent of divine deliverance, he is also the covenant mediator between the people and God, appointed by Yahweh and formally elected by the people. It is through Moses that God will make known his desires for this people, and in turn, Moses will be their official spokesperson before God. From now on, "to look to God meant to Israel to look to this man, to hear God to hear the word of this man, to obey God to follow his direction, to trust God to trust his insight."[8] From now on, "refusing belief in Moses is tantamount to refusing belief in Yahweh."[9]

Moses' response to the people's reaction at the foot of the mountain employs a subtle use of the word "fear": "Do not fear, for God has come to test you, so that the fear of him may be before your eyes, that you may not sin" (vs. 20). The first "fear" has to do with terror, the second with obedience. The purpose of the theophany, Moses suggests, has been to produce the second sense of fear. In the present text, fear as obedience is inseparable from the fact that the Decalogue interrupts the account of the theophany proper.[10] It is now impossible to understand the people's reaction apart from the declaration of the ten commandments. The overpowering presence of Yahweh is by no means an end in itself; rather, the theophany lends authority to the commands of God as they are revealed in the Decalogue. By the same token, the people's fear is not simply "a subjective emotion of terror, but the obedience of God's law."[11] "Holiness cannot be experienced without its power to command what we should be."[12]

The closing scene in chapter 20 points to the new identity of Yahweh. He is not only what he does, but also what he says. This correlation is suggested by Yahweh's first words to Moses after his formal confirmation as covenant mediator, again using a messenger formula: "Thus you shall say to the people of Israel: 'You have seen for yourselves that

I have talked with you from heaven' " (vs. 22). The parallel to 19:4 is obvious: "You have seen what I did to the Egyptians." Together, these two statements refer to the two "root experiences" of Israel—the experience of Yahweh's "saving presence" and of his "commanding presence."[13] Both of these experiences—the one in the form of deeds, the other in the form of commandments—are essential to Yahweh's identity.

Such a correlation of deeds and words in the identity of a person has an analogue in historic figures. For example, who Martin Luther King, Jr. was could be known from his active attempts to gain liberation for the black people of America. But King's personal identity was equally revealed by his speeches, and perhaps most of all by his rightly famous "I Have a Dream" speech. "I have a dream," he said, "that one day this nation will rise up and live out the true meaning of its creed: 'We hold these truths to be self-evident; that all men are created equal.' "[14] However much actions may speak louder than words, this dream of King's said as much about who he was and what he was about as did his deeds. Any narrative of his life that left out his "Dream" speech would exclude an essential aspect of King's identity. In the same way, the biblical text asserts that we know as much about who Yahweh is by his words as we do by his act of liberation. Yahweh's act and word belong intrinsically together as a definition of his identity—they cannot be separated, much less placed one over against the other.

There are numerous metaphors we could use to express the new identity of Yahweh, and the necessarily corresponding identity of Israel, but the one that is most appropriate to the text of Exodus is also well established in subsequent tradition—the Kingdom of God. Of course, the political aspect of Yahweh's character was already implicit in the promises of land and nationhood made to the Ancestors. But throughout the Ancestral Saga Yahweh appears primarily as the guide and protector of an extended family, "the God of Abraham, Isaac, and Jacob." In the first part of Exodus, on the other hand, Yahweh appears as a "man of war" (15:3) who fights against a political power for the liberation of an oppressed *people*, finally winning universal kingship (15:18). In the second part of Exodus the text represents the nature of the Kingdom Yahweh has established.

The Kingdom of Yahweh is represented initially by two distinct literary units: chapters 20—24 and 25—31. Taken together these two units constitute the polity of the Kingdom, in both senses of that term, namely the form of government of a social *and* of a sacral community.[15] While we shall discuss these two aspects of Israel's polity separately, following the order of the text, it is important to remember that they are complementary and inseparable. There is no "spiritual" or "religious" community apart from the "secular" or "political" community. Both aspects of the polity of the Kingdom are already visible in chapter 19, where Israel agrees to enter into a covenant with Yahweh by verbal commitment (vss. 3–8), and prepares for the encounter with God by liturgical sanctification (vss. 10–15).

The polity of the Kingdom as a social organization is presented by chapters 20—24. The primary content of this polity appears in the form of law: the Decalogue and the Book of the Covenant. While the content of these laws is, of course, of great importance in defining the nature of the Kingdom, and therefore the identity of Yahweh and Israel, we shall postpone any detailed discussion of the content until we come to the book of Deuteronomy. There much of the same material is repeated and interpreted theologically.

Our primary focus will be on the literary form of chapters 20—24. The sequence of the material is clear. At the opening of chapter 20, in a "preamble" to the Decalogue, Yahweh identifies himself as the God of Israel's salvation (vs. 2). He then pronounces the ten commandments, after which the people elect Moses as their official mediator. Moses then ascends the mountain to receive the detailed stipulations of the covenant (20:21—23:33). At the end of these stipulations is an admonitory section in which Yahweh warns of punishments for disobedience and promises rewards for obedience. The unit concludes with a ceremony in which the people ratify the covenant (chap. 24).

As numerous studies have shown, the formal sequence of these chapters substantially reflects the literary pattern of political treaties in the ancient Near East ("treaty" being a synonym of "covenant").[16] The particular pattern evidenced here is that between a superior king (a "suzerain") and one who is dependent on that king's support (a "vassal"). The major parallels between such treaties and Exodus 20—24 are: a historical prologue in which the suzerain recites his past acts of protection for the vassal; the stipulations of the treaty that the vassal must obey in order to remain in the "good graces" of the suzerain; deposit of the treaty document (cf. Exod. 25:16, 21); and a list of blessings and curses that will follow upon obedience or disobedience (cf. 23:20–33). While the correspondence between this treaty pattern and Exodus 20—24 is not exact, and important elements of the treaty form are missing, the resemblance is clear enough to warrant the conclusion that the biblical authors have employed a political model for their understanding of Israel's relationship to Yahweh. Yahweh is Israel's covenant lord, their suzerain; Israel is Yahweh's covenant people, his vassal. Surely one of the most profound (and at times revolutionary) implications of the Kingdom of Yahweh is that, if Yahweh is Israel's king, then all other kingships are relativized. Membership in the covenant community demands a "pledge of allegiance" to Yahweh that is absolute and unqualified: "You shall have no other gods before me" (20:3).

Just as the metaphor of the Kingdom of God signifies a new identity for Yahweh it also signifies a new identity for Israel, Yahweh's vassal. To be an Israelite now means to be a member of this *covenant* community. Israel is no longer a people in the strictly ethnic sense, the progeny of one family line, but a "holy nation" whose primary bond is one of covenantal polity rather than kinship.[17] The laws of the covenant represent the borders of Yahweh's Kingdom. To step outside those laws is to remove oneself from the protective sovereignty of Yahweh.

Similarly, to be an Israelite means to be a member of a covenant *community*. Each individual Israelite does not and cannot stand alone, but is also bound to the covenant brother or sister. The covenant code even demands a form of justice for the "alien" (sojourner) that is consistent with the covenant community's self-understanding (22:21). Ultimately there *is* no personal identity apart from one's covenantal identity, no "I" apart from "we." Thus the political metaphor of the Kingdom insists that "the inclination of humankind for community with God cannot become a reality without the community of each other."[18]

The second aspect of Israel's polity within the Kingdom of God is represented in chapters 25—31. After Moses has conducted the treaty ratification ceremony, he again ascends the mountain. The uniqueness of his office is emphasized when he actually enters the cloud that conceals the divine presence (24:18). Moses remains on the mountain forty days and forty nights, during which time he receives another set of instructions, now for the building of a sanctuary. We must not allow the technical detail of these chapters to detract from their narrative significance. Like the covenantal polity of Israel, the ecclesiastical polity is an essential part of the exaltation of Yahweh, soon to be consummated by the enthronement of Yahweh among the worshiping congregation. "Let them make me a sanctuary, that I may dwell in their midst" (25:8).[19]

The implications of this aspect of Yahweh's kingship are also far-reaching. Here we shall focus on two of them. First, as with the formation of the covenant community, the creation of the ecclesiastical community will provide a new way for righteousness between God and humankind. In fact, the language of "creation" is all the more appropriate here, for these chapters are framed by references which evoke *the* creation in Genesis 1. When Moses goes up the mountain to receive instructions for the tabernacle, the author tells us that the glory and cloud covered the mountain for six days, "and on the seventh day [Yahweh] called to Moses out of the midst of the cloud'' (24:16). Similarly, at the end of chapter 31, Yahweh concludes the tabernacle instructions with a commandment of Sabbath observance. Keeping the Sabbath is a "sign" of Israel's sanctification by Yahweh (vs. 13) and of Yahweh's creation of the world in six days, and his rest on the seventh (vs. 17).

For the Priestly author (who is at work in these chapters) this passage represents the culmination of a process that began with the covenant and sign of Noah (the rainbow) and Abraham (circumcision). All of world history has been driving toward this moment when Yahweh would open a new way for humankind through a new creative act. This act is quite literally a revolution in the relationship between God and humankind. For God to "dwell" with Israel is a reversal of the withdrawal of God's presence that figured so prominently in the Primeval cycle: Adam and Eve driven from the garden, Cain hidden from God's presence, or, on the other side, God's "coming down" not to dwell in community, but to "scatter" (Babel) and to destroy (Sodom, Egypt). In short, along with the movement toward *covenant* community, the exaltation of Yahweh also reveals a movement toward *sacral* community. "The book thus recounts the stages in the descent of the divine presence to take up its abode for the first time among one of the peoples of the earth."[20]

The second implication of Yahweh's enthronement as Israel's exalted king has to do with the ongoing life of the community. However much the covenant polity contained in chapters 20—23 may be constitutive for Israel's identity, the text recognizes that the people will need further guidance from Yahweh in the future. Since this community is defined by the words of Yahweh, there must be some way for it to hear those words afresh, and to hear new words in new situations. This is precisely one of the purposes of Yahweh's enthronement. The tabernacle, and more specifically the "ark of the testimony," is the place where Yahweh will "meet" with Israel through the representation of Moses: "There I will meet with you [Moses], and from above the mercy seat, from between the two cherubim that are upon the ark of the testimony, I will speak with you of all that I will give you in commandment for the people of Israel" (25:22).

Here is one of the clearest examples of how the two aspects of Israel's polity are in fact one. Yahweh's enthronement in the tabernacle provides the means by which the "commanding presence" can continue with the people on their journey through the wilderness and on into their future in the land. The king who dwells in the tabernacle is the God of the exodus and the covenant lord of Sinai, guiding his people with his *torah* that he reveals to them through Moses.

7. The Threat from Within (chaps. 32—34)

"Get up and make us a god who will go before us" (32:1). These are the first words of the people since the covenant ratification ceremony. The last time they spoke their words were quite different: "All that Yahweh has said we will do, and we will be obedient" (24:7). But the situation in which they now find themselves is also quite different. Moses has been on the mountain for a very long time—forty days and nights. For all the people know, when Moses entered the clouds at the top he also entered the "devouring fire," and that would be the last they would see of him.

In their long wait the people have had time to think of other things and, above all, to worry. They are thinking of the arduous and dangerous journey that lies ahead of them through the wilderness and of their ultimate destination, the land of Canaan. They are worried about the absence and apparent loss of their leader, Moses, and fearful (not without reason) that his absence means the absence of God as well. Thus what they demand of Aaron is a replacement for Moses and for the divine presence and guidance that has sustained them in the past.

The people's demand for a god who will "go before" them on the way to Canaan immediately calls to mind the concluding section of the Book of the Covenant (23:20–33). This passage in particular brings out the contextual irony of the story of the golden calf in terms of the major themes of the Pentateuchal narrative. The passage opens with a promise of divine presence and guidance on the way to the land. Yahweh will send an angel to bring the people "to the place which I have prepared" (cf. 15:17). The theme of blessing and curse also appears, both with respect to Israel and to the other peoples of Canaan. Although it is more militant, the formulation in verse 22 reminds us of Genesis 12:3: "I will be an enemy to your enemies and an adversary to your adversaries." Israel's enemies are thus placed under a curse, while Israel is explicitly promised blessing (vs. 25).

Of course, as we have already seen, the blessing of Israel is now dependent on covenant obedience—on Israel's responsibility to Yahweh as its suzerain. The greatest concern in this particular passage is to prevent the worship of other gods (vss. 24, 32–33), an act that would constitute the most serious breach of the treaty stipulations (20:3). In this context of covenant responsibility we now begin to see why the Canaanite peoples are so odious: their gods will be a temptation to Israel, and thus they will make Israel to "sin" against Yahweh (vs. 33).[21] The somber, admonitory tone of the passage serves to emphasize the conditionality of the covenant. There will be no pardon for disobedience (vs. 21).

In the present shape of the text, this conclusion to the Book of the Covenant represents the last words the people hear before they ratify the covenant: "All the words which Yahweh has spoken we will do" (24:3). If they will be true to *their* words, Yahweh will bless them and his angel will go before them to guide them to the promised land. At the conclusion of the covenant ratification, Moses ascends the mountain to receive the treaty document *and* the instructions for the tabernacle. Of the latter, the people know nothing. They are not aware of Yahweh's plan to provide a continual meeting place where they can learn of his will and benefit from his guidance. So far they know only of the covenant polity to which they have agreed. Now, after the long absence of Moses, they will provide their own medium of divine presence and guidance.

The first six verses report the construction of the calf and Aaron's pathetic attempt to remedy his error by proclaiming a feast to *Yahweh* (vs. 5). But his effort comes too late. Even if the calf is not intended to be an "other god" (20:3), it clearly constitutes a breach of the prohibition against a "graven image" (20:4–6). The people violate the treaty even before they have received the written document. Now in verses 7–14, composed entirely of speeches between Yahweh and Moses, a stunning movement takes place, one that goes to the heart of Israel's election, and indeed, to the heart of God.

First Yahweh refers to Israel as "your people" (vs. 7), implying that they are no longer "my people." Then he adds: "Now therefore let me alone, that my wrath may burn hot against them and I may consume them; but of you I will make a great nation" (vs. 10). In contrast to the rest of the story, this passage poses the problem and its solution in the most radical way possible. It is not a question of indiscriminate execution (vss. 27–28), or of a future punishment limited to the guilty (vss. 33–34), or of an immediate but limited curse by plague (vs. 35). Instead, here Yahweh is ready to destroy *the entire people*. Yahweh threatens to return the world to its pre-Abrahamic state of disorder, and to begin all over again with Moses. With a change in emphasis, the promise to Abraham is repeated word for word: "Of *you* I will make a great nation."

From the redactor's perspective, the severity of this decree does not suggest an excessive reaction, as it may to the modern reader. As we have already seen, within the covenant polity the people exists as a single corporate entity, not a collection of individuals. The terms of the covenant call for absolute obedience *as a people*, and the consequences of irresponsibility are equally comprehensive. The totality of the covenant polity was emphasized in the description of the ratification ceremony: "Moses came and told the people *all* the words of Yahweh and *all* the ordinances;

and *all* the people answered with *one voice*, and said, '*All* that Yahweh has spoken we will do' '' (24:3).

One of the great and enduring insights of Israel's political model for her relationship to Yahweh is that "a sinful deed is regarded as having objective *social* consequences, consequences menacing and even *fatal* not only to the doer of the deed but also to other members of his group, to his children and his children's children" (cf. 20:5).[22] To contemporary Western attitudes, so bereft of a sense of community and so enamored with individualism—in a word, so "narcissistic"[23]—such an ancient view seems "both immoral and primitive; but, unfortunately, it was also true."[24] While other texts will call into question the concept of corporate responsibility and punishment (e.g., Ezek. 18), it will remain throughout the Pentateuch (and much of the Hebrew Bible) as a permanent fixture in Israel's covenant polity. What is astounding to the author of verses 7–14, therefore, is not that Yahweh would threaten Israel's destruction; that was expected. What is astounding is that Yahweh finally "changed his mind" (vs. 14).

This is surely Moses' finest hour. His role of mediator, confirmed at the encounter before, is already tested to its limit. The boldness of Moses' reply is staggering. He reminds Yahweh of who he is and what his purpose is, and calls into question Yahweh's otherwise justifiable wrath. First Moses reflects Yahweh's classic self-introduction by lifting up before him "your people, whom you brought forth out of the land of Egypt." He then moves to Yahweh's purpose in a way that reminds us of the acknowledgment motif earlier in Exodus. If Yahweh destroys Israel, the Egyptians will claim that Yahweh's purpose with this people was "evil." Thus Moses demands (note the imperative) that Yahweh reconsider his decision of wrath.

Finally, Moses clinches his argument by reminding Yahweh of his promises of numerous descendants and of land to the ancestors. In fact, Moses refers specifically to the "oath" Yahweh swore to Abraham when Abraham was willing to sacrifice Isaac (vs. 13; cf. Gen. 22:16). Once again that moment of human righteousness has far-reaching consequences.

But our text is more concerned with the righteousness of God. Yahweh's agreement to "remember" the ancestors and to honor his promises to them discloses a dimension of his character transcending even his own standards of covenant righteousness that he has just revealed at Sinai. Righteousness, again, means being "in right relation with." For Yahweh this still means a relationship in which he elects Israel out of grace alone to be his people. There is a radical difference here, one that was glimpsed, perhaps, with a figure like the young Jacob, but that now appears to its fullest extent. It is not just that grace is not a reward for righteousness; it is that grace is offered *despite un*righteousness. Israel's failure to live

up to the conditions of the covenant means a failure to achieve sanctification, but it does not negate Israel's *salvation*. Yahweh is still willing to
call them "my people," as he was before they even knew of him (3:7–
10). That relationship is rooted in Yahweh's unqualified love for the people
and, in the light of the Primeval cycle, his love for the world, to whom
they have been appointed as a "kingdom of priests." As severe as the
punishment of this people under the divine curse may be, here and subsequently in the Pentateuch, the text will never suggest a final and complete abandonment of Israel by God. In effect, the golden calf story thus
represents an "identity crisis" within the heart of God. In order to be
true to that self that swore the oath to Abraham, Yahweh must suppress
that self that is the offended suzerain of Sinai.

What has happened between Moses and Yahweh makes the rest
of the story anticlimactic but certainly not insignificant. After all only we,
the readers, have been privy to this mountaintop decision. Israel knows
nothing of it. While the people are reveling in a blasphemous religious
frenzy, their fate is being determined on top of the mountain. They are
saved before they know they were damned.[25]

The rest of the story also points in the direction of a new and
different climax to the sin of the golden calf, suggesting that the full
significance of this story will appear only in the context of the following
chapters. When Moses comes down from the mountain and sees the
degrading spectacle, he angrily breaks the tablets of the covenant, thereby
symbolizing the broken *covenant* relationship between Yahweh and Israel.

Similarly, the end of the story and the beginning of chapter 33
suggest that the basis of Israel's *sacral* polity has also collapsed. The
promise of sending an angel before them now appears in the context of
a threat (vs. 34; cf. 23:20–21). In fact, in 33:1–3, Yahweh abruptly orders
Moses to begin the journey to the land of Canaan, again citing the "oath"
to the ancestors. Here too he promises to send an angel before the people,
but, he says, "*I* will not go up among you, lest I consume you in the
way"(vs. 3).

The people take these words as "evil tidings" (vs. 4), and rightly
so; although they remain God's chosen people, the relationship has been
pierced, as it were, on the horns of the golden calf. In effect, they are
now in the same position they occupied between Egypt and Sinai, only
made more tenuous by their sin. The covenant, under which they were
to enjoy the protective sovereignty of Yahweh and realize their very
identity as a people, lies shattered at Moses' feet. Moreover, although
they apparently know nothing of it, Yahweh has ordered Moses to leave
Sinai without first constructing the tabernacle, which was to have served
as the spatial medium for Yahweh's "dwelling" among them.

In the present context the "tent of meeting" described in 33:7–11 serves a provisional function. Although it represents God's continuing presence with Israel, it is virtually Moses' private institution that he has erected at his own initiative to serve as a temporary substitute for the tabernacle, the plan for which God has apparently abandoned in his order to begin the journey toward the promised land.[26]

Moses now directs his attention to an attempt to secure a pledge from Yahweh that Yahweh himself—and not just an angelic substitute—will go with his people. In an apparent attempt to bolster his office as mediator, Moses asks for a new revelation of Yahweh's character so that Moses may know him more fully, and he again asks Yahweh to "consider that this nation is your people" (vs. 13). Yahweh responds with the promise for which Moses had hoped: "I myself will go with you" (vs. 14).[27]

Now Moses presses his request even further by asking to see Yahweh's "glory," that is, to see God's essential nature. This, Yahweh says, is too much, even for Moses. No one can see his "face," his identity, and live. In unusually concrete language, Yahweh says that his glory will pass by Moses, but Yahweh will put his hand over Moses so that Moses can see only Yahweh's back.

How does God reveal his "glory"? Before Yahweh fulfils his pledge to proclaim his name to Moses, he issues an unexpected order: "Cut two tables of stone like the first; and I will write upon the tables the words that were on the first tables, which you broke" (34:1). Yahweh has decided to reinstate the treaty, and thus to reclaim Israel as his *covenant* people.[28] The renewal of the covenant itself is an act of divine grace, for in this decision Yahweh extends to Israel his protective and governing sovereignty, despite their breach of the original covenant. In fact, Yahweh's words—"I am making a covenant" (34:10)[29]—follow immediately upon Moses' final plea for pardon (vs. 9). The granting of the new covenant is at the same time the granting of pardon.

Yahweh has now reaffirmed his identity as Israel's suzerain, even though Israel is a rebellious vassal. Appropriately, in this context comes a new disclosure of the divine name (34:5–8). Following the covenant stipulations, the rest of chapter 34 proceeds to a reaffirmation of *Moses'* identity as mediator. In comparison with the previous covenant process (chaps. 19—24), the renewal of the covenant occurs with a significant omission: Israel plays no role whatsoever (vs. 27). Now the covenant is made through the agency of the mediator alone, without any consultation of the third party. In a sense, Moses not only "represents" Israel; he now *is* Israel, the faithful servant by whom alone Yahweh can reestablish his Kingdom.

Chapter 34 concludes with what appears to be an explicit contrast to Moses' earlier descent from the mountain (31:18). Again Moses stays on the mountain forty days and nights, and again he returns with the treaty document. His previous delay had driven the people to find a substitute for him, one that even made him comparable to a divine figure: "make us a *god* . . . for we do not know what has happened to this *man* Moses" (32:1). Now when he returns he is so physically transformed as almost to warrant the term "apotheosis." Moses' exaltation is a result of his talking with God (vs. 29), and now he mediates the divine words with a directness previously unknown.

> By placing the story in this form in its present position the author has given an interpretation of how he wants the entire Sinai tradition to be understood. God and the revelation of his will stand at the center. But Sinai is also the story of Moses, the mediator between God and Israel, who continued to function as a mortal man and yet who in his office bridged the enormous gap between the awesome, holy, and zealous God of Sinai and the fearful, sinful, and repentant people of the covenant.[30]

8. The Glory of Yahweh (chaps. 35—40)

Through the mediation of Moses and the grace of God Israel has been saved from death (chap. 32) and reinstated as Yahweh's covenant people (chap. 34). The final section of the book now turns to Israel as a sacral community. Chapter 34 represented a covenant *renewal*, but chapters 35—40 do not represent a renewal of the sacral community, for this community has not yet come into existence. Indeed, the text has never suggested that the people know of Yahweh's plan for the tabernacle.

What happens now is just as surprising as Yahweh's decision not to destroy Israel, and his decision to renew the covenant. This is the final movement of the divine presence, culminating in the enthronement of Israel's exalted king, but now that enthronement takes place "in the midst of" a "stiff-necked" people stained by "iniquity" and "sin" (34:9). For this reason, the allusions in the text to Genesis 1 which evoke the sense of a new creation—already noted at 24:16 and 31:12–17—now take on a deeper significance.[31]

A parallel to the latter passage, that concluded the original tabernacle instructions, now opens the story of the completion of the tabernacle (35:1–3). Moses assembles the congregation and issues yet another Sabbath commandment. The scene provides an ironic contrast to the opening scene in chapter 32, where the people assembled *against* Aaron and demanded the calf (vs. 1). In light of the previous Sabbath commandments (20:8–11; 34:21), another Sabbath commandment would seem unnecessary, but a reminder is in order because the construction of the tabernacle will be the *people*'s work, and that work must be done in strict conformity to the commandments of God. In addition, the Sabbath commandment reminds us of the orderly process through which the world came into being, with God speaking and everything happening "just so."

The people respond to Moses' instructions with what can only be called wild enthusiasm (35:20–29). "They came, every one whose heart stirred him, and everyone whose spirit moved him, and brought Yahweh's offering" (vs. 21). In fact they bring such enormous quantities of goods—from gold to goatskins—that Moses has to issue a restraint order (36:2–7)! Although the people are obviously responding to Moses' instructions, their "offerings" are technically not expiatory in nature (which one might expect), but "freewill offerings," which normally are "prompted solely by the impulse of the donor."[32] Thus the construction of the tabernacle represents not only a gracious condescension of Yahweh, but also a joyful "lifting up"[33] of the people's gifts to him. Now the "tent of meeting" is truly a meeting of the divine and the human will, and the story of its construction and sanctification continues the story of Israel's reconciliation to Yahweh.

As the work of the tabernacle comes to completion, the allusions to Genesis 1 return. As "in the beginning," so now all has taken place according to Yahweh's will: "Moses saw all the work, and behold, they had done it; as Yahweh had commanded, so had they done it" (39:43a; cf. Gen. 1:31). As "in the beginning" God had "blessed" his creation, so now Moses "blesses" the people (vs. 43b). As "in the beginning" God had "hallowed" the Sabbath day at the end of his creation, so now Yahweh orders Moses to "hallow" the tabernacle (40:9; cf. Gen. 2:3).

All that remains is for Yahweh himself to sanctify the tabernacle with his presence. Without that presence, the tabernacle—endowed as it is with the people's offerings of silver, gold, and precious stones—is no more than an empty shell, devoid of any theological significance. Thus the enthronement of Yahweh in his tabernacle constitutes the climax of the book, and indeed, of the Pentateuchal narrative up to this point: "Then the cloud covered the tent of meeting, and the glory of Yahweh filled the tabernacle. And Moses was not able to enter the tent of meeting, because the cloud abode upon it, and the glory of Yahweh filled the tabernacle" (40:34–35). In the context of the Pentateuchal narrative, the enthronement of the covenant lord of Israel in the tent of meeting provides a community of God and humankind that the world has not seen since the first man and woman were driven from Eden. "I will dwell among the people of Israel, and will be their God. And they shall acknowledge that I am Yahweh their God, who brought them out of the land of Egypt, that I might dwell among them; I am Yahweh their God" (29:45–46).

III
LEVITICUS—
In the Presence of Yahweh

1. Leviticus as Narrative

Many a pious vow to read straight through the Bible from cover to cover has foundered in the shoals of Leviticus. It is difficult to think of a book in the Bible that is less inviting to twentieth-century readers. This collection of ritual customs is not only soporific (two chapters one quarter hour before bedtime), but often seems utterly primitive as well. Consider the ritual in which a living bird, cedar wood, scarlet stuff, and hyssop are dipped in the blood of a slaughtered bird and then sprinkled on a person as a remedy for "leprosy" (14:4–7). Such passages conjure up the witches chant in *Macbeth*: "Lizard's leg, and howlet's wing; / For a charm of pow'rful trouble / Like a hell-broth boil and bubble" (IV.i.16–19).

Few people would want to revive such rituals, but even fewer have dispensed with the theological concerns those rituals express. Leviticus is a book about being in the presence of God. For the ancient world, at least, that situation was always an awesome experience, fascinating and terrifying at the same time—but always terrifying, because to be human meant to feel radically unworthy, indeed somehow "unclean," in the presence of holiness, and thus threatened by that presence.[1] Leviticus is a manual of instruction on how to remain fit for being in the presence of God, but it is also a major stage within the plot of the Pentateuchal narrative. When we consider the complementary functions of instruction (*torah*) and narration we shall find that the book represents an indispensable development in the characterization of Yahweh and of Israel.

Alongside the archaic customs in Leviticus, the major problem confronting the reader of the Pentateuch is the dearth of narrative. Only

---

In Leviticus read 1:1–9; 4:1–12; 8:1—10:3; 11:1–12; 13:1–8; 15:1–15; 16:1–34; 18:1—19:37; 25:1–17; 26:1–46.

chapters 8—10 (and 24:10–23) contain any action that qualifies as narrative in the ordinary sense. Clearly, the redactors did not arrange or compose the material in Leviticus with the purpose of rendering a realistic story. But here we must exercise extreme caution, precisely in our understanding of what it means to read the Torah as narrative. There can be little doubt that a major intention of the redactors of Leviticus was to compile ritual legislation that would meet their contemporary needs. It is also clear that they included the material here in the Torah in order to give it divine sanction; the legislation is represented as the revelation of Yahweh to Moses at Sinai. At the same time, the significance of the material also derives from its narrative context.

First, let us look at the incident in chapters 8—9. The first sacrifices take place here; thus this incident presupposes chapters 1—7, where the proper sacrificial procedures are specified. At first sight, chapters 1—9 might appear a mere appendix to the book of Exodus, one with which we could easily, even enthusiastically, dispense. But that is far from the case. In fact, these chapters represent the *completion* of the narrative sequence that began with Yahweh's command in Exodus 25:8, "Let them build me a sanctuary, that I may dwell among them." This command was enacted at the end of Exodus, when the "glory of Yahweh filled the tabernacle" (40:34).

However, the advent of the divine glory represented only a partial fulfilment of the instructions for the sanctuary. While the sacred space of worship was thereby legitimated, the time was not. In other words, the activities that take place in the sanctuary, and the people who perform these activities, were yet to be consecrated—the sanctification of the altar and the ordination of the priests who serve on behalf of the people. The ordination service is outlined in Exodus 29, but does not take place until Leviticus 8—9. Thus chapters 8—9 constitute the climactic moment at which the entire liturgical structure and activity of the people is consummated. Once again the "glory of Yahweh" appears, and now fire comes from Yahweh and consumes the first sacrifice (9:23–24). Just as the descent of the divine presence consecrated the tabernacle, now it consecrates the *ritual* of sacrifice and those who perform it.

But the significance of the event in chapter 9 is not exhausted with the constitution of the worshiping community. As we have already suggested, human finitude itself makes being in the presence of God an awesome and dangerous situation. In Israel's case, the narrative context of Leviticus 1—9 poses an even more threatening situation. For this is a sinful people—the people who, along with Aaron the priest, constructed the golden calf, as well as an unauthorized altar of sacrifice (32:5–6). It is this priest, on behalf of this people, who now approaches the legitimate

altar, and thus comes into the presence of God. While Yahweh has re-
scinded his verdict of annihilation for the sin of the calf (32:14), has
reinstated the covenant in response to Moses' plea for forgiveness (34:9–
10), and has sanctified the tabernacle with his presence, nowhere has the
text suggested that there was a complete reconciliation.[2] Indeed, that is
the irony of the conclusion of Exodus, where the Holy God descends to
the tabernacle and sanctifies *it*, even though the people and their priest
remain under the burden of their sin.

Such ironies the redactors of Leviticus do not like. While it was
probably not the original intention of chapter 9 to answer the problem of
the golden calf, in its present context it functions as the climactic resolution to that problem. In this chapter Aaron and his sons are ordained
and the altar of sacrifice is consecrated by a new manifestation of divine
presence. At the same time, the sacrifices Aaron performs at the command
of Yahweh mediated through Moses, secure "*atonement*" for him and
for the people (vs. 7). Had this event not taken place, Yahweh's presence
in the tabernacle would be in the midst of a "stiff-necked people," stained
by "iniquity" and "sin" (Exod. 34:9). Such a situation is intolerable. If
Exodus 40 represented the climax of the exaltation of Yahweh, it also
immediately introduced a new tension in the Pentateuchal narrative: how
could the Holy God dwell in the midst of a sinful people? That tension
is resolved in the first nine chapters of Leviticus, and only there. Thus,
to ignore these chapters would be to ignore an essential element in the
plot of the Pentateuch.

Secondly, there are a number of references within Leviticus to the
preceding narrative of Exodus, as well as to Israel's future. For example,
near the end of the chapter on dietary restrictions (chap. 11), Yahweh
asserts the authority of the laws and the motivation for obedience in terms
of the exodus story: "For I am Yahweh, who brought you up out of the
land of Egypt, to be your God; you shall therefore be holy, for I am holy"
(vs. 45). Similarly, the laws applying specifically to the land of Canaan
often begin with a reference to Israel's future occupation. On one level
such an introduction was necessary simply because these laws obviously
could not be in force until Israel entered the land. On another level the
introductory formulas fuse the literary genres of manual and story, and
even though no explicit references to the promises to the ancestors are
made, the manual has become a guide for the time when those promises
are fulfilled.

Thirdly, the final form of the entire book is, in fact, that of a
narrative, and not a manual. While narration in the usual sense occurs
only in chapters 8—10 and 24:10–23, the rest of the book is presented as
a series of divine speeches addressed to Moses (and sometimes Aaron).

At beginning and end, the redactors have provided a narrative framework: "Yahweh called Moses, and spoke to him from the tent of meeting, saying, 'Speak to the Israelites, and say to them . . .' " (1:1); "These are the commandments which Yahweh commanded Moses for the Israelites at Mount Sinai" (27:34). Periodically, the introductory framework is maintained by the shorter formula, "And Yahweh said to Moses" (4:1; 5:14; 6:1, 8, 19, 24, etc.).

The framework and connecting devices may seem artificial, and the resulting narrative may be difficult to describe as "realistic." After all, with the exceptions noted, nothing really "happens" in the book. But here we must remember our discussion of the Decalogue and the other laws in Exodus. There we concluded that Yahweh's identity and character are revealed as much by his words as by his deeds. However minimal the narrative structure of Leviticus may be, its presence makes a crucial difference for what the text represents.

How different the material in Leviticus would be, for example, if it were not in the Pentateuch at all, but somewhere else in the canon, and *without* the minimal narrative seams. Such a situation is hardly unthinkable (cf. Psalms and Proverbs), and in fact was commonplace in other ancient Near Eastern libraries, where cultic regulations do not appear in the context of a story, nor are they represented as divine commands.[3] The Near Eastern cultic laws were part of civil and criminal codes as they are in the Hebrew Bible, but they were promulgated by the king and thus served to undergird royal authority.[4] In contrast, the Levitical laws are represented as the words of Yahweh uttered within a narrative context, and thus further express the character of the God who is rendered by that narrative.

There is a symbiotic relationship between the narrative framework and the rules: the narrative converts the rules into the words, the speech, of Yahweh, and the speech tells us more about the person rendered by the narrative.[5] Here *torah* (instruction) cannot be understood apart from the narrative framework of *the* Torah; but at the same time those "narrative" portions *within* the Torah (i.e., those portions characterized by action), are also incomplete without the accompanying divine speeches. Words and deeds belong together, and only together do they fully render the person of Yahweh as represented in the Pentateuchal narrative.

What do these words of Yahweh say about him? Primarily, they say that the one who brought Israel out of Egypt, who became Israel's covenant lord, and who dwells in their midst in the tabernacle, is also the *holy* God whose presence demands holiness on the part of Israel. By now that may not seem very surprising, but the depth and breadth of this holiness as represented in Leviticus is one of the most distinctive contributions to the Pentateuchal description of God, and indeed, of Israel.

How different the character of God now appears from that of the one who ate at Abraham's tent and strolled with him as with a friend. After Leviticus, such an ingenuous portrait of the divine character will be both naive and virtually idolatrous unless it appears in tension with the one who says, "You must be holy, for I am holy" (11:45).

2. "You shall be holy"

The background for Israel as a "holy nation" was provided in Exodus 19 in connection with the awesome appearance of Yahweh. Before the advent of the holy God, the people were consecrated—"made holy" (qiddash)—they washed their clothes, avoided contact with the mountain, and abstained from sexual intercourse (vss. 10–15, 21–24). This cultic preparation provided a complementary counterpart to the covenantal preparation in verses 1–9.[6]

The basic meaning of "holiness" (qodesh) is "separation." For Israel to be a "holy nation" means to be "set apart" from all other nations. Holiness is not an intrinsic quality belonging to the people; rather, they become holy only with respect to Yahweh. Thus the text reads "You shall be to me . . . a holy nation" (Exod. 19:6). Leviticus emphasizes the same point: "You shall be holy to me, for I, Yahweh, am holy, and have separated you from the peoples, that you should be mine" (20:26).

Thus the people's holiness derives only from the relationship to Yahweh. This is because holiness in its primary sense, as an intrinsic quality, belongs only to Yahweh. In fact, holiness in this sense is virtually synonymous with divinity. Again, the connotation of separation is fundamental: God is by nature majestic, awesome, exalted, "high and lifted up," the "wholly other."[7] The holiness of God expresses the infinite qualitative distinction between divinity and humanity.

In the context of the book of Leviticus, the holiness of Yahweh is intimately associated with the worshiping community. This connection points again to the startling claim made at the end of Exodus: the "wholly other" God of Sinai, whose very holiness means separation from humankind, condescends to "camp" with his people. However, the resulting conception of divine presence is not as crude as it may first seem. God is not reduced to the level of a fellow Boy Scout on a camporee. The Hebrew verb for "camp" (shakan) implies an impermanent form of dwelling, one that can be moved from place to place.[8] The verb is obviously appropriate for the tabernacle or "tent of meeting," which moves with Israel on the way through the wilderness (cf. Exod. 40:36–38).

Theologically, the impermanence connoted by shakan suggests that God's presence in the tabernacle is not temporally final, ontologically complete, or in any way restricted or contained by the sanctuary. The tabernacle is sacred space only because Yahweh is present, and not vice versa. There is thus a radical contingency to the earthly sanctuary as the place where the presence of God is located: Yahweh's continued presence is conditional on Israel's continual holiness.

"You must be holy, for I am holy." On the one hand, Yahweh's presence is absolutely essential to the people's existence. It is this presence alone that sustains and guides them; it is the source of their blessing. On the other hand, the presence of the holy God in their midst means that any departure from the people's consecrated state will endanger their continued existence, because the holiness of God cannot coexist with what is *un*holy, what is impure or "unclean." The ambivalent character of the divine presence is clear from the juxtaposition of chapters 9 and 10. The divine fire that ignites the inaugural sacrifice and thus provides the means for atonement is the same fire that engulfs those who approach the divine presence in an unorthodox fashion (9:24; 10:1–2). Those who come into the presence of God while in a state of impurity will die, much as someone coming too close to nuclear radiation would die if unprotected. Moreover, there exists an even greater threat. If impurity spreads unchecked throughout the entire community, God will abandon the sanctuary, and thus the people.

Clearly Leviticus presents a new formulation of the theme of human responsibility before God. Apart from all the peoples of the world, the Israelites enjoy a unique intimacy with Yahweh. Unlike all other sacral communities, not only the king or the priests have access to the sacred precincts or to ritual instructions, but the people as a whole.[9] Yet, as with the covenantal polity, the people's privileged status brings with it a serious responsibility. The demand for holiness is another aspect of the demand for righteousness.

The way to remain holy is, of course, to abstain from sin. The predominant understanding of sin with respect to holiness has to do with what is usually called "defilement." Here the standard English connotations of defilement are instructive: dirtiness, pollution, uncleanness, contamination. Such connotations indicate immediately the strong physical or tactile dimension of defilement. Thus the most appropriate analogue for defilement is "stain."[10]

The nature of sin as defilement may, at first sight, appear strange to the contemporary reader, although many Americans often seem obsessed with a secular version of John Wesley's famous adage, "Cleanliness is next to godliness."[11] We are used to thinking of sin in terms of specific behavior. Consequently, we may speak of *a* sin or of sin*s* in the plural. A sin is a particular act (or the lack thereof). Sin is connected with *doing* something. Such an understanding of sin is by no means absent from Leviticus, which includes regulations governing stealing, lying, treatment of the alien, the poor, the disabled and aged, and business procedures, but the most distinctive construal of sin here is that of defilement.

The association between defilement and "uncleanness" also indicates that defilement is something that not only can but primarily does happen *to* someone. In most cases, sin as defilement is not the result of an act one commits but it is a state into which one is placed as a consequence of something beyond one's control. Sin is contagious. It can be "caught" by contact with an object that itself is unclean. As a result, sin can spread from one individual to the whole community, just as a stain may begin on a garment from a single drop of contaminant, but spread to a much wider area.

Why then are certain things or conditions considered unclean, and what is the relationship between uncleanness and holiness? Some interpreters think that the instructions concerning defilement or uncleanness are simply primitive forms of hygiene or public health laws. Thus the prohibitions against touching anyone with a disease, or the requirement that one who is unclean stay outside the camp would be intended to prevent the spread of the disease. Similarly, the dietary laws (chap. 11) could be intended to prevent various forms of illness, such as trichinosis from tainted pork.[12]

However, public hygiene is far from the major concern of these instructions. Instead, they represent a theological development of the biblical understanding of holiness within the context of the Pentateuchal narrative. As the anthropologist Mary Douglas has put it, "holiness is exemplified by completeness." Anything that strays from the perceived natural order is thus *un*holy, that is, "unclean."[13] For example, the pig is unclean because it does not conform to the dominant class of land animals which are cloven-hoofed *and* chew the cud. Shellfish and crabs are unclean because they do not conform to the typical manner of locomotion of sea animals. Leavened bread and wine, while not unclean, are prohibited from certain rituals and officiants because they are the products of altered natural states. Similarly, a garment that has mildewed, a person with a skin disease, a woman during her menstrual period, all are perceived as aberrations from the natural order, and thus are "unclean."

However strange or even harmful such notions may seem to us, we cannot fully understand them outside the symbolic system of which they are a part. As Douglas says of the dietary laws, they are "like signs which at every turn inspired meditation on the oneness, purity and completeness of God. By rules of avoidance holiness was given a physical expression in every encounter with the animal kingdom and at every meal."[14] The suggestion of Israel's conformity to the oneness and completeness of God also points to the narrative significance of these rules. By living according to the rules Israel lives in accordance with the created order, and therefore in harmony with that which the creator willed "in the beginning" (Gen. 1). Just as God made the universe in perfect harmony by separating light and darkness, waters and heaven, earth and waters, so God has created a sacral community by separating Israel from all the other peoples on the earth.[15]

The fundamental reason for obedience to the various ritual laws, therefore, is quite simply because Yahweh has commanded them, just as he commanded Adam and Eve not to eat of the tree of knowledge. Yet, in an ironic contrast to much of Genesis 1—10, Israel is *commanded* to be like God, *in the way that God has prescribed* (cf. 20:24–26).

For all of its resemblances to primitive notions of *taboo*, sin as defilement functions as a distortion of the relationship between Yahweh and Israel. The narrative context transforms defilement from a "pre-ethical" apprehension of holiness to one based on a covenantal ethic.[16] Uncleanness is not intrinsically sinful, nor are its effects necessarily harmful or lethal to the one who becomes unclean. For example, sexual intercourse renders a man and woman unclean for the remainder of the day on which it occurs (15:18). This does not mean that sexual intercourse itself is sinful. The culture that produced the lyric affirmation of sensuality in the Song of Songs could hardly make such a condemnation. The real problem with defilement is thus not that of a power that works automatically against the one who is unclean. Rather, the problem comes when the one who is unholy comes into potential contact with the sacred, for example, by entering the tabernacle precinct or partaking of consecrated food.[17]

The greatest threat of all is that impurity will penetrate the sanctuary and incur the wrath of Yahweh, and his abandonment. There are various ways this situation can be avoided. Numerous texts suggest that defilement runs its course, after which a person is again pure and creates no threat to the sanctuary. Other texts require that the offending party be "cut off from the people," which may refer to ostracism, capital punishment, or death by divine retribution.[18]

Clearly the primary means for ridding the community of the threat of impurity, however, is the ritual of sacrifice. If holiness exemplifies completeness, then impurity produces incompleteness and must be rectified by atonement—or, as it is often signified, at-one-ment. Sacrifice is the means to reconciliation between Yahweh and Israel.

Here the analogy of stain is again helpful. Atonement accomplished through sacrifice is to impurity as cleansing is to stain.[19] But the object of sacrificial atonement is not the community or the individual person; it is the *sanctuary*, the sanctity of which is threatened by the people's impurity.[20] As a result, sacrifice provides the means by which the tabernacle will continue to function as the place in which Yahweh continues to "tent" with Israel.

Precisely how the authors understood sacrifice to effect atonement remains unclear. Nowhere do we find an elaborate theological explanation of the process.[21] Almost certainly, there are magical vestiges involved, yet the ritual is not a mechanical device that can be manipulated at will. Its effectiveness is limited almost exclusively to unintentional violations and thus does not extend to such deliberate acts as murder, adultery, and apostasy.[22] The text insists that the ritual is a gift of God (17:11), not a human invention.

> As a result of the performance of certain rites, God grants expiation or atonement. In such instances, expiation, forgiveness, etc. are not the direct *physical effects* of the rites performed. Such acts are prerequisite, but not causational. It is God who grants the desired result![23]

As with the effectiveness of the ritual, so with its significance: it does not lie in the ritual itself, but derives from the narrative context in which the ritual is prescribed. As we have already seen, the first sacrifice on the altar secured the atonement for Aaron and the people (9:7). In its present narrative context, that event signified both the consecration of the sacrificial ritual and the consummation of the process of forgiveness for the sin of the calf that began in Exodus 32. The event happened once and for all.

At the same time, within the entire Pentateuchal narrative the sacrificial rituals of Leviticus provide the *first and only* means for reconciliation between God and humankind that is both formal and repeatable.[24] Thus the nature of the ritual as a divine gift is crucial to its meaning. Elsewhere Yahweh specifies punishments for breach of covenant; only here in Leviticus does he ordain a procedure that will protect the covenant community from its own sin. Of course, we must emphasize again that the sacrificial ritual is primarily the antidote to "unwitting" sins of uncleanness, and not to deliberate and malicious acts prohibited by the covenant laws. Nevertheless, within this limited scope, the laws of Leviticus offer the unique instance in which God issues commandments of how to live in a proper relationship with him, *and* offers a means by which that relationship may be restored once it has been broken.

In short, Leviticus offers not only a way in which righteousness may be followed, but also a way by which *un*righteousness may be remedied. It holds before Israel the command, "You must be holy," but also the promise, "atonement shall be made for you" (16:30). The new way of righteousness now includes a way out of sin.

3. "The land is mine"

If Israel is a "holy nation," it will live in a holy land. While the expression "holy land" does not occur in Leviticus, the theology of holiness imbues its entire understanding of the land. The holiness of Canaan is prominent in the two companion chapters 18 and 20. Since Israel is "separated" from the other peoples, Israel is not to live according to their customs, and particularly the customs of the present inhabitants of the land of Canaan (20:22–26). The nature of those customs is spelled out explicitly in the framework of chapter 18, where the Canaanites are identified with various forms of sexual immorality, which, of course, is understood in terms of defilement. Now we learn that the land too may become defiled (vss. 24–30). Again the physical connotations of defilement are salient; the uncleanness of the inhabitants means that iniquity has infected the land itself and the land must be purged. The result is literally physical revulsion—the land "vomits out" its inhabitants. Defilement is both poisonous and emetic. Thus Israel is warned to avoid those native customs that cause defilement, lest Israel too be vomited out of the land.

This personification of the land also appears in the legislation for the sabbatical year and the year of jubilee (chap. 25).[25] The primary purpose of the former (every seven years) is not to provide rest for human beings, but rather for the land (vs. 4). In this year there is to be no sowing of crops or even pruning of vines. Thus the land can "rest" from the work it has done in providing food for human beings, and it is thus protected from ruthless exploitation. As with the dietary laws, we must be careful not to interpret this instruction in purely practical terms, although it would clearly have some ecological benefit. In the first place, it is not clear to what extent the custom was practiced,[26] and in the second place a fundamental theological issue is at stake. While we may detect some associations with relatively primitive understandings of the land in relation to divine powers of fertility in the soil, the literary context has suppressed such views. At the outset (vss. 1–2) the law is rooted in the narrative setting of a gift from Yahweh to Israel at Sinai. As with the people themselves, the sanctity of the land is not intrinsic, but derives from the relationship rendered by this narrative. Just as the people represent God's new community on earth by conforming to the order of nature and the pattern of rest established by the creator, [27] so must the land be allowed its sabbath to conform to this pattern as well.

The tripartite relationship of God, land, and people appears much more succinctly in verse 23: "For the land is mine, for you are resident aliens and sojourners with me." This is a truly remarkable statement, especially when one realizes the meaning of the expressions "resident alien" and "sojourner." As we have seen before, these terms refer not to permanent, native inhabitants, but to temporary residents. Ever since Abraham and Sarah, the Israelites have been resident aliens, with only a burial plot to call their own. Now in a startling reformulation of the Pentateuchal theme, the text insists that Israel's status in the land will *always* be that of an alien! The point, of course, is that Israel's possession of the land is a lease, and Yahweh may terminate the lease if Israel proves to be an undesirable tenant. This text thus represents the first explicit statement of a conditional formulation of the land promise, one that becomes more prominent in chapter 26 and in the rest of the Pentateuch. As an alien, Israel does not possess the land as an inalienable right.

The statement of Israel's alien status in verse 23 serves as the motivation for the central commandment of the Jubilee year (every forty-nine years): since the land belongs to Yahweh alone (vs. 23), it cannot be bought and sold like any other commodity; it is not private property.[28] On the other hand, particular plots of land are understood to belong to particular families (or at least extended families), and while that property, in a sense, may be leased, it belongs to that family forever, and at each Jubilee year they may reclaim it. Presumably this ownership goes back to the original gift of the entire land of Canaan by Yahweh to Israel, which in verse 38 is portrayed as the purpose of Israel's release from Egyptian bondage. The land was to be parceled out by lot, with each tribe receiving an "inheritance," which, in turn, would be subdivided among the individual families within the tribe. The legislation of the Jubilee year thus intends to protect this gift of Yahweh to each family. As a gift of God, it is not to be commercialized, for this would deny its very character as gift. The land as gift also suggests why the above contradiction is more apparent than real; the land of Canaan as a whole belongs to Yahweh alone, and is his to give (or retract), but individual segments of that land are given as "property" to individual tribes. Thus the individual tribes may be understood as landed tenants, even while the nation as a whole retains the tenuous status of "resident alien." "The aim of jubilee is the restoration of the position as it was of old: free persons living on free land."[29]

The contingency of the people's relationship to the land becomes all the more radical when it appears in terms of blessing and curse. We have already seen indications that the sacerdotal view of the "holy nation" in Leviticus understands the sanctuary as the locus of blessing, mediated to the people by the priests. Thus at the climactic consecration of the sacrificial altar and the priests at the end of chapter 9, the blessing pronounced on the people by Aaron and Moses has a prominent role (vss. 22–23). However, seen in the larger context of the whole book of Leviticus, the sanctuary and priests are not an automatic or unconditional source of divine blessing; rather, that blessing—or its opposite, the curse—is determined by obedience or disobedience within the covenant relationship between Yahweh and the people. The elaboration of this contingency of blessing and curse, and thereby of the relationship of the people to the land, is spelled out in graphic detail in chapter 26.

Chapter 26 would be a more fitting conclusion to the book than chapter 27, and perhaps was originally intended as such. In fact, the summary statement in 26:46 seems to include all of Exodus 19 through Leviticus, namely the time that Israel spent at Sinai (cf. 27:34). It is true that Israel does not leave Sinai until Numbers 10, but, as we shall see in the next chapter, Numbers 1—10 really has a different focus than Leviticus (it is interested in "Israel on the march"), and thus is rightly separated from it. Moreover, since a list of blessings and curses traditionally concludes a treaty, chapter 26 fits here at the end of that time in which Yahweh promulgated the statutes of his treaty with Israel. If the entire Sinai period is in view at the end of the book (27:34), then the legal process of covenant-making has become the structure for the plot of the narrative.

Ultimately, Leviticus directs the reader not only to the hoary past, when Yahweh spoke to Moses from the tent of meeting at Mount Sinai, but also to the far distant future, beyond the occupation of the land, to a time when the promises of nationhood, land, and blessing all will have been both fulfilled and then destroyed by sin and the resultant curse (26:27–39). Thus the text projects an Israel which waits in exile "beyond the Jordan," just as the Israel *within* the narrative has yet to reach the Jordan. Yet it also projects, even in that situation, a synchronic movement of human repentance and divine forgiveness which together point to a horizon of hope (26:40–45). For even though Yahweh may unleash the curse in all its fury, he will not break his covenant. Yahweh will remain Israel's king.

IV
NUMBERS—
In the Wilderness

1. Numbers as Narrative

     Numbers contains a bewildering variety of literary materials: on the one hand, detailed regulations, lists, and rules (most of chaps. 1—10 and 26—36); on the other hand, dramatic stories of a woman miraculously turned into a leper, an earthquake that engulfs a surly mob, a rod that produces almonds, and a charismatic wizard with his talking ass (within chaps. 11—25).[1] Thus in the present text narrative material is framed on either end by what we might call "legislative pronouncements." However, as we have already seen in the latter part of Exodus and in Leviticus, such a distinction cannot be made without qualification, for there is also legislative material imbedded within chapters 11—25 (cf. chaps. 15, 18, 19), and stories within the otherwise non-narrative texts (e.g., 9:1–8 and chap. 32). Moreover, as William Hallo notes, "the legislative portions of Numbers are set in and directly derived from the narrative context to an extent found nowhere else."[2] In fact, materials that are not technically legislative—such as the census lists in chapters 1 and 26—also are part of the warp and woof of the narrative, so much so that they provide structure and meaning to the whole book *as a narrative*.

     That Numbers deserves to *be* a book may at first sight appear questionable. There are so many connections with Exodus and Leviticus that Numbers might seem to be little more than an addendum. All three books share similar cultic regulations and concerns. Large portions of Exodus and Numbers, as well as the whole book of Leviticus, take place "in the wilderness of Sinai." And some of the controversy stories in Numbers appear *déjà vu* after Exodus.[3] These stories at some point were

---

In Numbers read 1:1–3, 47, 54; 2:1–2; chaps. 9—14; 16:1—18:7, 22–23; 19:11–13; 20:1—26:2; 27:12–23; chaps. 32 and 34; 36:13.

placed within two units (Exod. 15:11—18:28; Num. 11:1—20:13) to form a framework for the massive Sinai narrative that comes in between (Exod. 19—Num. 10).

However, despite all of this overlapping, there is a salient transition at Numbers 10:11–13 where a redactor has given us a precise date for the day on which the people of Israel broke camp and started on their journey *away from* "the wilderness of Sinai." This turning point in the narrative has influenced the whole book of Numbers; in fact, it clearly provided the theme around which a collection of often disparate literary traditions *became* a "book." That theme we may designate as "the way to the land." The book of Numbers is essentially the story of what happened to the people of Israel in between the wilderness of Sinai and the promised land. It is for this reason—that is, primarily on the basis of narrative structure— that we have three books (Exodus, Leviticus, Numbers), and not two or even one.[4] The three books in their canonical shape have distinctively different orientations: Exodus concentrates on the liberation from Egypt and the constitution of the covenant and sacral community of Israel; Leviticus focuses on the detailed instructions for the sacral community, highlighted by the ordination of the priesthood and consecration of the sacrificial altar (chaps. 8—9); and Numbers emphasizes those events encountered by Israel on the march from Sinai to Canaan. Whereas Leviticus focuses on the *order* of holiness for the sacral community, Numbers focuses on that community in terms of its *marching* orders.

Numbers thus deals with space and time that is in between—in between Egypt and Canaan, slavery and full citizenship, promise and fulfilment. The Hebrew title to the book (taken from 1:1) is most appropriate: "in the wilderness." The very barrenness of this land, and the strange animals that inhabit it, make it an object of dread. It is a "great and terrible wilderness,with fiery serpents and scorpions, and thirsty ground where there is no water" (Deut. 8:15). In short, it is "a land through which no one can pass" (Jer. 2:6). Yet it is precisely this land through which Israel now must pass on the way to the promised land.

It is no wonder, therefore, that the departure from Sinai is fraught with a sense of danger, and that numerous passages betray anxiety over the provision of guidance for such a perilous journey. Perhaps it was to mark this anxiety that the redactors placed an account of the Passover celebration near the end of the opening unit (9:1–14), for that ritual dramatizes the people's liminal situation in between the past and the future.[5] The way to the land is not only a geographical journey, it is also a spiritual journey, and the wilderness is both a place and a condition. The rigors of this journey will test the integrity and endurance of the people and their leaders such that the "wilderness journey" will become a companion metaphor for the "dark night of the soul."

Just as the redactors had good reason to constitute Numbers as a "book," so they provided it with four sections, each with a distinctive integrity, yet each linked to the preceding to produce a narrative with impressive literary artistry and theological depth:

chaps. 1—10   Mustering the Troops
11:1—20:13   Mutiny and Doom
20:14—25:18   Blessing Turned to Curse
chaps. 26—36   The Inheritors of the Land

2. Mustering the Troops (chaps. 1—10)

The distinct focus of Numbers is evident in the opening verses. As in Leviticus, Yahweh speaks to Moses from the tent of meeting, but the concern is not with cultic offerings. Yahweh's order is for a draft registration of "all in Israel who are able to go forth to war" (vs. 3; cf. 20, 22, etc.). Whereas Exodus and Leviticus focused on Israel as a vassal and a congregation governed by the commanding and sanctifying presence of Yahweh, Numbers focuses on Israel as a military force marching behind Yahweh as vanguard. Israel is an *army* about to take the field. The primary purpose of chapters 1—9 is the mobilization of this fighting force for the departure from Sinai and the "order of march" (10:28) through the wilderness.[6]

The result of the military census in chapter 1 is impressive—603,550 fighting men! While this may not have been the original figure, in the present text the number represents a formidable array.[7] In addition, when we add women and children, the number clearly suggests that Israel has indeed been fruitful and multiplied.[8] Israel begins the march to Canaan as a people blessed and an invincible army.

Of course the sacral dimension of this army is not lost in Numbers— if anything, it is accentuated. The tribe of the Levites is singled out as the custodian of all the appurtenances of the tabernacle (1:47–54; cf. chaps. 3—4; 8). The entire camp of the people is to be in the form of a concentric circle, with the tabernacle in the center, then the Levites around it, and then each of the other tribes, with all tents facing inward toward the tabernacle. Consequently, when camp is broken those tribes on the east of the camp will depart first, then those on the south, followed by the Levites bearing the tabernacle, the tribes on the west and finally those on the north. The camp and order of march reflect the centrality of the divine presence. Moreover, as with the laws of holiness in Leviticus, the "perfect ordering of the people around God's dwelling place is a realization of the created order in history."[9]

Just as Numbers emphasizes the tabernacle as the center of a military camp, so it focuses on the divine presence as military escort.

The cloud and fire that led Israel through the sea and defeated the Egyptians will now lead Israel through the wilderness: "So it was continually; the cloud covered [the tabernacle] by day, and the appearance of fire by night. And whenever the cloud was taken up from over the tent, after that the people of Israel set out; and in the place where the cloud settled down, there the people of Israel encamped" (9:16–17).

Although much of the material in chapters 1—10 may not make for exciting reading, the redactors have constructed the unit to drive toward a dramatic moment—the departure of Yahweh's army from Sinai:

> In the second year, in the second month, on the twentieth day of the month, the cloud was taken up from over the tabernacle of the testimony, and the people of Israel set out by stages from the wilderness of Sinai; and the cloud settled down in the wilderness of Paran. They began their march at the command of Yahweh by Moses (10:11–13).

For the author, this moment was as exciting as the launching of the lunar spacecraft was for many Americans. After all, what is being "launched" from Sinai is, in effect, the new model of human community before God. The manifestation of Yahweh's presence that began with the burning bush (Exod. 3), wrought victory at the sea (Exod. 13:21—14:31), confronted the people at the sacred mountain (Exod. 19—34), "encamped" in the tabernacle among the people (Exod. 40), and sanctified the sacrificial cult (Lev. 8—9), now has stirred once again. The cloud lifts up over the tabernacle and moves off in the direction of Canaan. If there had been any question that Yahweh belonged only to "the mountain of God,"[10] it is now negated: Yahweh will be with his people as protector and guide.

Such is the picture of Israel that we gain in the first unit of Numbers: the "holy nation" is now the army of Yahweh, hundreds of thousands strong, marching rank on rank, led by the cloud of the Holy Warrior who overthrew Pharaoh and all his host. It is a community completely ordered by the divine will and responsive to its human leadership, for it begins its march "at the command of Yahweh by Moses" (10:13). What enemy could possibly defeat such a mighty force? How could such an army fail? We cannot help but approach the second unit of Numbers with such questions in mind.

3. Mutiny and Doom (11:1—20:13)

The contrast between the mighty force described in chapters 1—10 and the sniveling, recalcitrant mob whom we now meet is overwhelming. Chapters 11—20 present a series of rebellions in the Israelite camp, each of which depicts the people in a very negative light, yet each of which might be understandable if not excusable. However, the context of chapters 1—10 foils any attempt to sympathize with the people. The discrepancy is perhaps nowhere greater than at the immediate juncture. In 10:36 we hear Moses' typical call to the divine warrior to return from his victory over Israel's enemies: "Return, Yahweh, to the ten thousand thousands of Israel!" Yet immediately in 11:1 we confront what is typical of the whole second unit: "Now the people complained in the hearing of Yahweh about their misfortune."

It is significant that this otherwise obscure incident (11:1–3) was placed here at the beginning of the second unit. It is an etiology of the place name Taberah, but it does not tell us what "misfortune" is the subject of the people's complaint. Thus what internally is already puzzling becomes in context completely inexplicable, and the divine judgment that follows appears to be unquestionably justified. Finally, the intercessory role of Moses is also crucial; only his intervention prevents Yahweh's fiery wrath from enveloping the entire camp. This brief and enigmatic passage thus functions as a paradigm for the stories that follow: Israel complains, Moses intervenes, Yahweh's care is elicited, or his righteous indignation curtailed.

After the introductory episode in 11:1–3, the narrative takes on a much more serious quality when the people question the adequacy of the gracious gifts of Yahweh and implicitly charge that Moses' mission has failed. They are tired of the manna, the "bread from heaven" which Yahweh had provided for their sustenance (see Exod. 16). Now they want a good steak—"Who will give us meat to eat?" (vs. 4). Moreover, the bland and Spartan diet of the wilderness makes them long for the succulent vegetables and subtle flavors of Egyptian cuisine. Apparently those who are now free but poorly fed would rather be slaves and well-fed—"for it was well with us in Egypt!" (vs. 18). The fear of the wilderness and the understandable need for food have aroused a romantic idealization of the past. Fear has blinded them from seeing Yahweh's presence, resulting in an unthinking distortion of divine grace, and Moses rightly uncovers the theological dimensions of their complaint: "You have rejected Yahweh, who is among you . . . , saying 'Why did we come out of Egypt?' " (vs. 20). Nevertheless, the people's rebellion here is only implicit, only expressed in the form of a surly question, and thus at this stage it represents only a foreshadowing of what is to come (chaps. 13—14). Thus, although the provision of quail carries with it an ironic consequence (even a delicacy can become nauseating after a month; vs. 33), these negative results of their stubbornness are incidental to the rest of the story. Instead, the rest of the incident turns on the question of Moses' leadership.

If the people's querulous refusal to recognize divine grace has a familiar ring to it (cf. already Exod. 14:10–12), so too does the way in which it involves Moses' role as leader. This is the primary focus of the second narrative thread in chapter 11. Moses' appeal to Yahweh in light of the people's complaint is as bold as it is pathetic (vss. 10–15). "Why have you dealt ill with your servant? And why have I not found favor in your sight, that you have laid the burden of all this people upon me?" (cf. Exod. 5:22–23). Moses' lament has a tone of desperation that we have not seen before, and he closes his appeal with the wish to die.

There follows a reaffirmation of Moses' leadership as well as a demonstration of his magnanimity. The cloud appears at the tent of meeting and some of the prophetic spirit that resides with Moses is transferred to others (vs. 25). Precisely how this is to help Moses out of his predicament is not made clear (especially given its ephemeral nature; end of vs. 25), but what is clear is that Moses is the fountainhead of the prophetic spirit.

The questions surrounding divine presence and human leadership are hardly resolved in chapter 11, notwithstanding the miraculous arrival of a flock of quails and the great charismatic awakening in the camp. In chapter 12 these questions are again couched in the form of prophetic legitimacy. Here the challenge to Moses' leadership is more direct. While the role of Moses' wife in the incident (vs. 1) remains ambiguous, the question posed by Miriam and Aaron is quite clear: "Has Yahweh indeed spoken only through Moses? Has he not spoken through us also?" (vs. 2). The issue concerns the authoritative media of revelation, the legitimate spokespersons of Yahweh—in short, an issue similar to that in chapter 11, the extent of the prophetic office.

The story wastes little time in reaffirming Moses' authority. First, in a rare biographical comment, the narrator tells us that Moses was the most humble man on earth (a comment notoriously difficult to square with the Mosaic authorship of the Pentateuch!). Then Yahweh once again appears in the cloud at the tent of meeting and rebukes Miriam and Aaron. Whereas Moses was the fountainhead of the prophetic spirit in chapter 11, here his authority goes beyond that of the prophet, for only Moses speaks with Yahweh "mouth to mouth" (an unusually bold metaphor), and only Moses is addressed by Yahweh as "my servant" (vss. 6–8). Moreover, while the emphasis in Yahweh's speech is on the "word" shared between them,[11] the end of the story also demonstrates Moses' authority when his intercession saves Miriam from permanent leprosy.

One would think that these indications of Yahweh's presence among the people, and direct divine confirmations of Moses' leadership, would prevent any further complaining. But in chapters 13—14 the complaining escalates into full-scale revolt and a crisis develops that can be compared only with the flood story (Gen. 6:5–8) and the golden calf incident (Exod.

32). "Now Yahweh said to Moses, 'Send men to reconnoiter the land of Canaan, which I am about to give to the people of Israel.' " (13:1–2). Israel stands at a watershed which separates the past from the future, the wilderness from the land of promise. To look behind is to look through the beginnings of the march on the way, through all the preparations of the camp, through the epochal events at Sinai and in Egypt, through three generations of the ancestors, all the way back to those words spoken to Abram at the very beginning of Israel's story: "Go from your land . . . to the land that I will show you" (Gen. 12:3). Now that charge and promise, whose fulfilment had at best been adumbrated to the ancestors, is about to be realized.

Numbers 13 thus presents us with what was to have been Israel's D-Day, yet it proves to be a day of infamy and defeat, a day that sealed the doom of the whole wilderness generation of Israel. The reason is not difficult to find; it is the same reason that stood behind the incident of the golden calf. Israel's greatest enemy was not the Canaanite force, not even the giants among them (13:32–33); Israel's greatest enemy was the enemy within—Israel's lack of trust. This threat from within does not emerge until the spies have returned with their report. There is no problem with the land itself, for "it flows with milk and honey," and they have brought an enormous cluster of grapes to demonstrate its fertility. But the cities are heavily fortified, and the spies even saw the descendants of Anak—the legendary giants—there. The sudden disquiet in the camp is momentarily silenced by Caleb (one of the spies), who is certain of Israel's superior military capability. But the other spies quickly dispel Caleb's confidence; now the mighty army of Yahweh seems "like grasshoppers" in the face of the Canaanite force (13:33). This "bad report" triggers the usual complaint from the people, but this time their utter panic drives them into outright mutiny: "Let us choose a captain and go back to Egypt!" (14:4).

As in the account of the golden calf in Exodus 32, the seriousness of Israel's disobedience leads to the threat of total destruction. Yahweh announces that he will annihilate the people and begin again with Moses. In both cases Moses' intercession prevents Yahweh's wrath from running its full course. Nevertheless, here Yahweh appears to execute the punishment he had postponed in Exodus 32:34[12]. Israel as a nation will survive, but the entire wilderness generation will die outside of the land of promise (except for Joshua and Caleb, and, presumably, Moses and Aaron). Perhaps the punishment in Numbers 14 is also much more severe than in Exodus 32 not only because here we have the crescendo of repeated rebellions, but also because here there is an attempt to reverse completely Yahweh's earlier act of liberation. In Exodus 32 they may commit idolatry, but at least they want gods to lead them on their way; now they want to reverse that way by electing a captain to lead them back to Egypt. Accordingly, a "measure for measure" punishment dominates the section in 14:26–35. Those who complained that they would die in the wilderness *will* die in the wilderness, yet their children—whom they thought would die—will live and enter the land; the spy mission that took forty days will have its counterpart in a new "wilderness wandering" of forty years. Throughout the section the redactor hammers out a stark contrast between death in the wilderness and life in the land.

Once the wilderness generation has brought about its own doom, one would think that the spy story would have run its course, but there is yet another incident that adds a note of irony. When the people are informed of their fate, they suddenly become as courageous as they had before been cowardly. Now they think that a confession of sin will turn them into conquerors (14:40). Moses warns them that precisely what they unjustifiably *feared* was the case before, *is* the case now: "Yahweh is not among you. . . . Yahweh will not be with you" (vss. 42, 43). Nevertheless, the people set out on a campaign into the land, unaccompanied by the ark (the representation of divine presence) or Moses (their legitimate human leader). The result is a decisive defeat. In this final act of foolishness, the people justify the sentence Yahweh had already declared; theirs is not to be the generation of the land. What they persistently and stupidly described as divine *purpose,* has now become the *result* of human irresponsibility: Yahweh has brought them out to die in the wilderness (Exod. 14:11; 16:3; 17:3; Num. 14:2).

To summarize: in their present shape chapters 11—14 resume a thematic tension that began as early as Exodus 3. In almost all cases, the immediate question has to do with the people's refusal to recognize Moses as their legitimate leader. Due to the mixture of traditions, the focus shifts from the relationship between Moses' authority and the prophetic office (chap. 12) to Moses' abilities as a field commander (chap. 14). Correlated with this challenge to Moses' authority, and indeed inseparable from it, is an increasingly bitter and ultimately irrational refusal to recognize Yahweh's saving presence among them. Here the very identity of Yahweh as defined by the preceding narrative ("I am Yahweh your God, who brought you out of the land of Egypt") is radically distorted. In fact, at the very moment of potential fulfilment of the promise of the land, the people throw that promise into question: "Why does Yahweh bring us into this land, to fall by the sword?" Thus the denouement of this episode ("How long will they not trust in me?"; vs. 11) stands in stark contrast to that in Exodus 1–14, where the people finally "trusted in Yahweh, and in Moses his servant" (14:31). Moreover, within the context of Numbers

1—14, chapters 11—14 betray an additional irony. It is the people who set out on the way to the land "at the command of Yahweh by Moses" (10:13) who in the end "transgress the command of Yahweh" (14:41). It is the invincible force of "ten thousand thousands," led by the ark and Yahweh of hosts (10:35-36) who in the end see themselves "as grass-hoppers" and are abandoned by the ark and Yahweh and defeated by their enemy (14:44-45). Such is the wilderness generation, the generation who must die outside the promised land.

It is tempting to suggest that Numbers 15 was placed in its present position simply to allow the reader to recover from the devastating con-clusion of chapters 11—14. At first it is difficult to discern any other reason for the insertion of this collection of regulations. But the contextual sig-nificance of the chapter is striking; immediately after the wilderness gen-eration is doomed to die outside the land, Yahweh gives instructions to Moses for life *in* the land (vss. 2, 18).[13]

With chapters 16—20 the redactor has shaped material of unusually complex and diverse origins into a narrative unit with impressive integ-rity.[14] To do so he seized on recurrent catchwords in order to enhance a thematic homogencity, not only in chapters 16 and 17, but to the end of the unit at 20:13. While some of these catchwords are more obvious in the Hebrew, most are apparent even in English:

"to draw near" (*qarah*), 16:5, 9, 10, 40; 17:13; 18:3, 4, 7, 22
"holy" or "sanctify" (*qadash*), 16:3, 5, 7, 37, 38; 18:9, 10, 32; 20:12, 13
"to choose" (*bahar*), 16:5, 7; 17:5
"to die/put to death" (*mwt*), 16:13, 29, 41, 48; 17:10, 13; 18:3, 7, 22, 32; 19:11, 13, 14, 16, 18; 20:1, 3, 4

Taken together, these catchwords produce the central theme of the unit: holiness and death.

The narrative that begins at 16:1 contains what is now one incident relating generally to Moses' alleged lack of leadership (16:12-15). In one of those incredibly ironic accusations (cf. 14:3), Dathan and Abiram sug-gest that Moses has led them "*out* of a land flowing with milk and honey," in order to kill them in the wilderness. At the same time, they accuse him of pretending to be "prince over us" without authority. Such complaints, of course, resume the controversy which can be traced all the way back into the book of Exodus (cf. Exod. 2:14 and Num. 16:13). However, when we look at the unit 16:1—20:13 as a whole, we find that the controversy has taken on a peculiar configuration. General complaints about Moses' leadership have been subsumed under the more specific topic of Moses'—and Aaron's—relationship to the priesthood, and, eventually, their rela-tionship to the holy God of Israel.

The unit gets under way with the initial challenge to Moses and Aaron: "You have gone too far! For all the congregation are holy, every one of them, and Yahweh is among them; why then do you exalt yourselves above the assembly of Yahweh?" (16:3). To this Moses responds that Yahweh "will show who is his, and who is holy" by choosing the one who is to "come near" to him, referring to the one who is to have immediate access to the holy God of the sanctuary. Others may *not* so approach, and those who do so without divine authorization will die. Consequently, in the ensuing narrative, the leaders of the rebels perish in an earthquake, and fourteen thousand seven hundred of the congregation die by plague. It is no wonder that the whole people then fears death (17:12–13).

The narrative thread is maintained well into chapter 18, where the issue of the priestly authority of Moses and particularly of Aaron is finally resolved, both with respect to contentious groups (the Levites), as well as the whole people. The redactor has also linked the material in chapters 16—18 with the final incident in 20:1–13 by using the key word "perish" in a strategic retrospective reference (*gw'*, 17:12–13 and 20:3). We may thus construe the whole unit as a narrative expression of an issue central to the preceding book of Leviticus: the ultimate danger inherent in the presence of holiness—the presence of Yahweh—among the people. Holiness cannot bear what is *un*holy, either by defilement, or by unauthorized encroachment on the divine sphere (cf. again Exod. 19:12–13; Lev. 10:1–7). In such a confrontation, either the holy one must withdraw, or the unholy must die, and it is clearly the latter alternative that is taken in Numbers 16—18.

It is also this intrinsic connection between holiness and death that provides the reason behind the insertion of chapter 19 into its present position. Since the priests emerge in chapters 16—18 as the "inner circle" who prevent the congregation from encroaching on the realm of the holy and thus from inviting death, what better place to insert legislation in which the priests are the manufacturers of a substance that counteracts the effects of contact with the dead? This is particularly the case if we understand death as the ultimate form of defilement and thus the extreme opposite of holiness.[15]

We may now turn to the final incident in the unit, the story about "water from the rock" in 20:1–13. Apparently Moses and Aaron are faulted here because they disobey Yahweh's order to *speak* to the rock, and angrily *strike* it instead with the rod. While to us the fault may seem trivial, and the punishment unnecessarily severe, from the author's perspective, Moses is entrusted with the responsibility of mediating the divine will with a directness unique to him, and thus his failure to execute Yahweh's command to the letter meets with a correspondingly serious punishment.[16] But our purpose is to focus on the way in which the sentence handed down to Moses and Aaron provides a surprising conclusion to the unit 11:1—20:13.

Looked at internally, one can easily see that 16:1—20:13 ends in a bitter irony, one that is directly connected to the interplay of holiness and death. The challenge of the rebels to Moses and Aaron ("everyone is holy—why do you exalt yourselves?") at first leads to the death of the rebels and to the exaltation of the leaders (along with *their* party, the priests). But in the end, the controversies lead to the humiliation of Moses and Aaron, and to a divine verdict of death outside the land of promise, a verdict that is seen as necessary because the holy ones (16:5, 7) failed to sanctify *the* Holy One (20:12–13).

The irony is all the more salient when we compare this unit with the preceding one (11:1—14:45; chap. 15). As already indicated there, the initial unit turns, not on controversies involving leadership and priesthood, but on disputes regarding leadership and *prophecy* (cf. 11:26–30 and esp. 12:6–8). Seen in this light, the complaint in 12:2 is the precise thematic counterpart to that in 16:3: "Has Yahweh indeed spoken only through Moses? Has he not spoken through us also?" (12:2); "all the congregation are holy . . . , why then do you exalt yourselves above the assembly of Yahweh?" (16:3). Moreover, whereas the initial unit issues in a verdict of death outside the land for the whole *people* (except their children, of course, and Caleb and Joshua; chaps. 13—14), the final unit issues in a verdict of death outside the land for the *leaders*. The contrast is highlighted by a glance at the motif of "trust" (*'amen*). Whereas in the first unit it is Moses who is "entrusted with all Yahweh's house" (12:7), and it is the people who refuse to trust in Yahweh (14:11), in the final unit it is Moses and Aaron who do not trust in Yahweh (20:12). Thus the theme of holiness and death, which constitutes a distinct thread uniting 16:1—20:13, ultimately links this unit with the preceding in the form of an ironic contrast.

The story of water from the rock has a dramatic effect on the portrait of Moses in the subsequent Pentateuchal narrative. All the endeavors of Moses that follow—and those endeavors will be considerable—will be achieved in the face of and in spite of the inevitable doom that hangs over his life. Despite all he will do to deliver the Israel of the future to the banks of the Jordan River, he himself will not be allowed to cross over into the land of promise. Thus, for the figure of Moses, the rest of the Pentateuchal narrative is marked by a note of tragedy. "The tragic hero has normally had an extraordinary, often a nearly divine, destiny almost within his grasp,"[17] only to prove himself all too fallible a human being. So it is with Moses.

4. Blessing Turned to Curse (20:14—25:18)

The third unit in the book has been sewn together in part by the use of itinerary notices (e.g., 20:22; 21:4, etc.), which take Israel all the way from Kadesh in the "Wilderness of Zin," to "the plains of Moab beyond the Jordan at Jericho" (20:1; 22:1).[18] Thus, at the end of this unit, and indeed, *throughout* the remainder of the Pentateuch, Israel stands at the door to the promised land, on the east bank of the Jordan river (cf. Num. 36:13; Deut. 1:1–5).

The unit opens with a subsection (20:14—21:35) that seems to suggest that Israel is *really* "on the way." Despite being repulsed by the Edomites, and despite yet another questioning of their mission (the incident of the serpents), the section as a whole presents at last an Israel victorious over her foes, the king of Arad, and Sihon and Og. Thus Israel's *military* confrontations in the passage through the peoples are relatively successful: no defeats, one retreat, and three victories. Yet Israel has at best gained a foothold on territory that will have an ambiguous status vis-à-vis Canaan.[19] The promised land still lies ahead, and the rest of the unit presents two quite different kinds of confrontations between Israel and the peoples, one in which—unbeknownst to Israel—the enemy attempts to employ a powerful secret weapon (a sorcerer's curse), and one in which the *same* enemy appears as a religious subversive, inviting Israel to an ecumenical festival of worship. As we shall see, it is the second confrontation that proves to be the more insidious, and spells disaster.

Initially, the story of Balaam in chapters 22—24 presents a confrontation between the power of Yahweh and the power of a pagan "diviner," one who theoretically could discern the will of the gods, especially through the examination of the organs of sacrificial animals. Balaam is represented as a diviner of considerable reputation and ability, for he is brought all the way from his homeland in Mesopotamia, and Balak, his Moabite employer, expresses his confidence in Balaam by saying, "he whom you bless is blessed, and he whom you curse is cursed" (22:6). Thus the Pentateuchal theme of blessing and curse is posed quite sharply, and in the form of a challenge to the blessing that the reader knows resides with Israel. This challenge is not unprecedented, for Balak reminds us of the Pharaoh when he fears that Israel is "too mighty for me" (22:6; cf. Exod. 1:9–10), and the employment of a diviner recalls the magicians of Pharaoh's court. Moreover, as in Exodus, the outcome of the plot is predetermined; there will be no contest because, in the very first words he utters, Balaam avers that he will do and say what *Yahweh* tells him![20] What a striking coincidence: here is the pagan sorcerer, brought by the enemy, Moab, to curse Israel, and the sorcerer declares at the outset that he follows the orders of the *God* of Israel. It would be somewhat like asking the ambassador of the United States to help plan the attack on Pearl Harbor. Moreover, in his first consultation with God Balaam is told explicitly, "You shall not curse the people, for they are blessed" (22:12). With this, the plot of the story is hardly disclosed before its outcome is decided. The deck is stacked in Israel's favor. The one whom Yahweh has blessed cannot be cursed—at least, not without Yahweh's approval.

There are other indications that Balaam steps to the beat of a different drummer. While his reputation seems to be that of a diviner, and he orders the customary sacrifices (22:40; 23:1, 29), his decisions are not based on such ritual procedures but on direct communication with Yahweh (cf. 23:1–7). In fact, it seems to be part of the redactor's purpose to emphasize Balaam's status as a spokesperson—indeed, a prophet—of Yahweh! Thus in the end any pretense of the use of omens is abandoned, and Balaam, overwhelmed by the Spirit of God, delivers oracles of what he has seen and heard in a direct, visionary encounter (24:1–4).

The way in which the character of Balaam changes from pagan sorcerer to charismatic prophet of Yahweh suggests that the story does have a movement, even if the outcome of the plot is predetermined. After Balaam's initial encounter with Yahweh, the reader is relieved of the necessity of maintaining the question, "Will Israel be blessed or cursed?" and is increasingly prompted to raise a different set of questions: "What is the nature of the blessing that is Israel's, and what is to happen to Israel's enemy, Moab?" These two questions, of course, are inextricably intertwined. Moving through the four oracles there is a gradual development from the possibility of a curse placed on Israel by the enemy, to the likelihood of a blessing on Israel, to the confirmation of a blessing on Israel and a curse on the enemy (which also includes Edom, 24:18). From a self-confident employer of an internationally famous sorcerer, Balak becomes a compromising and ultimately impotent pawn in a cosmic game, forced to stand by outraged and helpless as his hireling turns the curse upon him and his own people. Thus Balak is at first shocked by the implicit blessing upon Israel (23:11), then, after the second oracle, he makes a desperate attempt at least to keep Balaam neutral—" 'Even though you cannot curse them,' said Balak to Balaam, 'at least do not bless them!' " (23:25; NAB). But his plea goes unheeded, and, as we have implied, the third oracle becomes even more explicit—"Blessed be every one who blesses you, and cursed be every one who curses you" (24:9). With this, Balak becomes furious, and orders Balaam to flee, only to hear him turn the curse explicitly against his own people, the Moabites (24:10—14).

Undoubtedly we are intended to read the Balaam story with a sense of humor. Here is a diviner who, at one point, is less capable of discerning the divine will than his donkey. Here is a shrewd king whose lavish bribes and elaborate magical rites reveal him to be a fool. But the meaning of the story is obviously not limited to such comic twists. The most obvious function of the story can be seen in the way it serves as an extended illustration and confirmation of the blessing originally placed on Abraham and Sarah, a blessing that again involves political sovereignty over Moab, Edom (traditionally the descendants of Lot and Isaac respectively), and other peoples. Here we have a clear resolution to the question that has arisen a number of times in the Pentateuchal narrative: what is to happen to the offshoots of the Abrahamic line? Edom (Num. 20:14–21) and Moab (Num. 22—24) have both proved to be inimical to Israel, the people blessed by Yahweh, and thus *have brought upon themselves* the curse. Their refusal to seek their own blessing through the blessing placed on Abraham (Gen. 12:3) also stands in ironic contrast to the attitude of Balaam, who echoes the ancestral blessing and wishes it upon himself: "Who can count the dust of Jacob, or number the fourth part of Israel? Let me die the death of the righteous, and let my end be like his!" (Num. 23:10; cf. Gen. 13:16; 28:14).[21]

A second function of the Balaam story is perhaps less obvious, namely the way in which it illustrates once again that the blessing on Israel is completely derived from unmerited grace. Here the meaning of the story lies in its immediate literary context, especially its juxtaposition with chapter 25, and will involve us again with the Pentateuchal theme of the problem of Israel's responsibility. Indeed, this aspect of the Balaam story provides the major focus for the entire unit, 20:14—25:18.

Perhaps the perspective that will best illuminate the contextual meaning of the Balaam story is that provided by the narrator at the moment when Balak and Balaam first join forces: "The next morning, Balak took Balaam and brought him up to the Heights of Baal, and from there he saw the nearest of the people [of Israel]" (22:41). Picture, for a moment, this scene, portrayed with the barest of details. Here is the Moabite king and his hired sorcerer, standing on a high ridge named for the pagan god Baal, looking down on the encampment of Israel, which is so vast that only a portion is visible. What is most interesting about this scene (and about the entire story which follows) is that only the two characters— and we, the readers—know it is happening. Israel knows nothing. Nestled in their camp in the valley, apparently safe and secure from all danger, the people are not aware that a drama is being played out on the heights above, a drama whose outcome will destine them to either blessing or curse, life or death. In fact, even once the drama has run its course, and Balaam and Balak return to their respective homes, Israel is not informed of what has happened. The people are blessed without even knowing the danger of the curse.

The irony of the Balaam story, and indeed of Israel's stay "in the plains of Moab" as a whole, thus turns on the contrast between the blessing Yahweh has pronounced upon Israel without the people's knowledge, and the curse the people bring down upon themselves. When God's work is done, Israel's is begun (chap. 25). When Yahweh was confronted with the Moabites, Yahweh turned their curse into a blessing on the victim, and a curse on the culprit. When the Israelite people are confronted with the Moabites, they turn their own blessing into a curse.

The story needs only a brief review; in fact, its scope is already fully apparent in the opening lines: "While Israel dwelt in Shittim [the place of their encampment in the plains of Moab] the people began to play the harlot with the daughters of Moab. These invited the people to the sacrifices of their gods, and the people ate, and bowed down to their gods. So Israel yoked himself to Baal of Peor." Here the Israelite men succumb to the pandering of the pagan women, and join in some kind of sexual ritual. Once again there is an outrageous breach of covenant. What was to have been Israel's passage *through* the peoples has become Israel's immersion *in* the peoples. Thus the explicit warning of the covenant law regarding mixing with the native population has been disregarded: "Take heed . . . lest you make a covenant with the inhabitants of the land, and when they *play the harlot* after their gods and *sacrifice* to their gods and one *invites you*, you *eat* of his sacrifice, and you take of their *daughters* for your sons, and their daughters play the harlot after their gods and make your sons play the harlot after their gods" (Exod. 34:12, 15–16).[22]

The holy nation has become defiled by participation in pagan "abominations" (cf. Lev. 18). In light of this sin, there is no wonder that "the anger of Yahweh was kindled against Israel" (Num. 25:3), and the result is the death of 24,000 by plague. But in the wider narrative context, death by plague involves a further irony. Such physical afflictions are primary ways in which punishment for breach of covenant is accomplished. In other words, plague is the physical form of Yahweh's curse (cf. Deut. 28:58–62; 29:22–28). Thus the juxtaposition of the Balaam story with that of Baal Peor is drawn even more sharply. Unknowingly redeemed from the curse of the Moabites that would have brought defeat and death, Israel mixes with the Moabites (the text bluntly calls it fornication, 25:1) and brings on the curse of the covenant. Such is the bitter end of Israel's passage through the peoples. The greatest threat in that passage is not the *armies* of the peoples, but rather their religion and culture.

From the incident of the golden calf at the foot of Mt. Sinai, to the incident of Baal Peor at the door to the promised land, the story of Israel as the covenant people is the story of repeated *breach* of covenant, a wanton, reckless, and ultimately disastrous invocation of Yahweh's curse, in defiance of the blessing originally pronounced on Abraham and held out to the covenant people as the possibility of their future. It is for this reason that the rest of the Pentateuchal narrative—from Numbers 26 to the end of Deuteronomy—will portray the people of Israel as if frozen in space and time, encamped "in the plains of Moab by the Jordan at Jericho" (36:13). It is this Israel of the broken covenant who must now be reassessed, recommissioned for the task of entering the land and, above all, instructed in *how* to go into the land which Yahweh swore to Abraham, Isaac, and Jacob.

5. The Inheritors of the Land (chaps. 26—36)

The final literary unit in Numbers is dominated by rather arcane matters having to do with cultic and civil legislation, but it is clear from numerous references to the preceding units that the redactors were self-consciously adding to an ongoing *narrative*, and not simply compiling lists. The primary concern of this material involves the danger Israel's past behavior poses for the possession of the land by the next generation. This concern is immediately evident in the redaction of the census list in chapter 26. Originally, the list probably began with verse 4b: "The people of Israel, who came forth out of the land of Egypt, were . . . ." To this superscription the redactor added verses 1–4a, creating some literary awkwardness. The purpose of this editing is clearly to tie the taking of the census to the immediately preceding incident of Baal Peor (chap. 25), and to explain that the census was of "all in Israel who are able to go forth to war" (vs. 2b). What this already implies is made even more explicit at the end of the census, verses 63–65: "But among these there was not a man of those numbered by Moses and Aaron the priest, who had numbered the people of Israel *in the wilderness of Sinai*" (vs. 64). In effect, this serves as a corrective to verse 4b. The census is *not* of those "who came forth out of the land of Egypt," but rather of the *new* generation who has reached the age of military conscription (20 years; vs. 2). Thus an originally *independent* census has been altered to fit the narrative context; it is a *new* census that is to be understood as the counterpart to that taken in Numbers 1 (note esp. 1:3).

The reason for the alteration in Numbers 26, of course, was also provided by narrative necessity. All of the exodus generation had died, in fulfilment of Yahweh's punishment for the mutiny at Kadesh (Num. 13—14 and esp. 14:29; cf. 26:65). Only the new generation can be the inheritors of the land (26:53); only a new commander can lead them into the land (Josh. 27:12–23). This is the major justification for our determination of the final unit of the book as chapters 26—36. Both this unit and Numbers 1—25 begin with a military census, but the latter leads ultimately to the death of the entire wilderness generation, whereas the former creates a completely new literary horizon. The one focuses on the past, and how Israel's sin led to disaster; the other focuses on the future, and how renewed obedience to Yahweh can lead to the fulfilment of the promise. In short, the one represents the grim reality of Yahweh's curse; the other offers the possibility of Yahweh's blessing.

This relationship between the past as warning and the future as possibility—and both with reference to the promise of land—dominates the redaction of chapters 26—36. Here, perhaps more than anywhere else in the Pentateuch, the redactors go beyond their role as narrators and become commentators as well; that is, they speak directly to the reader, and offer a theological interpretation of the events within the narrative. Thus in 26:63–65 the redactors explain *why* there was a new census, and in 26:9b–11 the redactor not only inserts a narrative summary of the sin of Dathan, Abiram, and Korah, but also steps outside the narrative mode and directly admonishes the reader that the story serves as a pedagogical *sign* (vs. 10b). The RSV appropriately translates the word "sign" as "warning." The sin of the past has become a warning for the future.[23]

The sin of the wilderness generation and its legacy for the future is not limited to the corporate inheritors of the land, but also extends to the individual leaders, Moses and Aaron. One of the clear indications of redaction as we near the end of the Pentateuchal narrative is the way time is being stretched, that time in which Israel encamps "in the plains of Moab," looking over to the promised land. The most poignant effect of this stretching of time can be seen in the fate of Moses. In 27:12–14 and again in 31:1–2 the reader receives the clear impression that Moses' death outside the land is imminent. In the former passage, Moses is reminded by Yahweh of his breach of faith (Num. 20:1–13), and in the latter the reader is led to expect Moses' death at the end of the chapter, after revenge has been taken on the Midianites. And yet, Moses' death does not occur there; in fact, it does not occur until the very end of the Pentateuch, in Deuteronomy 34.

The reason that the apparently imminent death of Moses has been prolonged in the Pentateuchal redaction is twofold. First, a successor (Joshua) had to be appointed for Moses, just as there had been one (Eleazar) for Aaron (for the latter, cf. 20:23–29). But this actually takes place already in 27:15–23.[24] Thus the major reason for the prolongation of Moses' death has to do with the preparation of the people as a whole—the new generation—as the inheritors of the land. This is the reason Moses' death could not come at the end of Numbers 31, or even at the end of the book. Even aside from the admonitory passages discussed above, most of chapters 26—36 has to do with instructions for how to live in the land of the promise: the army that is to take the land (chap. 26), rules of inheritance of the land (27:1–11; chap. 36), a festival calendar for the land (chaps. 32; 34), Levitical cities and cities of sanctuary in the land (chap. 35). Given the way in which Israel's past history has been, over and over again, a history of the broken covenant, and the way in which the continued breaking of covenant led Israel to the brink of destruction, here "in the plains of Moab" it is absolutely crucial that the *new* Israel be instructed as to the way that lies ahead. That way is not simply geographical—the way across the Jordan River, into the land of Canaan. That way also is and always has been theological—the way of *torah*. Thus the time Israel spends "beyond the Jordan" is, without exaggeration, the most critical time in the Pentateuchal narrative. It is truly an hour of decision, in which Israel stands in between promise and fulfilment, in between blessing and curse, in between the wilderness and the new land. Within the Pentateuchal narrative there was only one individual who possessed the stature and authority to instruct Israel in this way of *torah*, the one through whom the *torah* had been given to Israel in the first place, the one who knew Yahweh "face to face," the one who talked with Yahweh "mouth to mouth," the prophet without equal—Moses, "the servant of Yahweh."

V

DEUTERONOMY—
Beyond the Jordan

1. Deuteronomy as Narrative

Sometimes one can understand a great deal about people by knowing what stories out of their past they remember, which stories they choose to retell, and the way they go about the retelling. In the opening chapters of Deuteronomy, the authors have repeated several stories from Israel's past that they obviously consider crucial to Israel's identity. That they have retold these stories in a separate book, rather than editing the original versions *in situ*, suggests the self-consciousness with which the authors were working as *interpreters*.[1] As a result, Deuteronomy is both the conclusion of the Pentateuchal narrative and the definitive commentary on that part of the narrative that precedes it. As *the* Mosaic Torah, Deuteronomy is "the hermeneutical key to the Pentateuch as a whole."[2]

As the epilogue to the Pentateuchal narrative Deuteronomy presents us once again with a rather strange notion of what "narrative" is, for there is very little action in the book. Moses delivers several lengthy speeches, his leadership of the people is transmitted to Joshua, and then Moses dies. The dearth of events is reflected by the reticence of the redactors to speak in the narrative mode. In fact, the redactors *as narrators* come to the fore in only a few passages in the beginning and near the end (note esp. 1:1–5; 4:41—5:1a; chaps. 27—34 *passim*).[3] Even here the content of the narration (with the notable exception of chap. 34) is little more than a reminder of who is speaking—"Then Moses said" (e.g., 29:2; 31:1, 7, 9–10). *Indirectly* through Moses' comments, or from a rare comment by the narrator, we learn that a few other things happen: the people pledge their allegiance to Yahweh (26:16–19), and the Levites

---

In Deuteronomy read 1:1—2:37; 3:23—10:22; 11:26–28; 12:1; chaps. 15, 24, 26, and 28; 29:10–15; chaps. 30—32 and 34.

receive a copy of the covenant law (31:9). But these little scenes are momentary at best, and some of them do not even occur "on stage." If one were to dramatize the book, one would need really only one actor— the rest of the cast would be walk-ons. Indeed, even God would enjoy only a bit part, appearing just a few times at the end. The show really belongs to Moses alone.

In dramatic terms, therefore, Deuteronomy is essentially a soliloquy, just as most of Leviticus was a soliloquy, but here it is a man and not God who is talking. The difference is striking. Whereas Leviticus opens with Yahweh speaking to Moses from the tent of meeting, and the phrase "Yahweh said to Moses" occurs repeatedly throughout, Deuteronomy opens with Moses speaking to Israel and, with few exceptions (all at the end), Yahweh never speaks.[4] The reason for this remarkable shift from divine to human speech lies in the Deuteronomic emphasis on Moses' office established at Mt. Sinai (or Horeb, in Deuteronomic parlance). In chapters 4—5 the Deuteronomist repeats the story from Exodus 19—20, adding an interpretation of the significance of the events. In chapter 4 the emphasis falls on verse 12: "Yahweh spoke to you out of the midst of the fire; you heard the sound of words, but saw no form; there was only a voice." The rest of the chapter is a passionate homily on this verse. Since the people saw no form in Yahweh's self-revelation, they should make no form, no physical representation (the second commandment, cf. 5:8–10). The only way to re-present the reality of Yahweh is to recite Yahweh's words (and deeds); the only appropriate *response* to this reality is obedience to the words.

In the context of the wider Pentateuchal narrative the emphasis on Yahweh's words rather than on a visible form takes on a greater significance. From the moment Israel left Egypt until the end of the book of Deuteronomy (31:15), Yahweh's guidance has been marked by the visible phenomena of cloud and fire. But those phenomena will cease when Israel crosses the Jordan. Then there will be only the ark of the covenant, the ark that contains Yahweh's words.[5] As much of Deuteronomy will insist, the future of Israel—either for good or for ill—will be determined by the extent to which they follow the guidance (*torah*) of these words. Thus the traditional Hebrew title for the book is highly appropriate: "these are the words" (1:1).

Chapter 5 describes the revelation of the Decalogue and, just as importantly, the legitimation of Moses' office. At the height of the theophany, the people draw back and ask Moses to be their mediator: "Go near, and hear all that Yahweh our God will say; and speak to us all that Yahweh our God will speak to you; and we will hear and do it" (vs. 27). Again, the author repeats an incident from Exodus (20:18–19) but amplifies it, here with a divine speech in response (vss. 28–31). The divine affirmation of the people's election of Moses accentuates the authority he now bears, and thus authorizes the words of Moses that follow *in the rest of the book*. In fact, the "commandments, statutes, and ordinances" that Yahweh had earlier given to Moses on Mt. Sinai (vs. 31), Moses is only *now* delivering to Israel (chaps. 6—26).[6] Because Moses is the spokesperson for Yahweh, Moses' words *are* Yahweh's words, and the following speeches of Moses are fresh revelations of Yahweh.

So far we have concluded that Deuteronomy is essentially a series of speeches by Moses. In fact, the redactors have divided the book into four speeches.[7] Chapters 4 and 5 are placed at the juncture of the first and second speeches as conclusion and introduction respectively. Obviously the story of Yahweh's self-revelation at Horeb, of the gift of the covenant and the Decalogue, is of central importance to the authors. In fact, it is possible to construe the book more in terms of a legal document than a narrative. Thus the core (chaps. 12—26) is a law code dealing with everything from the covenantal responsibility of the king to whether or not one may eat a buzzard. Moreover, the form of the book can be compared to the form of a treaty, moving from historical prologue (chaps. 1—5) to blessings and curses (chaps. 27—28).[8] Similarly, the book reflects the *liturgical* order of a covenant-making or renewing ceremony (cf. 29:10–15). In fact, since chapters 6—26 represent newly disclosed commandments of Yahweh, and since at the end of the pronouncement of these commandments the people accept them (26:16–19), we can understand Deuteronomy as the *completion* of a covenant-making process stretching back to the original events at Sinai.

Still, the legal delineations do not sufficiently consider the framework of the book or the dominating presence of the figure of Moses. As much as Deuteronomy may be compared to Exodus 19—24, and may even be a completion of a process begun there, the redactors have set it apart as a distinct document: "the book is cast in the form of Moses' last will and testament."[9] More specifically, the book is the *story* of how Moses pronounced his last will and testament. In effect, Deuteronomy as a whole seems to be a combination of two traditional forms—the deathbed blessing and the charge. A clear precedent occurs in the portrayal of Jacob's deathbed pronouncements at the end of Genesis, marking a major transition in the Pentateuchal narrative.[10]

In Deuteronomy, however, the "charge" is not limited to the specific command regarding the deposit of the "book of the torah" (31:26, *tsivah*), but in fact extends to all of chapters 1—33. This indicated in part by the inordinate number of references to Moses' impending death, beginning with 1:37.[11] The Deuteronomist has a very different understanding of why Moses was not allowed to enter Canaan from that given in Numbers 20 (the fault lies with the people, not with Moses),[12] but the effect of the repeated references to Moses' imminent death is to emphasize not so much *why* Moses may not enter as *that* he may not enter. Particularly in the opening chapters, the references impress upon Moses' audience that these are Moses' *final* words of instruction. When the people enter the land, they will no longer have Moses with them—they will have only his words. Just as Yahweh's words now replace his previous guidance in the forms of fire and cloud, so now "the Torah is actually *a replacement for Moses himself* in his capacity as the greatest mediator of divine words to Israel."[13]

Thus the greatest significance of Deuteronomy as a book derives from its configuration as the *narrative* of Moses' farewell address, the address that constitutes his last will and testament to the new generation of Israel, the people who wait "beyond the Jordan" for the fulfilment of the promise. On the one hand, ever since the "fall" of Adam and Eve, the Pentateuch has been a search for the genuinely righteous person, the human being who comes as close as humanly possible to representing the divine will. Moses is that person. Yet it is not Moses himself, but Moses' *words,* his *torah,* that arrests our attention and claims our allegiance.

2. Narrative and Torah

One way to construe the structure of the book is as follows:

Prologue: 1:1—4:43
General Commandments: 4:44—11:32
Statutes and Ordinances: chaps. 12—26
Ceremony of Curses and Blessings: 27:1—29:1
Concluding Exhortations: 29:2—30:20
Transmission of the Mosaic Legacy: chaps. 31—33
Death of Moses and Concluding Eulogy: chap. 34

We cannot, of course, discuss all the material in detail. Instead we shall focus on the way the redactors have used paradigmatic stories in conjunction with *torah* at key points within the first three units.

The introduction to the first address of Moses (1:1—4:43) provides the key for unlocking the combination of *torah* and narrative that pervades the entire book. In the opening verses, a redactor has set the scene of the book as Moses' testamentary address "beyond the Jordan, in the land of Moab," almost forty-one years after Israel left Egypt. On this occasion, the redactor says, "Moses undertook to explain this *torah,* saying. . . ." What is the "*torah*" Moses sets out to explain? It is not *torah* in the strict sense of "law." Moses is not expounding here the "commandments, statutes, and ordinances." Moses is retelling a portion of the preceding Pentateuchal narrative (to begin with, the rebellion at Kadesh, Num. 13—14). At the same time, Moses' narration is intricately laced with interpretation and commentary on the story's meaning for his present audience. He is not simply retelling, but also "explaining" the *torah*. Moses is both a skilled storyteller and a passionate preacher. As a result, the narration itself *is torah*, a form of instruction.[14]

Yet it is more than that. It is significant that the redactor uses the word *torah*, and not some other word for teaching (e.g., *limmad*, as in 4:1, 5, etc.). In the context of what will unfold in Deuteronomy, the retelling of the story as instruction makes a *demand* of Moses' listeners, for narrative as *torah* cannot be understood apart from the covenantal context of Moses' testament. In fact, the basic purpose of his narration, as we shall see, is to lead up to the "Great Commandment" that Yahweh as the covenant lord places upon Israel, the covenant people.[15] Ultimately, the telling of the story demands that the audience either accept or reject this Great Commandment, and the covenant itself. Thus listening to the story cannot be (from the redactor's point of view) a passive act; it *demands* a response. One cannot listen to the story and simply conclude that it is interesting, or even that it is profound. After hearing the story, one must respond in either of two ways: "Because of this story, I accept the covenant," or, "Despite this story, I reject the covenant." Acceptance or rejection will finally determine whether one receives blessing or curse, hence the gravity of the response that is demanded. The significance of the narration in Deuteronomy is eviscerated if this demand for responsibility is ignored.

Moses' explanation of *torah* and its relationship to narrative (i.e., the Pentateuchal narrative) is by no means limited to the first address, crucial as the interpretive key in 1:6 may be. In fact, all of chapters 1—11—which leads up to the specific covenant stipulations in chapters 12—26—is anchored in stories from Israel's past which serve as the motivation for Israel's future, and thus are *"torah"* (cf. 4:44).[16] The context stretches from creation (4:32) to Yahweh's oath to the ancestors (e.g., 4:31; 6:23), to the exodus (e.g., 6:21; 7:8), to Israel's present situation. Moreover, the placement of the stories is also significant. A story of rebellion opens and closes chapters 1—11 (Kadesh, chap. 1, and the golden calf, 9:6—10:11), while the encounter at Mt. Sinai stands in between the two subsections (chaps 4, 5). In addition, the specific laws themselves are studded with references to previous stories, and the collection concludes with a liturgical recitation summarizing events from Genesis 12 up to that time in the future when Israel will have entered the land (chap. 26). *Because* these stories provide the stuff of Israel's identity they are the *torah* for her future.

3. The Great Commandment (chaps. 1—11)

Chapter 1 opens with a grim warning, creating a sense of urgency that remains unrelieved throughout the rest of the book. The redactor wishes us to read Moses' testament in light of the story that brought Israel to the brink of destruction and condemned both the wilderness generation and Moses to die outside the promised land—the story of the rebellion at Kadesh (Num. 13—14). At the outset, the author emphasizes how this story *could* have ended in the fulfilment of the promise to the ancestors: "Look, I have set the land before you; go in and take possession of the land which Yahweh swore to your ancestors, to Abraham, to Isaac, and to Jacob, to give to them and to their descendants after them" (vs. 8). Similarly, Moses affirms in verses 10–11 that the blessing on Abraham has been fulfilled ("You are this day as the stars of heaven for multitude"), and that an even greater blessing awaits Israel in the future. But by an artful rearrangement of the narrative sequence, the author also provides an interpretation of why the promise of land and blessing came to ruin: Moses reports the rebellion of the people immediately after the good report from the spies, and before any indication of the opposing military forces (vss. 25–28). The point is to illustrate a fatal lack of trust in the God who had led them through the wilderness (vss. 32–33) that results in an irrational fear and disastrous rejection of the ancestral promise and of Yahweh. In a shocking formulation the author even has the people turn their redemption into damnation: "Because Yahweh *hated* us he has brought us out of the land of Egypt!" Thus the Deuteronomic retelling of the story has rightly been labeled as the representation of an "anti-exodus" and an "anti-holy war."[17]

The Deuteronomist has naturally retained that element of the story in which the people who came out of Egypt are doomed to die outside of the land. That, after all, is the major thrust of the message for the *present* generation, Moses' audience. The situation throughout Deuteronomy is thus comparable to that at the end of Numbers (chaps. 26—36). The old generation has died (Deut. 2:14–16), and the new generation stands in their place, full of hope, but also confronting the same temptations to which their parents succumbed. Although the "you" whom Moses addresses would often seem to be the old generation (e.g., frequently in chaps. 1—10), it is in fact the new, for they, along with every subsequent generation, are included with those who stood at Sinai and received the covenant (cf. esp. 5:3; 29:10–15).[18] Israel has also stood at the door to the land before—as Moses' audience does now—and refused to go in, or tried to go in on their own terms (1:41–46). The rest of the book is Moses' final instruction on *how* to go into the land as responsible heirs of the promise. From here to the end, the subject of "when you go into the land" is always to be read in light of this harrowing story, and is thus a subject to which the Deuteronomist returns again and again with the utmost seriousness (e.g., 6:1, 3, 10; 7:1; 8:7, etc.).

In between the story of Kadesh and the story of Horeb, Moses recounts Israel's passage through the peoples—chapters 2—3 (cf. Num. 20:14 —25:18; chap. 32). Close comparison with the accounts in Numbers reveals some striking differences. The Deuteronomist has subjected his material to a systematic interpretation upholding Yahweh's beneficent attitude and promises to the extra-covenantal ancestors of Abraham—the Ammonites, Moabites, and Edomites. They too possess a specific geographical territory as a divine gift (2:5, 9, 19). There are now, in effect, *four* promised lands, each of which is to remain inviolate, a fulfilment of the promise to Abram that, in conjunction with the blessing pronounced upon him, at least these peoples also will receive blessing. The Kingdom of Yahweh is not geographically limited to Israel's land, even though Israel may be the only *covenant* people of Yahweh. It is ultimately Yahweh who establishes the boundaries of all peoples, because all of humanity, and all of the earth, are his (cf. Deut. 32:8–9; Exod. 19:5). At the same time, there are those, such as Sihon and Og (2:24—3:11), who unknowingly seek a curse because of their hostility to the chosen people. They will be dispossessed of their lands. And there are those who now inhabit what is to be Israel's land. They too will be dispossessed, for reasons explained in chapter 7 (and already in Exod. 23:23–33).

After recounting his appeal to enter the land, and Yahweh's denial (3:23–28), Moses brings his audience full circle, back to that spatial and temporal "now" that is so fraught with theological urgency (3:29—4:1). The opening speech has taken us from Horeb to Kadesh to the east bank of the Jordan, and now to Horeb again (chap. 4). The second part of the prologue (4:44—11:32) also begins and ends with Horeb, and thus with an obvious irony; the story of covenant-making opens the section (chap. 5), while the story of covenant-breaking closes the section (9:7—10:11). Accordingly, the prologue as a whole begins with the disaster of Kadesh and ends with the golden calf—the covenant of Horeb stands in the center.

As we have seen, chapters 4 and 5 authorize Moses' words as a continuation of Yahweh's self-revelation. Thus, what immediately follows is of the utmost importance. All of chapters 1—5 have been a preparation for this revelation, and all that follows *in the rest of the book* can be understood as a development of this revelation.

After an exhortative introduction (vss. 1–3), Moses pronounces what is appropriately called the *Great* Commandment, the commandment which, above all others, stands at the theological center of his testament.

It is the traditional "Shema" of Judaism (the Hebrew word means "hear"), and the basis of the "great commandment" of Jesus (Matt. 22:34–40, etc.): "Hear, O Israel! Our God is Yahweh, Yahweh alone! And love Yahweh your God with all your heart, with all your life, indeed with all your capacity!"[19] The Shema has two primary foci: first, the confession that only Yahweh can be *Israel*'s God (rather than that Yahweh is the only God), and secondly, that this confession carries with it the demand to love Yahweh (hence the continuation of the imperative mood in vs. 5). "Love" here is in no sense sentimental; although it connotes endearment, it is also technical treaty language for loyalty. And that is precisely what the Great Commandment commands—undivided loyalty to Yahweh. This is the heart of the covenant, the bedrock of Israel's responsibility to Yahweh. The exclusivity of the demand is accentuated by the final phrase: "with all your heart, with all your life, indeed with all your capacity!" With climactic progression, the Shema emphasizes that the total person— and the total community—must pledge its allegiance to Yahweh, and to no other. The words of the Shema are of such central importance that they must be communicated constantly, day and night, bound on one's forehead, and written on every doorpost and city gate (vss. 6–9).

Clearly, if the Shema is the Great Commandment and the heart of the covenant, it must also be the heart of *torah*—perhaps even the heart of *the* Torah. What, then, is the relationship between this, the greatest commandment, and the Torah as narrative? This question is answered as we come to the end of the chapter, where it is posed in a different form by a child: "What is the *meaning* of the testimonies and the statutes and the ordinances which Yahweh our God has commanded you?" (vs. 20). In other words, "What is the meaning of the Great Commandment, and, indeed, what is the meaning of *torah*?" The child is asking for no less than the ground of all ethical behavior, the ethos of the community called Israel.

What response does Moses have the parent give? He does not provide a philosophical or systematic argument on the meaning of *torah*, nor merely authoritarian custom—"Because Yahweh said so, it is enough to do it." Instead Moses suggests that the parent do what he himself has been doing all along in his testament; he suggests that the parent tell the child a story. Of course, it is not just any story, it is *the* story that provides Israel's communal identity, the story that begins, "We were Pharaoh's slaves in Egypt." This is also the narrative that renders the identity of the one who is confessed, witnessed to, in the Shema. To say, "Yahweh is our God" and "We were Pharaoh's slaves in Egypt" is to state Israel's identity in exact correspondence to *Yahweh*'s identity: "I am Yahweh your God, who brought you out of the land of Egypt, out of the house of bondage" (Deut. 5:6; Exod. 20:2).

Nowhere is the relationship between *torah* and narrative put so succinctly. The connection between the narration (plus interpretation) in Deuteronomy 1—11 and the laws in chapters 12 and following suggests what is, without exaggeration, *the* most important aspect of the understanding of *torah*. *Torah* is not heteronomous, an imposition of divine will "out of the blue." Rather, as Paul Ricoeur puts it, *torah* is "connected to the founding events" in such a manner that "the legislative genre is in a way included in the narrative genre. And this in turn signifies that the memory of deliverance [from Egypt] qualifies the instruction in an intimate way."[20] The meaning of *torah* lies in the narrative itself, and the narrative (if one genuinely *responds* to it) leads to the responsibility of *torah* (vs. 24). It is not primarily a responsibility *to torah*—this is the significant addition in verse 25—but to *Yahweh*, who is the ultimate subject of the narrative. It is this responsibility to Yahweh, manifested in obedience to his commandments, that Moses designates as "righteousness." To be righteous is to live out the implications of one's narrative identity ("We were Pharaoh's slaves in Egypt") in response to the one who is the primary agent of that narrative ("I am Yahweh your God, who brought you out of the land of Egypt"). The reciprocity of law and story is now transparent; obedience to law is rooted in the recital of and identification with a story, an identification that is vacuous without obedience to law.

The rest of the prologue is preoccupied with three future situations when the Israelites will be in the land and will be tempted to forget their narrative identity and abandon absolute allegiance to Yahweh. In each case, *remembering* the story is posed as the only means to avoid disloyalty and the resultant punishment (cf. 7:17–18; 8:17–18; 9:4, 7). In the first case, the Israelites will be tempted to forget their status as Yahweh's holy people and instead to fuse indistinguishably with Canaanite culture (7:1–11). If the motivation for cultural assimilation is, in part, fear of the Canaanites' military superiority, Israel must remember the story of Yahweh the Holy Warrior and his victory over the Egyptians (7:17–26).

In the second case (chap. 8), Israel is warned against the presumption of self-sufficiency, as if the land and all its rich blessings were a result of human achievement alone. Affluence is not inherently evil, but it is inherently dangerous. The way to avoid an attitude in which materialism replaces allegiance to Yahweh is to remember the story of the wilderness journey, and especially the provision of manna. Israel's greatest treasure is not gold and silver, but the memory of a time of poverty that demonstrated God's love and humankind's dependence.

The third case is almost a reverse of the first: the Israelites are warned against the assumption that their imminent victory over the Canaanites will be a sign of their relative "righteousness" (9:4). In contrast, Moses calls them to remember the story of the golden calf that exemplifies their *un*righteousness "from the day you came out of the land of Egypt until you came to this place" (9:7). Thus, in terms of narrative referents, the prologue concludes with that story that brought Israel to the brink of destruction (9:8, 14, 19), just as it began with that story that described the doom of the entire wilderness generation. If the concluding story of the golden calf is not sufficiently negative reinforcement to instill obedience to the specific laws that follow, the larger context provides more, for Israel's narrow escape resulted only from Moses' intervention with Yahweh, but when Moses has finished with his testament, Israel will have him no more. They will have only his words.

The transitional material in 10:12—11:32 reiterates the paramount call of the Shema (10:12–13), but also introduces a completely new aspect that will dominate much of chapters 12—25. The Great Commandment demanding the love of Yahweh also demands the love of other people; it has a horizontal as well as a vertical dimension. Israel is to love Yahweh because Yahweh first loved Israel (10:15), but Yahweh also loves the poor, the weak, and the defenseless (the widow, the orphan, and the resident alien ["sojourner"]), and therefore Israel is to love them too (10:18–19). The later Jewish, Christian, and Muslim correlations of the love of God and neighbor have their origin here. The transitional material intends to move us from the Great Commandment to the Great Society, for these two belong together just as, and for the same reason that, narrative and *torah* belong together.

4. Memory: A Poor Man's Coat and a Basket of Fruit (chaps. 12—26)

We have seen that the transitional material introducing the legal corpus provides a sociological extension of the Great Commandment. Israel is commanded not only to love Yahweh, but also to love the widow, the orphan, and the resident alien. These three categories of people are often mentioned together because they constitute the clearest examples of those who were helpless in the ancient world. References to these people, as well as to others within Israelite society who are helpless (the poor, the hired servants), are concentrated in a series of laws in 24:10–22. Here we also find repeated what is crucial for our understanding of the commandment to "love the sojourner" in 10:19—the motivation attached to the commandment: "for you were aliens in the land of Egypt." We have noted in passing a similar injunction in Exodus 22:21. While other ancient Near Eastern law codes protected the widow and the orphan, only in ancient Israelite law was there legislation on behalf of the alien.[21] The reason has to do with the central core of Israel's narrative identity. What chapter 24 adds to the earlier motivation in Exodus is the specific command to *remember:* "remember that you were a slave in Egypt" (vss. 18, 22; cf. 5:15; 15:15).

There are many motivations for obedience to *torah* in Deuteronomy and elsewhere: sanctions, such as capital punishment (24:7); the promise of reward (22:7), often closely associated with divine blessing (15:6); the threat of a divine curse (chaps. 27—28); requirements due to Israel's "holiness" (14:1–2); and appeals to humanitarian concern (24:6). But the basic motivation for obedience to *torah* is remembering the narrative that provides Israel's identity: "You were Pharaoh's slaves in Egypt." We have seen this to be the case in a more strictly theological dimension with the narrative that renders the meaning of *torah* and the Great Commandment in 6:20–25. Now we see it applied explicitly on the horizontal level.

The specific commandments to remember suggest that the narrative providing Israel's communal identity is also the bedrock for *justice* in the wider society. There is an inherently ethical dimension to remembering the story, and to the love of Yahweh that results from that memory. As Paul Tillich has written, "Justice is the structural form of love without which it would be sheer sentimentality."[22] Israel cannot genuinely love Yahweh without also loving the widow, the orphan, the resident non-Israelite, the poor, and the hired servant. The reason for the motivation is imbedded in the meaning of the narrative: because *you* were once resident aliens or slaves in Egypt, and were the beneficiaries of divine justice (redemption), therefore you must be agents of justice in society. The way this works out in specific circumstances can include not only proscriptions of injustice, but also prescriptions of the way in which the helpless are to be treated. A hired servant must be given his or her wages on the day they are earned (24:15); Israelites must leave part of their crops for the poor to glean (24:19–22); in making a loan to a widow, an Israelite may not demand her "garment" (the basic overcoat) in pawn (24:17); Israelites may not demand interest on *any* loans to fellow Israelites (23:19); and one law may even suggest that the loan itself (i.e., the principal) is cancelled every seven years (15:1–2). However much we may emphasize the motivation for such laws, we must not ignore their substance: "From the topics and terms of the instructions we are able to derive *an actual socioeconomic content* for Israel's understanding of 'deliverance from bondage' or 'national liberation.' "[23] Obedience to these *laws* is as much an expression of Israel's identity as remembering the *story*—indeed, helping the helpless is the ethical form of memory.

The connection between law and motivation is the connection between *torah* and narrative. That connection, and the way remembering the story impinges on every aspect of society having to do with justice, has been eloquently expressed by André Neher: "It is as though the law, in a desire to prevent the petrification of the Exodus and its relegation into past history, demanded from man when faced with his neighbour, that he put himself back in the situation when the breach was first made: to rediscover the experience of passing from degradation to dignity in all its freshness."[24] Being a sojourner is not simply an aspect of who Israel *was;* it is a permanent aspect of who Israel is (cf. Lev. 25:23). This is the horizontal dimension of *torah* and narrative; identification with the ancient story of oppression requires identification with the oppressed in any age. Genuine response to the story entails not only love of Yahweh, but also active pursuit of human rights for all. If ever human beings are properly to attempt to be "like God" (Gen. 3—11) it is in this imitation of divine redemption.

"Justice, and only justice, you shall follow, that you may live and inherit the land which Yahweh your God gives you" (16:20). In the chapters preceding the corpus of laws, we have seen that the inheritance of the land is conditional on a number of basic attitudes, all of which are part of a proper righteousness: trust, loyalty, gratitude, humility. While the laws in chapters 12—26 contain a great deal of other meanings that we have not pursued, one of the basic concerns is to demonstrate that inheritance of the land is also conditional on the maintenance of justice in society. "It will be righteousness for you" when the story is properly remembered and loyalty to Yahweh is maintained (6:20–25). Just so, "It will be righteousness for you" when a poor man is not denied his coat overnight (24:10–13).

We turn now to the conclusion of the legal corpus in chapter 26. The final verses (16–19) represent the completion of the laws as well as the covenant agreement between Yahweh and Israel. The latter covenant-making process is extended by the ceremony at Shechem (chap. 27), blessings and curses (chap. 28), final covenant instructions (chaps. 29—30), and deposit of the covenant document (chap. 31). Then comes Moses' "song" in chapter 32, his formal blessing of the tribes in chapter 33, and his death in chapter 34.

The position of 26:1–15 is thus pivotal, coming at the end of the treaty stipulations and leading into the declaration of covenant agreements. The two ceremonies described here have to do with the agricultural produce of the land. We shall focus on the first-fruits ceremony in verses 1–11. The centrality of the land is quite clear in the passage, not only because of the agricultural content, but also because the passage as a whole is provided with a framework that focuses the reader's attention on the land as Yahweh's gift to Israel. The passage opens with a temporal clause—"When you come into the land which Yahweh your God is about to give you"—and closes with a suggested invocation—"Look down from thy holy habitation, from heaven, and bless thy people Israel and the ground which thou hast given us, as thou didst swear to our ancestors, a land flowing with milk and honey." Moreover, six times in verses 1–3 and 9–11 the passage emphasizes that the land is Yahweh's gift *(natan)*.

The central focus on the land is matched by a renewed emphasis on the relationship between *torah* and narrative. The *ritual action* commanded for the celebration of the first harvest (vss. 1–4) is supplemented by another commandment, that the participants recite the *narrative* which provides their identity as the covenant people (vss. 5–10a). The story that the participants are to recite is, in effect, a summary of the entire Pentateuchal narrative from Genesis 12 to the end. In fact, it goes beyond the end, for it deals with a time in the future of Moses' audience when they can say, in the past tense, "Yahweh brought us into the land" (vss. 9–10). The ritual law is also intended to apply to all subsequent generations who will celebrate the festivals of first fruits and agricultural tithes.[25]

Here we shall focus not so much on the credo in verses 5–9, but on the shorter declaration in the ceremony in verses 1–4. On presenting the first fruits, the participants are to say, "I declare this day that I have come into the land" (vs. 3b). Here the native becomes an immigrant, re-enacting the entry into the land. Moreover, the effect of the opening temporal clause ("When you come into the land," vs. 1) is to accentuate the temporal and spatial tension that underlies and is intrinsic to ritual participation. Whereas in the *ceremony* the declaration expresses fulfil ment ("I have come into the land"), in the *text* the introduction expresses promise ("When you come into the land"). In other words, by projecting into the future what has already occurred long ago, the entrance formula catapults subsequent generations back to a time and place "beyond the Jordan." Entrance into the land becomes a perennially *potential* reality, even though the participant declares that the reality has already been realized—"I have come into the land."

The text as a whole therefore revolves around the opening temporal clause and the declaration within the entrance ceremony: "When you come into the land . . . ; I have come into the land." This tension between introductory formula and liturgical confession must not be broken. In particular, the declaration cannot and must not ignore the temporal clause. The experience of "now" (vs. 10) cannot be valid without the remembrance of "when" (vs. 1). In short, the effect created by the opening clause is the placing of the liturgical festival within a temporal, as well as narrative nexus. This, to be sure, is accomplished also by the credo in verses 5–9, but while the credo moves from past to present, it does not *suspend* that movement as does the entrance formula. The tension introduced by this formula is both temporal and spatial, summoning Israel to recognize the inseparable relationship among past, present, and future, and between life in the wilderness and life in the land. The tension is thereby theological as well, for the festival's location within historical narrative serves as a reminder that the festival is rendered solely to the God who is the subject of that narrative, the God who is "about to give" the land, that is, "Yahweh alone."

Thus, like the social law protecting the alien, this ritual law also prevents the "petrification" of Israel's story into merely past history. Liturgy is another form that gives shape to narrative memory. Indeed, the ritual and ethical bond is reflected by the juxtaposition of verses 12–15, where the third year tithe of produce from the land is given "to the Levite (landless priests), the alien, the fatherless, and the widow." Memory is the fulcrum for theology (chaps. 1—11), for ethics (chaps. 12—25), and for worship (chap. 26).

Both the social and the ritual laws we have examined introduce a subtle aspect of inconclusiveness to Israel's narrative identity. Israel is the community of the redeemed, but only if also a redemptive community. Israel is the people who will soon possess the land, but only if they continue to recognize and remember their status as aliens. This sense of inconclusiveness is not incidental to these laws; on the contrary, it pervades the book of Deuteronomy, and is nowhere more striking than at its end.

Conclusion

THE WAY OF TORAH

The meaning of a story is often significantly determined by the way it ends, and this is certainly the case for the Pentateuchal narrative. What meaning should we infer from the fact that the Pentateuch concludes with the picture of all Israel standing "beyond the Jordan," looking over to the promised land? Why did the editors, along with subsequent tradition, opt for a Pentateuch rather than a Hexateuch? Why does the narrative that establishes Israel's identity not include the occupation of the land that has been a driving motivation ever since Genesis 12?[1]

"All plots have something in common with prophecy, for they must appear to educe from the prime matter of the situation the forms of a future" (Frank Kermode).[2] Commenting on the deposit of the "book of the *torah*" in the ark (Deut. 31:26), William Moran suggests that "the *torah* itself becomes prophetic."[3] While by *torah* he did not mean the Pentateuch, the extension is appropriate. Perhaps it is not merely coincidental that "the Law" ends with an encomium to Moses as the unique prophet of Israel (34:10–12), whereupon the collection which tradition knows as "the former prophets" begins with Joshua. In other words, perhaps at its end the redactors of the Pentateuch are saying that this narrative—so much of which relates Moses' words and deeds—is, in fact, the *source* from which all other "prophetic" books derive, much as Moses' prophetic spirit was the source of communal prophecy in the wilderness (Num. 11:25).[4]

Moran's categorization of the *torah* as prophetic is based in part on the way it is construed as a "witness" for the future (Deut. 31:26; cf. vss. 19, 21 referring to the song of chap. 32). As a prophetic document, the Torah does not simply recount ancient history; it opens up a path for each new generation. On the other hand, as prophecy the Torah is not merely a crystal ball; rather, it performs a *critical* function within the ongoing life of the people. It provides the criterion by which their present is informed and judged in terms of their past, and the way their future is determined by that critical evaluation. The end of the Torah thus points us toward the *way* of *torah*.

Two preliminary observations are in order. First, there is no indication anywhere in the Pentateuchal narrative that would lead us to suspect that the end of the Pentateuch results in an annulment of the themes we have traced—especially the theme of land and nationhood. For example, many Christian hymns refer to heaven in such terms as "Canaan's fair and happy land." While the symbolic extension is not inappropriate, any suggestion that the Pentateuchal theme of the land refers *only* to an other-worldly realm would turn the narrative into an allegory.[5]

Second, our emphasis throughout this book on the meaning of the text apart from continual references to authorial situations does not mean that we can ignore that situation in which the Pentateuch as a separate document almost certainly came into existence. I refer, of course, to the exile of 587 B.C.E. and its aftermath. With the exile came the loss of land and nationhood, and the apparent onslaught of God's curse, understood as a result of Israel's irresponsibility to the divine will. While a significant number of the exiles would return to the land within a generation, there would be no independent state for four hundred years. Moreover, never again would those who called themselves Israelites—or, more properly now, Jews—be limited to the land of Canaan. The exile marked the beginning of the Diaspora, the spread of Jewish communities of increasing size and importance from Babylon to Alexandria and beyond. In the context of this tumultuous epoch—from about 600 to 450 B.C.E.—the Pentateuch was born.

The inconclusiveness of the Pentateuch made it immediately applicable to those who had experienced the exile, and subsequently to those who lived outside the land or even those who had returned to the land, but not as an independent nation. "Wherever exilic Jewry opens the Pentateuch it finds itself."[6] Moreover, all future generations who also stand "beyond the Jordan" can identify with the Torah. Because of the way the story of the Pentateuch ends (or does not end), the story is *about them,* not just about ancient Israel. Even more remarkable, the resultant process of identification with the Israel in the Torah was not one of doleful resignation. On the contrary, to identify with the Israel who stood "beyond the Jordan" was to grasp one's election as God's chosen people from among all the peoples of the world. Thus, "through the Torah, Israel passed from a nation in destitution to a religious community in dispersion which could never be destroyed.''[7] In fact, we can extend the application beyond the implied Jewish community and say that, largely (but not only) because of the way the story ends it is also about everyone. That is, the story *can* be about all human beings because it remains open-ended, and this open-endedness evokes a dimension of the human condition. In short, perhaps the most remarkable feature of the Torah is its correspondence to "the narrative quality of experience," the way in which every human being *is* an uncompleted story, a nexus of past, present, *and* future. Personal identity is a combination of "the chronicle of memory and the scenario of anticipation."[8]

The inconclusiveness of the Pentateuch emerges in a context that has appeared at a number of key places within the narrative—the context of departure. A quotation from Frank Kermode's *The Sense of an Ending* will prove helpful here in considering the end of the Pentateuch as a moment of departure:

> All . . . plotting presupposes and requires that an end will bestow upon the whole duration and meaning. To put it another way, the interval must be purged of simple chronicity, of the emptiness of *tock-tick*, humanly uninteresting successiveness [i.e. *chronos*]. It is required to be a significant season, *kairos* [a pregnant moment] poised between beginning and end. It has to be, on a scale much greater than that which concerns the psychologists, an instance of what they call "temporal integration"—our way of bundling together perception of the present, memory of the past, and expectation of the future, in a common organization. Within this organization that which was conceived of as simply successive becomes charged with past and future: what was *chronos* becomes *kairos* (46).

In terms of "departure," we shall emphasize two key phrases from the above quotation—an "interval . . . poised between beginning and end," and a way of "bundling together perception of the present, memory of the past, and expectation of the future."

The Pentateuch does not end with an arrival, but with a suspension of the moment before departure. The suspension of such a moment is not unique to the end of the narrative. The bridge between the Primeval cycle and the Ancestral Saga of Genesis (12:1–3) is constructed on the foundation of Yahweh's charge to Abram before his departure from Haran. Jacob becomes the heir to Abram's promise on the night before his escape from Esau (28:10–17); he receives the name "Israel" and a divine blessing on the night before his return to Canaan (32:22–32); and he receives a renewal of the promise of nationhood on the night before his departure for Egypt (46:1–7). The traditional name of the book of Exodus ("a going forth") speaks for itself, and includes not only the departure from Egypt, but the *expectation* of Israel's departure from Sinai (chaps. 32—33), an expectation realized in Numbers 10. Similarly, Israel stands on the verge of departure from the wilderness to the promised land in Numbers 13—14, only to step back in diffidence and defeat.

As we have previously seen, the Passover celebration represents a liturgical expression of the suspended moment of departure, a classic *rite de passage,* and we may now see it as suggesting a sense of the end of the Pentateuch.[9] Passover is "a night of watching by Yahweh" (Exod. 12:42), and, by extension, it is a night of watching by Israel. Passover celebrates salvation, but not by placing the celebrants on the other side of the Sea; the celebrants are poised on the night in between slavery and freedom. Even while it *celebrates* salvation as past, it *portrays* salvation as future. This sense of departure as *kairos,* as an urgent moment full of hope as well as danger, pervades the end of the Pentateuch. As in the Passover liturgy, the Israelites (and we the readers) are not deposited on the other side of the Jordan, but suspended "beyond the Jordan," waiting to enter the land. The Torah leaves the reader at a moment of temporal tension, not only at the end, but also at the beginning, of an adventure.[10]

On the other hand, one can make too much of the inconclusiveness of the Pentateuch. This happens when one distorts its narrative dimension by construing it apart from its political dimension. At the same time that the themes and plot render a story, they also render *torah*—instruction, guidance, and law. If the end of the Pentateuch is inconclusive, it is not premature but, in fact, entirely appropriate to the function of the Pentateuch as *the* Torah, the "guide book" of Israel. As both story *and* law, the Pentateuch is inconclusive but not incomplete, and the resultant tension is an essential part of its significance.

From the moment God drove Adam and Eve from the garden, the Pentateuch has portrayed Yahweh as a deity in search of community, a God whose primary purpose is the restoration of the order among creator, creature, and world that existed before the first human beings broke the first commandment. The Pentateuch is a narrative description of that process of restoration—or better, re-creation—as it took shape in the sacral community known as Israel. At the end of the Pentateuch, that community—*as a possibility*—is now complete. Through the agency of Moses, God has finished the work that he began with the charge to the ancestors, continued with the salvation of Israel from Egypt, and completed in the formation of the covenant community gathered around the tabernacle. Israel is a people with a divinely given polity, "a constitutional theocracy with a complete system of government (cf. esp. 17:8—18:22)."[11] Near the end of Moses' last will and testament, therefore, Moses can declare: "this day you have become the people of Yahweh your God" (27:9). The Israel that stands "beyond the Jordan" represents a complete model of reality, the way in which human beings can live in conformity to the will of God.

With this description of the new community of God, the Pentateuch has reached its true end—its *telos*—its goal and purpose. The Pentateuchal narrative renders a new world. But as it was "in the beginning," so it is now; while that world exists as a reality in terms of what God has done, it exists only as a possibility in terms of what Israel will do. The Torah ends very much the way it began. Just as God placed the earth before Adam and Eve and offered it to them as their dominion, so God places the land of Canaan before Israel and offers it to them. Just as God provided for Adam and Eve a commandment, obedience to which would mean continued blessing, but disobedience to which would entail a curse, so God has blessed Israel as his special people, but warned them of the curse that leads to death. Just as Adam and Eve could be genuinely human only in responsibility to the divine will, so Israel can be God's holy nation only in responsibility to God's *torah*.

Here again the Pentateuch is at once complete and open-ended. Although it renders the new world created by God—the work God has finished, the covenant community that is "very good"—it ends with the death of Moses, and with the challenge of his testimony. The Torah ends with a charge, and thus with a question: will Israel *be* the new community God has created, or not? The way of Torah lies open, but it is a straight and narrow path:

> I call heaven and earth to witness against you this day, that I have set before you life and death, blessing and curse; therefore choose life, that you and your descendants may live, loving Yahweh your God, obeying his voice, and cleaving to him; for that means life to you and length of days, that you may dwell in the land which Yahweh swore to your fathers, to Abraham, to Isaac, and to Jacob, to give them (Deut. 30:19–20).

Notes

INTRODUCTION

1. Jacob Neusner, *The Way of Torah: An Introduction to Judaism* (The Religious Life of Man, ed. F. J. Streng; Belmont, CA: Dickenson, 1970).
2. Cf. Clines, *The Theme of the Pentateuch*, 97–98; Cross, *Canaanite Myth and Hebrew Epic*, 325; for a later date, see Widengren in Hayes and Miller, *Israelite and Judaean History*, 514–15, 536–37.
3. The classic work that attempts to demonstrate the original orientation of Deuteronomy is that of Martin Noth, *The Deuteronomistic History, JSOT Suppl*, 15 (Sheffield: JSOT, 1981 [1967]).
4. At the end of his translation of Martin Noth's *A History of Pentateuchal Traditions* (Englewood Cliffs, NJ: Prentice-Hall, 1972), Bernhard Anderson has provided a convenient chart showing the division of literary sources throughout the Pentateuch.
5. *The Vitality of Old Testament Traditions*, 38. For an extended treatment of J, see Peter F. Ellis, *The Yahwist: The Bible's First Theologian* (Notre Dame: Fides, 1968).
6. " 'The Ancestress of Israel in Danger' in Danger," *Semeia* 3 (1975): 82–83.
7. On "E" see P. Volz and W. Rudolph, *Der Elohist als Erzähler: Ein Irrweg der Pentateuchkritik? BZAW* 63 (1933) and more recently the treatment of Gen. 20—21 by John Van Seters in his *Abraham in History and Tradition*. For the theory of larger independent literary units rather than continuous narrative sources see Rendtorff, *Pentateuch*; for critique of Rendtorff's study, see the entire issue of *JSOT* 3 (1977). For the two views on the dating of "J" see respectively Fretheim, *Creation, Fall, and Flood*, 15–16 and Van Seters, *Abraham in History and Tradition*, 271–72 (in general, 148–53).
8. *The Eclipse of Biblical Narrative: A Study in Eighteenth and Nineteenth Century Hermeneutics* (New Haven: Yale, 1974), 9 (emphasis mine).
9. Ibid., 11 (emphasis his). Cf. M. Weiss, "Einiges über die Bauformen des Erzählens in der Bibel," *VT* 13(1963): 459, and Frye, *Anatomy of Criticism* (Princeton: Princeton University, 1957), xvii, 315. On the tension between the historian and the literary critic see Frank Kermode, "The Argument About Canons" in *The Bible and the Narrative Tradition*, ed. Frank McConnell (New York: Oxford, 1986), 78–96, esp. 88.
10. For a brief overview associated with the "new criticism" see D. Robertson, "Literature, the Bible as, "*IDBSup*, 547–51; for structuralism, see Robert Polzin, *Biblical Structuralism: Method and Subjectivity in the Study of Ancient Texts* (Philadelphia: Fortress, 1977); for rhetorical criticism (coined by James Muilenburg) see J. Jackson and M. Kessler, eds. *Rhetorical Criticism: Essays*

in Honor of James Muilenburg (Pittsburgh: Pickwick, 1974); current "canonical criticism" is divided by those who continue to emphasize the significance of the *process* by which the text achieved its present shape (James Sanders—for an overview see his "Hermeneutics," *IDBSup* 402–407) and those who stress the final *product* (Brevard Childs, *Introduction to the Old Testament as Scripture*).

11. For representative studies, see Bernhard W. Anderson, "Tradition and Scripture in the Community of Faith," *JBL* 100 (1981): 5–21 and "From Analysis to Synthesis: The Interpretation of Genesis 1—11," *JBL* 97 (1978): 23–39; Kenneth Gros Louis, ed. *Literary Interpretations of Biblical Narratives* (Nashville: Abingdon, 1974); Jacob Licht, *Storytelling in the Bible* (Jerusalem: Magnes, 1978), 14–15, 144–49; Edward L. Greenstein, "Biblical Narratology" (a bibliographical essay), *Prooftexts* 1 (1981): 201–208.

12. For the former metaphor see Brueggemann, *Vitality*, 17; for the latter, Alter, *Art of Biblical Narrative*, 13–14.

13. See James Barr, "Story and History in Biblical Theology," *JR* 56 (1976): 1–17; Frye, *The Great Code*, 39–50, 64–65; Brian Wicker, *The Story-Shaped World*.

14. *The Torah*, xxiii; for a similar call for balance, cf. Polzin, *Biblical Structuralism: Method and Subjectivity in the Study of Ancient Texts* (Philadelphia: Fortress, 1977), 201; Richard Friedman, *The Creation of Sacred Literature: Composition and Redaction of the Biblical Text* (University of California Publications: Near Eastern Studies 22; Berkeley: University of California, 1981), 1.

15. Robert Scholes and Robert Kellogg, *The Nature of Narrative* (London: Oxford, 1966); Stephen Crites, "The Narrative Quality of Experience," *JAAR* 39 (1971): 291–311; George W. Stroup, *The Promise of Narrative Theology: Recovering the Gospel in the Church* (Atlanta: John Knox, 1981), and his bibliographical essay in *TTod* 32 (1975): 133–43.

16. In general see also Peter Miscall, "Literary Unity in Old Testament Narrative," *Semeia* 15 (1979): 29 and n.2; Norman Wagner, "Response to Rendtorff," *JSOT* 3 (1977): 22.

17. The phrase is Frye's (*The Great Code*, 211; cf. 216). On the general relation between law and story see Sanders, *Torah and Canon*, 1–4; Friedman, *The Creation of Sacred Literature*, 2; Rendtorff, *Pentateuch*, 167; Krister Stendahl, "The Bible as a Classic and the Bible as Holy Scripture," *JBL* 103 (1984): 3–10.

18. For example, see the anthology edited by Roland Frye, *The Bible: Selections from the KJV for Study as Literature* (Boston: Houghton Mifflin, 1965), which leaves out most of Leviticus, Numbers, and Deuteronomy. Even the study by Joseph Blenkinsopp and John Challenor entitled *Pentateuch* completely ignores the books of Leviticus and Numbers (Scripture Discussion Commentary, 1; Chicago: ACTA Foundation, 1971).

19. *Mimesis*, 14–15. Cf. Wicker, *Story Shaped World*, 4; Frye, *Anatomy of Criticism*, 352 and *The Great Code*, 62–63, 71; Fokkelman, *Narrative Art*, 6, who speaks of "a world-in-words"; and Clines, *The Theme of the Pentateuch*, 102.

20. Still the best short introduction to Hebrew narrative art is Auerbach's classic discussion of Gen. 22 in *Mimesis* ("Odysseus' Scar," 3–23). For a full-scale development of Auerbach's approach see Alter, *The Art of Biblical Narrative*.

21. Reynolds Price, *A Palpable God: Thirty Stories Translated from the Bible, with an Essay on the Origins and Life of Narrative* (New York: Atheneum, 1978), 11.

22. *The Art of Biblical Narrative*, 126. Cf. Scholes and Kellogg, *Nature of Narrative*, 166–67, 171; Licht, *Storytelling in the Bible*, 31–33.
23. Alter, *The Art of Biblical Narrative*, 154.
24. *Mystery and Manners*, ed. Sally and Robert Fitzgerald (New York: Farrar, Straus & Giroux, 1961), esp. 103, 153, 202–203.
25. Cf. Alter, *Art of Biblical Narrative*, 33.
26. *Mimesis*, 22–23.
27. Ibid., 18.

GENESIS: THE PRIMEVAL CYCLE

1. See Ricoeur, *The Symbolism of Evil*, 3–10, 161–74; Brevard Childs, *Myth and Reality in the Old Testament* (Studies in Biblical Theology, 27; London: SCM; 1960); Fretheim, *Creation, Fall, and Flood*, chap. 3; Howard N. Wallace, *The Eden Narrative* (Harvard Semitic Monographs, 32; Atlanta: Scholars, 1985), chaps. III and IV.
2. All of these texts are found in J. B. Pritchard, *Ancient Near Eastern Texts Relating to the Old Testament* (Princeton: Princeton University, 1950). Commentaries that devote considerable attention to these texts include Nahum Sarna, *Understanding Genesis* (New York: Schocken, 1966); and Speiser, *Genesis*. For recent overviews of each of the books of the Pentateuch in relation to ancient Near Eastern literature, see the essays by William W. Hallo in Plaut, *The Torah*.
3. The contrast here is quantitative. Cf. Clark, "The Flood and the Structure of the Pre-Patriarchal History," *ZAW* 83 (1971): 184–88; Thorkild Jacobsen, "The Eridu Genesis," *JBL* 100 (1981): 513–29; Michael Fishbane, *Text and Texture: Close Readings of Selected Biblical Books* (New York: Schocken, 1979), 28–30.
4. Cf. Susan Niditch, *Chaos to Cosmos: Studies in Biblical Patterns of Creation* (Chico, CA: Scholars, 1985), 63.
5. For a similar view, see Fishbane, *Text and Texture*, 38. Note also Childs, *Introduction to the Old Testament as Scripture*, 152–53.
6. The phrase is that of Wicker, *The Story-Shaped World*.
7. The numbering and function of these formulae is open to debate. See D. W. Baker, "Diversity and Unity in the Literary Structure of Genesis," in Wiseman and Millard, eds. *Essays on the Patriarchal Narratives*, 196; Fretheim, *Creation, Fall, and Flood*, 28; Redford, *The Biblical Story of Joseph*, 3–14; and Cross, *Canaanite Myth and Hebrew Epic*, 301–305 and n.3; Olson, *The Death of the Old*, 98–114.
8. This is essentially the division followed by Plaut, *The Torah*, ix–xi.
9. Cf. Clines, *Theme of the Pentateuch*, 76–78.
10. The traditional chapter divisions are late (i.e., Christian) additions to the text.
11. See Rendtorff, "Genesis 8:21 und die Urgeschichte des Jahwisten," *KD* 7 (1961): 75; Claus Westermann, *The Promises to the Fathers* (Philadelphia: Fortress, 1979), 54–55, his *Genesis 1—11* (Minneapolis: Augsburg, 1984), 63; and B. Anderson, "From Analysis to Synthesis: The Interpretation of Genesis 1—11," *JBL* 97 (1978): 39. For other responses to Rendtorff's article, see Clines, *Theme of the Pentateuch*, 71–72.
12. For further discussion of the command-execution pattern in Priestly theology see Westermann, *Genesis 1—11*, 5–6, 11–14, and Blenkinsopp, *Prophecy and Canon*, 60.

13. *The Art of Biblical Narrative*, 143–44.
14. For a delineation of the theme of the land throughout the Hebrew Bible and into the New Testament, see Walter Brueggemann, *The Land* (Overtures to Biblical Theology, 1; Philadelphia: Fortress, 1977).
15. On blessing in general, see Westermann, *Blessing in the Bible and the Life of the Church* (Philadelphia: Fortress, 1978). On blessing in the Pentateuch, see Goldingay, "The Patriarchs in Scripture and History," in Wiseman and Millard, eds. *Essays on the Patriarchal Narratives*, 11–42.
16. My use of the term *theme* is different from that of tradition-critics such as von Rad and Noth (e.g., Noth, *A History of Pentateuchal Traditions*, chap. 7; von Rad, *Genesis*, 13–27). On the other hand, I obviously do not agree with Clines (*The Theme of the Pentateuch*, 20) when he insists that there can be only *one* theme to a work. For him that theme is the partial fulfilment of the promise to Abraham. Since that promise is a triad of posterity, divine-human relationship, and land, we are in close agreement despite our theoretical differences. For a similar approach that focuses on blessing as the central theme, see Goldingay, "The Patriarchs in Scripture and History," 26–34.
17. *Prolegomena to the History of Ancient Israel* (Cleveland: World, 1957), 304.
18. When *adam* occurs with the article (*ha*) or as a proper name (2:20; 3:17) in the Eden story the word refers to Adam as a male, not to humankind (male and female) as in chap. 1.
19. See also Fretheim, *Creation, Fall, and Flood*, 76–77 (where he sees the same problem with Cain, Lamech, and the tower of Babel, on which see below); Patrick D. Miller, Jr., *Genesis 1—11* (Sheffield: University of Sheffield, 1976), 21; and Niditch, *Chaos to Cosmos*, 37.
20. Friedman, "Sacred History and Theology: The Redaction of Torah," in *Creation of Sacred Literature*, 26. Cf. Alter, *The Art of Biblical Narrative*, 141–47.
21. See Westermann, *Genesis 1—11*, 295.
22. Cf. the literary form of Exod. 21:15–17 and Num. 3:19.
23. For the parallels to the Sethite genealogy in chap. 5 (P), see Plaut, *The Torah*, 54. Note that J refers to the Sethite line in abbreviated form in 4:25–26.
24. *Genesis*, 108.
25. A list of antediluvian figures leading up to the protagonist of the flood story is also known from Mesopotamian sources (e.g., the "Sumerian King List"). See Speiser, *Genesis*, 41–42, and Plaut, *The Torah*, 54.
26. The name Enosh (the son of Seth) is a synonym for Adam ("humankind").
27. Usually thoughts are rendered by speech (e.g., vs. 7, 1:26; 8:21; 11:6). See Alter, *The Art of Biblical Narrative*, chapter 4.
28. For the wider theological implications of this understanding see the concept of "divine pathos" as developed by Abraham Heschel, *The Prophets* (New York: Harper & Row, 1962), 26 and frequently elsewhere.
29. On "character" and narrative, see Stanley Hauerwas, *A Community of Character: Toward a Constructive Christian Social Ethic* (Notre Dame, IN: University of Notre Dame, 1981), esp. 62, 69.
30. On this sacrifice, see J. Milgrom, "Sacrifices and offerings, OT," *IDBSup*, 769.
31. On the role of law here see von Rad, *Genesis*, 129, and Westermann, *Genesis 1—11*, 64–65. Westermann suggests a difference from later covenants in that the law here is given as part of the blessing, not the covenant (vss. 8–17). Contrast Cross, *Canaanite Myth and Hebrew Epic*, 296.

32. One of the more obvious problems is that it is Ham who sees the nakedness of his father, but Ham's son, Canaan, who is cursed.
33. See Westermann, *Genesis 1—11*, 66–67. Along with other scholars, Westermann sees here an originally independent story of a Noah different from that of the flood story.
34. For a probing analysis of how the characterization of Yahweh in the wider context of the Pentateuch rules out such an interpretation, see Wicker, *Story-Shaped World*, 88–91.
35. For a summary of the most prominent interpretations, see Plaut, *The Torah*, 83–84.
36. Sarna, *Genesis*, 77. My interpretation is also in basic agreement with that of Fokkelman (*Narrative Art*, 14–17).
37. With few exceptions (including 10:18). See Ezek. 11:17; 20:41–42; 28:25; 29:13; 34:12–13.
38. So also Sarna, *Genesis*, 67 and 72; Fokkelman, *Narrative Art*, 18 n.12; and Isaac M. Kikawada and Arthur Quinn, *Before Abraham Was: The Unity of Genesis 1—11* (Nashville: Abingdon, 1985), 69, 71, 81 n.16.
39. Cf. Fokkelman, *Narrative Art*, 17; and Miller, *Genesis 1—11*, 24.
40. Cf. most recently Kikawada, *Before Abraham Was*, 51–52.
41. The first phrase here ("so be a blessing") is actually verse 2b, and is usually translated "so that you will be a blessing." The verb, however, is pointed as an imperative, and I have translated it accordingly. Read that way, it continues the force of the initial imperative in verse 1, on which see below. Cf. Samuel Terrien, *The Elusive Presence: Toward a New Biblical Theology* (New York: Harper & Row, 1978), 74–75.
42. Von Rad, *Genesis*, 155.
43. Jack Sasson, "The 'Tower of Babel' as a Clue to the Redactional Structuring of the Primeval History (Gen. 1—11:9)," in *The Bible World*, ed. Gary Rendsburg, et al. (New York: KTAV, 1980), 216.
44. For this construction using the imperative mood see Thomas O. Lambdin, *Introduction to Biblical Hebrew* (New York: Charles Scribner's Sons, 1971), 119 (section 107b). For a particularly close analogy see 1 Kings 1:12.

GENESIS: THE ABRAHAM CYCLE

1. I am using the term to designate an extensive redactional unit rather than individual stories in terms of form-criticism. Actually, the entire book is really a saga in this sense. So also George Coats (*Genesis*, 5–7, 28–29, 14–15), who sees the whole Pentateuch as a saga since he terms Exodus-Deuteronomy as "The Moses saga." The use of the term "saga" is hardly without debate, however. See Gunkel, *The Legends of Genesis*; Claus Westermann, *The Promises to the Fathers*; Clark, "The Biblical Traditions," in Hayes and Miller, eds. *Israelite and Judaean History*, 133–35; von Rad, *Genesis*, 30–42; Karl Barth, *Church Dogmatics*, III/1 (Edinburgh: T. & T. Clark, 1956), 81–90; Childs, *Myth and Reality in the Old Testament*, 31–59; Van Seters, *Abraham in History and Tradition*, 131–38; and Fokkelman, *Narrative Art in Genesis*, 238–39.
2. For a convenient collection of recent discussions on the thematic unity of Gen. 12—50, as well as the historical issues involved, see the articles of Baker,

Goldingay, Wenham, and Wiseman in D. J. Wiseman, and A. R. Millard, eds. *Essays on the Patriarchal Narratives.*

3. Sören Kierkegaard, *Fear and Trembling* (New York: Doubleday, 1954), xvi, 89–90.
4. Cf. Seth and Noah (4:26; 8:20), who also represent a new beginning.
5. Clines, *Theme of the Pentateuch*, 46.
6. Van Seters, *Abraham in History and Tradition*, 306.
7. For other connections see Norbert Lohfink, *Die Landverheissung als Eid: Eine Studie zu Gn 15* (Stuttgarter Bibelstudien, 18; Stuttgart: Katholisches Bibelwerk, 1967), 85.
8. Speiser, *Genesis*, 115.
9. Apparently Eliezer could be Abram's legal heir, but verse 2b is muddled and notoriously difficult to decipher. See the commentaries.
10. Cf. Jer. 7:1; 11:1; 18:1; Num. 12:6; 24:4, 16; 2 Sam. 7:4, 17.
11. Cf. 20:18; 29:31; 30:2; 1 Sam. 1:5.
12. With the possible exceptions of chaps. 23 and 36, which are usually attributed to P.
13. For a recent study of the full "covenant formula" to which these verses are related ("I will be your God and you shall be my people"), see Good, *The Sheep of his Pasture*, 65–85.
14. For this translation see Speiser, *Genesis*, 122. The covenant offer of verse 2 is also seen as a reward by Van Seters, *Abraham in History and Tradition*, 288.
15. Van Seters, *Abraham in History and Tradition*, 293.
16. Note that the mission of the angels originally had nothing to do with Lot but was intended only for judgment against the cities (cf. 18:20–22).
17. Since apparently ten righteous people were not to be found, it is not Abraham's negotiation with Yahweh that brings about Lot's rescue, but God's remembrance of Abraham as the agent of his blessing (19:29).
18. The word is *yada*, the basic meaning of which is "to know." Compare its use in Amos 3:2.
19. Cf. von Rad, *Genesis*, 208–09, and Walter Brueggemann, *Genesis* (Atlanta: John Knox, 1982), 171.
20. See Van Seters, *Abraham in History and Tradition*, 71–76, 167–75. For a "synchronic analysis" of the same texts (which include 26:6–11) see Robert Polzin, " 'The Ancestress of Israel in Danger' in Danger," 81–97.
21. Verse 15, where the verb used is *yashav*, which often connotes a more permanent settlement than *goor*, "to sojourn." However, note that both verbs are used in verse 1.
22. See the commentaries for discussion of the possible legal backgrounds to Abraham's claim.
23. Cf. the same verb in Isa. 30:28; 63:17; Ps. 107:40; Prov. 12:26; and esp. Jer. 50:6.
24. Note the parallels to "time," "old age," and "laughter" in 17:17, 21; 18:11, 13–15. Note also the emphasis in verses 1–2: "as he had said," "as he had promised," "of which God had spoken."
25. See the classic analysis of Eric Auerbach, *Mimesis*, 3–23.
26. Brueggemann, *Genesis*, 187.
27. Speiser, *Genesis*, 161. The identical phrase is used in verses 7 and 11, each with a different nuance determined by the context.

28. Quoted from an unpublished manuscript in Plaut, *The Torah*, 153 (my italics).
29. See 24:7; 26:3; 50:24; Exod. 13:5, 11; Num. 14:16, 30; 32:11; Deut. 1:8, 35; 6:10, etc. See Rendtorff, *Pentateuch*, 75.
30. The verb for "made over" in verse 17 is used in legal real estate transactions in Lev. 25:30; 27:14, 17, 19.
31. Von Rad, *Genesis*, 245.
32. Chap. 27; 47:29—49:33; and 50:24–26 respectively. Note esp. the same custom of taking an oath in 24:1–4 and 47:29–31.
33. Except 20:13, which, however, does not refer specifically to the promises and even appears to be critical of Yahweh's guidance (see the discussion and accompanying note above).
34. Cf. Exod. 34:11–16; Deut. 7:1–5.
35. So Plaut, *The Torah*, 161, in contrast to Redford (*The Biblical Story of Joseph*, 247) who suggests that the search involves not only "religious" but also "racial exclusiveness."
36. Cf. Van Seters, *Abraham in History and Tradition*, 243–46.

GENESIS: THE JACOB CYCLE

1. Verse 22. The root *rss* usually means "crush." Here it is often translated by "struggled together," which is appropriate but does not convey the more violent connotations of the root.
2. The text assumes that this is the same Abimelech as in chap. 20. The connections with 12:10–20 and chaps. 20–21 are usually understood as evidence for the existence of two alternative traditions of the same incidents, now lodged in two literary sources (J in chaps. 12; 26, E in chaps. 20; 21). A different approach would see in chap. 26 a deliberate commentary on the earlier stories rather than an independent tradition. For the former view, see the standard commentaries; for the latter, see for example Van Seters, *Abraham in History and Tradition*, 167–82.
3. On this compare also von Rad, *Genesis*, 38; Rendtorff, *Pentateuch*, 58; and Fokkelman, *Narrative Art*, 122.
4. *Art of Biblical Narrative*, 45.
5. *The Great Code*, 182. Cf. Fokkelman, *Narrative Art*, 111, 115–121; and Herbert Schneidau, "Biblical Narrative and Modern Consciousness," in *The Bible and the Narrative Tradition*, ed. Frank McConnell, 145–47.
6. Fokkelman (*Narrative Art*, 75–76) argues with considerable cogency that verse 21b ("Yahweh shall be my God") belongs with the conditional clauses of verses 20b–21a, and not with the following result clauses of verse 22.
7. Fokkelman, *Narrative Art*, 74.
8. Benno Jacob as quoted in Plaut, *The Torah*, 207.
9. Note the explicit terms "younger" (*tsa-eer*) and "first-born" in verse 26. Also the root for "deceive" (*ramah*) in verse 25 is the same as that for "deception" in 27:35.
10. Verses 19, 20 ("outwitted" = "stole the heart"), 30, 32, 39.
11. With the final verse, the speech also sounds like a song of thanksgiving or vindication. Compare Ps. 7:3–5; 94:16–17. Verse 40 has an exact parallel in Jer. 36:30 in the context of a divine curse.
12. Neutral, 1 Sam. 10:5; friendly, Isa. 64:5; hostile, e.g., Josh. 2:16; Judg. 8:21; 15:2.

13. Cf. 32:30b; 16:13; Exod. 33:20. As Fokkelman notes (*Narrative Art*, 220) the expression of deliverance in 32:31b represents a fulfilment of the prayer in 32:11, but this does not obviate the ambivalence, as Fokkelman suggests. Cf. Plaut, *The Torah*, 219–20.
14. Jacob has already purchased a piece of land outside the city, according to 33:18–20.
15. While their actions seem clearly to be irresponsible and certainly do not receive authorial approval, it is possible that later writers in the Pentateuch would applaud their behavior (e.g., Deut. 7:2). However, the two texts deal with very different situations and involve radically different theological motivations.
16. Simeon and Levi have already incriminated themselves in 34:25–31 as the ringleaders of the Shechem massacre.
17. Cf. Exod. 19:10, 14; Isa. 2:3; Jer. 31:6.
18. Verses 1 and 7 refer to 28:10–22; verse 3 refers to 32:8; and in context, at least, verse 5 may refer to 34:30.
19. The latter verses clearly conflict with 28:19 and 32:28 in that the names "Bethel" and "Israel" are introduced as if previously unknown. Verses 9–15 are usually assigned to P (sometimes without vs. 14).

GENESIS: THE JOSEPH CYCLE

1. On these and other connections, see most recently Alter, *Art of Biblical Narrative*, 10–11, 163; and Seybold, "Paradox and Symmetry in the Joseph Narrative," in *Literary Interpretations of Biblical Narratives*, ed. Gros Louis, 67–69.
2. See Alter, *Art of Biblical Narrative*, 3–12; Redford, *Story of Joseph*, 18 and 139, n.1.
3. Alter, *Art of Biblical Narrative*, 10.
4. The term is often used in contexts involving "Israelites" and non-Israelites; e.g., Exod. 1—2, 1 Sam. 4; 13; 14.
5. Note also that the word for "pledge" in verse 9 is derived from the same root *'rb* as the "pledge" in 38:17.
6. On the collision of narratives in the formation of identity, see Stroup, *Promise of Narrative Theology*, 171–75.
7. A reference to the land of Goshen. For this use of "remnant" with land, see Isa. 15:9; Jer. 47:4–5; Ezek. 25:16.
8. Alter, *Art of Biblical Narrative*, 112–13; cf. also 32–34, 176–77. Cf. George Coats, *From Canaan to Egypt: Structural and Theological Context for the Joseph Story* (Washington: Catholic Biblical Association, 1976), 89–90; and Mary Savage, "Literary Criticism and Biblical Studies: A Rhetorical Analysis of the Joseph Narrative," in *Scripture in Context: Essays on the Comparative Method*, ed. Carl D. Evans (Pittsburgh: Pickwick, 1980), 93–94. Contrast Redford, *Story of Joseph*, 251.
9. "Bring you up" could refer to Jacob's burial in Canaan, but that is unlikely. Cf. 28:15 ("I will not leave you until I have done that of which I have spoken to you") which also seems to apply to Israel of the future (i.e., given the content of the divine words in verses 13–14).
10. This passage (along with vss. 5–6) appears to be an insertion within an otherwise self-contained story (48:1–2, 8–22).

11. Cf. Rendtorff, *Pentateuch*, 75–77.

EXODUS 1—15

1. Indeed, George Coats has suggested that the figure of Moses binds together the entire Pentateuch. See, most recently, his *Genesis*, 5–7, 14–15. The term "saga" is also used by Martin Buber, *Moses: The Revelation and the Covenant*, (New York: Harper, 1958), 13, 17, not only to designate the individual stories in Exodus, but also "the Biblical narrative" of Exodus through Deuteronomy as "a continuity of events."

2. William W. Hallo originally suggested this typology in a joint study with J. J. A. van Dijk, *The Exaltation of Inanna*, Near Eastern Researches, 3 (New Haven: Yale, 1968), chap. 6: "The Typology of Divine Exaltation." I have used the typology in *Divine Presence and Guidance in Israelite Traditions: The Typology of Exaltation*, Johns Hopkins Near Eastern Studies, (Baltimore: Johns Hopkins University, 1977), esp. chaps. 5–7. For Hallo's more recent view, see his comments regarding Exodus in Plaut, *The Torah*, 372–77.

3. This clearly contradicts much of the book of Genesis, but it may accurately reflect the background of some groups within "Israel" who had never heard of Yahweh until they encountered the God of the Exodus story.

4. Even though there are no explicit cross references here to Genesis, I cannot agree with those who argue that Exod. 1:7 represents "a separate and independent narrative motif." So Claus Westermann, *Promises to the Fathers*, 22; cf. Rendtorff, *Pentateuch*, 70. For a view similar to mine, but with connections drawn to Genesis that I often find forced, see Ackerman, "The Literary Context of the Moses Birth Story (Exodus 1—2)," in *Literary Interpretations of Biblical Narratives*, ed. Gros Louis, 74–79. For a thorough discussion of Exod. 1:1–14 see George Coats, "A Structural Transition in Exodus," *VT* 22 (1972): 129–42. See below on the references to the land of Canaan in Exod. 13.

5. See Childs, *Exodus*, 8–10; Irwin in Hayes and Miller, *Israelite and Judaean History*, 200–03; Hallo in Plaut, *The Torah*, 368–70.

6. I have paraphrased the classic formulation of Gressmann (quoted by Childs, *Exodus*, 54): "The discoverer (*Entdecker*) has become the discovered (*Entdeckte*)." Gressmann's comment referred to the development of the tradition within Exod. 3, not to the material in 2:23–25, but the effect is the same.

7. Cf. my discussion of the syntax of Gen. 12:1–3 in the previous chapter. In the received text of Exod. 3:10 the verb "and bring out" is an imperative. That Moses is the subject of this verb is stunning, since it often signifies the exodus as *Yahweh's* act of deliverance (e.g., 20:2).

8. The literature is enormous. See Childs, *Exodus*, 60–70, 74–76; Cross, *Canaanite Myth and Hebrew Epic*, 60–75; Plaut, *The Torah*, 404–06, and other commentaries (including discussions of 6:2–8).

9. As quoted by Sean McEvenue, *The Narrative Style of the Priestly Writer*, *AnBib* 50 (1971): 141–42.

10. Hugh White, "French Structuralism and OT Narrative Analysis: Roland Barthes," *Semeia* 3 (1975): 113.

11. For example, see Childs, *Exodus*, 170–75 and, more recently, Robert Wilson, "The Hardening of Pharaoh's Heart," *CBQ* 41 (1979): 18–36; Plaut, *The Torah*, 416–17.

12. On this motif see my earlier study in *Divine Presence and Guidance*, 134–39; also von Rad, "Beobachtungen an der Moseerzählung Exodus 1—14," *EvTh* 31 (1971) 587–88; H. H. Schmid, *Der sogenannte Jahwist: Beobachtungen und Fragen zur Pentateuchforschung* (Zürich: Theologischer Verlag, 1976), 105; Rendtorff, *Pentateuch*, 71, 155; and J. Halbe, *Das Privilegrecht Jahwes, Ex. 34, 10–26*, 290–97.

13. Even at chaps. 19—20 the extent to which the people hear Yahweh's *words* will not be completely clear; cf. Deut. 5:4–5, 22–27, and see the discussion below.

14. Actually the first plague begins at verse 14, and verses 8–13 resemble 4:1–5 (the "signs"). However, in the present text a more natural break comes in between 7:7 and 8. For a recent survey of the possible literary patterns in the cycle see Plaut, *The Torah*, 430.

15. On this motif see also Ziony Zevit, "The Priestly Redaction and Interpretation of the Plague Narrative in Exodus," *JQR* 66 (1976): 197. The classic study of "I am Yahweh" was done by Walther Zimmerli in 1953 (in German). For a recent and brief statement of his views in English see his *Old Testament Theology in Outline*, (Atlanta: John Knox, 1978), 20–21.

16. The verse consists of two nominal clauses without any finite verbs; thus the tense must be determined on the basis of context.

17. For an assessment of the critical implications of the land promise in chap. 13, see Rendtorff, *Pentateuch*, 77. In 12:25, 13:5, 11 references to the land of Canaan clearly connect with Yahweh's "oath" in Genesis. In contrast, other references (e.g., 3:8) appear to derive from completely different traditions or authors.

18. George Coats, "The Yahwist as Theologian? A Critical Reflection," *JSOT* 3 (1977): 31.

19. See my *Divine Presence and Guidance*, 123–30. Some of the most original and creative work on this and related texts has been done by Cross, *Canaanite Myth and Hebrew Epic*, 112–44.

20. This term was introduced by Buber (*Moses*, 101), originally with reference to the Sinai covenant of chap. 19.

21. The peoples mentioned here correspond to some of the major characters in the Ancestral Saga: the Philistines, Edom, Moab, and the Canaanites. Here they are perceived as potential enemies, or at least as those who may stand in the way of Israel. Cf. also 23:23–33; 34:11–16; Lev. 18; Num. 20—25; Deut. 2—3.

22. The complicity of the people is suggested by 1:9, the plural verbs following in verses 11–14, and "all his people" in verse 22. In contrast, it is possible to understand the midwives as Egyptians, although they are more likely Hebrews. Exod. 1—15 thus provides a case in which blessing remains a major theme of the Pentateuchal narrative even though explicit use of the word is limited to one verse (12:32). On this verse and its relation to Gen. 12:3 see Wolff, "Kerygma of the Yahwist," in Brueggemann and Wolff, eds., *Old Testament Traditions*, 60–61, and, in opposition to any connection, Rendtorff, *Pentateuch*, 154, n.6.

23. Thus I would also argue, in conjunction with the previous note, that the corollary theme of curse pervades this literary unit despite the complete absence of the word, especially since plague is one of the most prominent manifestations of divine curse, as are the destruction of crops, the spoiling of water, and the death of first-born offspring—all obviously connected to

fertility or its opposite, sterility. Cf. the covenant curses in Lev. 26:14–26; Deut. 28:15–68 and note in the latter the explicit references to the Egyptian plagues in verses 27, 60. When the Egyptians threaten to murder all male Hebrew children, they thereby threaten to exterminate the blessing itself (Gen. 1:28; Exod. 1:7).

24. See 7:13–14, 22; 8:15, 19, 32; 9:7, 34.
25. Richard Friedman, "Sacred History and Theology: The Redaction of Torah," in *The Creation of Sacred Literature*, 31–32.
26. Concentrated in previews and in the final four plagues: See 4:21; 7:3; 9:12; 10:1 (which resembles the preview texts in scope), 20, 27; 11:10; 14:4, 8, 17 (in the last occurrence the object is the heart of the Egyptians, i.e., the troops). In addition, the motif with Yahweh as subject is concentrated in the later literary strata. See Wilson, "The Hardening of Pharaoh's Heart," and Friedman, "Sacred History and Theology," 31–34.
27. G. von Rad, *Old Testament Theology* (New York: Harper & Row, 1965), II, 153.
28. Plaut, *The Torah*, 454.
29. Emil Fackenheim, *God's Presence in History: Jewish Affirmations and Philosophical Reflections* (New York: New York University, 1970), 25.
30. *Understanding Exodus* (New York: Behrman House, 1969), 181.

EXODUS 16—40

1. E.g., Exod. 13:20; 14:2; 15:22, 27; 16:1; 17:1; 19:1. For further discussion of the redactional function of the itinerary notices see below in the introduction to the book of Numbers.
2. The manna story about food stands in between two stories about thirst (15:22–27 and 17:1–7). In addition, the latter two are preceded and followed respectively by stories about military threats (chaps. 14—15; 17:8–16).
3. This particular formula occurs only three other times in the Pentateuch (3:14, 15; 20:22). It resembles the "prophetic messenger formula" ("Thus says the Lord"), which in the Pentateuch is limited to Exod. 4—11 (and 32:27).
4. For a different view see R. W. L. Moberly, *At the Mountain of God: Story and Theology in Exod 32—34* (JSOT Suppl, 22; Sheffield: University of Sheffield, 1983), 226, n.4.
5. For this translation (JPS) see Plaut, *The Torah*, 522.
6. Ibid., 541.
7. The word "thunder" in verse 19 can also mean "voice." On whether or not the people heard the words of the Decalogue, see below.
8. Karl Barth, *Church Dogmatics*, IV/1, 430.
9. George Coats, "The King's Loyal Opposition: Obedience and Authority in Exodus 32—34," in *Canon and Authority*, ed. Coats and Burke O. Long (Philadelphia: Fortress, 1977), 95.
10. See Plaut, *The Torah*, 535–36, and the extensive discussion of Childs, *Exodus*, 351–60, 370–71.
11. Childs, *Exodus*, 373.
12. Paul Tillich, *The Dynamics of Faith* (New York: Harper & Row, 1957), 56.
13. The expressions are those of Emil Fackenheim, *God's Presence in History*, 14.

14. "I Have a Dream," in *The Voice of Black America*, ed. Philip S. Foner (New York: Simon & Schuster, 1972), 971–75.
15. See Langdon Gilkey, "The Political Dimensions of Theology," *JR* 59 (1979): 154–68 (esp. section II).
16. George Mendenhall, "Law and Covenant in Israel and in the Ancient Near East," *BA* 17 (1954) 26–46, 49–76. For more recent studies see the bibliographies of Childs, *Exodus*, 385–86. For a brief review, see Plaut, *The Torah*, 525 and the example from a Hittite treaty on p. 528; see also the more extensive discussion of Hallo in the same volume, 374–76.
17. Cf. the comments of Mendenhall as quoted in Plaut, *The Torah*, 537. Note also Good, *The Sheep of his Pasture*, 52.
18. W. Pannenberg, "Zur Theologie des Rechts," *Zeitschrift für evangelische Ethik* 7 (1963): 17–18 (my translation).
19. See Cross, *Canaanite Myth and Hebrew Epic*, 93–111, and Plaut, *The Torah*, 612.
20. See Moshe Greenberg, *Understanding Exodus*, 16–17.
21. Again the political model must be kept in mind. The "other gods" are to Yahweh what other kings were to a human suzerain. Allegiance to the latter prohibited any agreements with others, and violation of this arrangement often met with ruthless punishment. Ancient Israel's history was punctuated by such breaches of covenant involving capitulation to Canaanite religion and culture, and it is the danger of this capitulation that has influenced the anti-Canaanite thread that runs throughout the Pentateuch, beginning with the curse on Canaan (Gen. 9:25). One of the most violent of such statements occurs in Deut. 7. Clearly this fear, at times bordering on xenophobia, stands in tension with the potential blessing of other peoples that comes through Israel (cf. Deut. 2—3).
22. Gilkey, "The Political Dimensions of Theology," 160 (emphasis added).
23. Christopher Lasch, *The Culture of Narcissism* (New York: Warner Books, 1979); Robert Bellah, *Habits of the Heart: Individualism and Commitment in American Life* (New York: Harper & Row, 1985).
24. Gilkey, "The Political Dimensions of Theology," 160.
25. Cf. Childs, *Exodus*, 562–63.
26. In its original conception, the "tent of meeting" almost certainly reflects a history of tradition different from that of the tabernacle. Compare the role of the tent in Num. 11:16, 26; 12:4. For a different view, see Moberly, *At the Mountain of God*, 171–77.
27. For this translation of *panim* (literally, "face"), cf. 2 Sam. 17:11. For further discussion, see Mann, *Divine Presence and Guidance*, 157.
28. See the discussion of Childs, *Exodus*, 604–09. Contrast Moberly, *At the Mountain of God*, 83–106, 157–61, who argues that the text presented a covenant renewal from the outset.
29. The verb is a participle, and could also be translated "I am about to make."
30. Childs, *Exodus*, 619.
31. On this and what follows, see Hallo in Plaut, *The Torah*, 377, where he cites a study (in Hebrew) by Moshe Weinfeld; note also the comments of Plaut on p. 688. See also Blenkinsopp, *Prophecy and Canon*, 62–63.
32. T. H. Gaster, "Sacrifices and Offerings, OT," *IDB* 4: 149.
33. This is the literal meaning of the *terumah* ("offering"), e.g., 35:5.

LEVITICUS

1. The classic analysis of this phenomenon is that of Rudolf Otto, *The Idea of the Holy* (New York: Oxford, 1958). For examples of the phenomenon see Gen. 28:17; Exod. 3:5; 19:24 (see below); and Isa. 6:1–5.
2. I am following Jacob Milgrom, "Atonement in the OT," *IDBSup*, 81b.
3. See the ritual texts in Pritchard, *Ancient Near Eastern Texts*, 325–26, 331–53.
4. Hallo in Plaut, *The Torah*, 746–47.
5. This symbiosis is most apparent as *redaction* in those collections using the third person ("If anyone . . . he"; e.g., chaps. 4, 5). Here the introductory framework (vss. 1–2a) converts the rules into speech. But in many of the other codes, the relationship between rules and speech is intrinsic by virtue of the use of first and second person. The latter codes thus virtually presuppose a narrative context, whereas the former (without their redactional introduction) do not.
6. Corresponding to Exod. 20—24; 32—34 (covenantal), and 25—31; 35—40 (cultic).
7. The latter phrase was coined by Otto (see n.1 above).
8. On this term see Cross, *Canaanite Myth and Hebrew Epic*, 299.
9. Jacob Milgrom, "Sacrifices and Offerings," *IDBSup*, 765; Plaut, *The Torah*, 733–34 along with Hallo, 745, 748.
10. Ricoeur, *The Symbolism of Evil*, 33–40.
11. As Will Herberg has suggested, the "American Way" as a religion has "an extraordinarily high moral valuation of—sanitation!" (*American Civil Religion*, ed. Russell E. Richey and Donald G. Jones [New York: Harper & Row, 1974], 79).
12. For a recent presentation of this view, see Ronald E. Clements, *Leviticus*, The Broadman Bible Commentary, 2 (Nashville: Broadman, 1970), 33–34. He also emphasizes a religious significance.
13. *Purity and Danger* (London: Routledge & Kegan Paul, 1966), 53.
14. Ibid., 57.
15. Cf. J. R. Porter, *Leviticus*, Cambridge Bible Commentary on the New English Bible (Cambridge: Cambridge University, 1976), 11, 84. Cf. the role of the Sabbath and creation in Exod. 35—40.
16. See Ricoeur, *The Symbolism of Evil*, 28.
17. Milgrom, "Atonement in the OT," *IDBSup*, 79a.
18. See Bamberger in Plaut, *The Torah*, 786.
19. See B. Levine, *In the Presence of the Lord* (Leiden: Brill, 1974), 57.
20. Milgrom, "Atonement in the OT," 79a.
21. Interpreters often appeal to 17:11 and suggest a substitutionary understanding of sacrifice. For a refutation of this interpretation of the text, see Milgrom, "A Prolegomenon to Leviticus 17:11," *JBL* 90 (1971): 149–56, and "Sacrifices and Offerings in the OT," *IDBSup*, 770.
22. Levine, *In the Presence of the Lord*, 90–91; Bamberger in Plaut, *The Torah*, 768 and 861; Porter, *Leviticus*, 37. In addition, as Milgrom notes ("Atonement in the OT," 80), repentance on the part of the worshiper is a precondition in the ritual texts.
23. Levine, *In the Presence of the Lord*, 65–66.
24. With the exception of the ritual described in Deut. 21:1–9.

25. Cf. Exod. 21:1–6; 23:10–11; Deut. 15:1–18; 23:19–20; Jer. 34:8–22. On the uniqueness of the sabbath and the sabbatical and jubilee years in the light of Near Eastern parallels see Hallo in Plaut, *The Torah*, 747–48.
26. See Bamberger in Plaut, *The Torah*, 941 for positive evidence regarding the second temple period and the Common Era. Cf. also B. Z. Wacholder, "Sabbatical year," *IDBSup*, 762–63.
27. Gen. 2:1–3; Exod. 31:12–17; 35:1–3, and see the discussion at the end of the previous chapter.
28. Thus there is a parallel with the slave law in chap. 25 where Israelites are forbidden to own fellow Israelites since they belong to Yahweh alone as his "slaves" (cf. vs. 42).
29. A. van Selms, "Jubilee, year of," *IDBSup*, 497a.

NUMBERS

1. For a recent survey of interpretation and bibliography see B. Levine, "Numbers, Book of," *IDBSup*, 631–35; Childs, *Introduction*, 190–201. A more recent study which emphasizes the final form of the text is Dennis T. Olson's *The Death of the Old and the Birth of the New*. Olson and I have arrived independently at similar conclusions regarding the key role of the census lists in chaps. 1 and 26.
2. Hallo in Plaut, ed. *The Torah*, 1019–20.
3. Manna and quail, administrative assistants (Exod. 16; 18; Num. 11); water from a rock (Exod. 17:1–7; Num. 20:1–13).
4. Cf. Clines, *Theme of the Pentateuch*, 87.
5. For the redactor, apparently the literary context of the passage is more important for its significance than chronology (cf. 9:1; 10:11; 1:1). For bibliography and discussion on the liminal significance of the wilderness stories see Robert Cohn, *The Shape of Sacred Space* (Chico, CA: Scholars Press, 1981), chap. 2.
6. On the divine vanguard motif, see my *Divine Presence and Guidance in Israelite Traditions*. Chap. 8 deals specifically with Num. 1—10.
7. It appears that the number originally was 6,000; the word formerly thought to mean "hundred" probably means "platoon (of ten men)". Cf. Hallo and Plaut in *The Torah*, 1019, 1034–35. On the other hand, I would agree with Walter Harrelson, "Guidance in the Wilderness," *Int* 13 (1959):28; that the authors were aware of the incredibility of the figure, but used it for irony— "A fighting force of more than 600,000 men has been entirely cowed by the report of ten scouts."
8. So also D. Kellermann, *Die Priesterschrift von Numeri 1,1 bis 10,10 BZAW* 120(1970): 16. Cf. Exod. 1:7; Deut. 1:10–11.
9. Fretheim, *Creation, Fall, and Flood*, 26.
10. Cf. Exod. 32:1, 34; 33:1–6. See my *Divine Presence and Guidance*, chap. 9.
11. The root *dabar* is used four times here for "word," "speak," and "speech."
12. There Yahweh had promised to send his angel before the people to Canaan, but also had warned that, at some time in the future, punishment would be invoked for the sin of the calf.
13. The peculiarity of chap. 15 is accentuated by the redactional slip in vss. 22–23, where the editor refers to Moses in the third person in the context of a direct address by Yahweh to Moses.

14. For more details, see my study, "Holiness and Death in the Redaction of Num. 16:1—20:13," in *Love and Death in the Ancient Near East* (Essays in Honor of Marvin Pope; Guilford, CT: Four Quarters Publishing Company, 1987), 181–90.
15. Ibid., and n.30.
16. See my "Theological Reflections on the Denial of Moses," *JBL* 98 (1979): 481–94.
17. Northrop Frye, *Anatomy of Criticism*, 210. Cf. also H. Barzel, "Moses: Tragedy and Sublimity," in *Literary Interpretations of Biblical Narratives*, ed. Gros Louis 120–40; also George Coats, "Legendary Motifs in the Moses Death Reports," *CBQ* 39 (1977): 33–44.
18. The itinerary notices begin at 1:1, then resume at 11:3, 34–35; 12:16, etc. While some interpreters use the itinerary notices as indicators of the structure of the book, they do not function that way in the final redaction. See Olson, *The Death of the Old*, 34–35.
19. See chap. 32 and Josh. 22:7–34.
20. See 22:8, 19, 38. Cf. Exod. 3:19–20; 7:1–5.
21. Cf. J. Halbe, *Das Privilegrecht Jahwes*, 157–60, 304–05, 313.
22. See Halbe, *Privilegrecht Jahwes*, 304–05. Note the parallels to the italicized words in Num. 25:1–2; cf. also Exod. 20:3; 23:24; and the militant warning in Deut. 7.
23. Cf. 16:40, where the same incident is described as a "reminder." Note also 32:7–15.
24. Note the variant tradition in Deut. 31:14–15, 23 which now appears to *confirm* Joshua's appointment.

DEUTERONOMY

1. Of course, every Pentateuchal redactor was an interpreter, but this is more overtly the case with the Deuteronomic editors. For example, P apparently embellished a J narrative in the manna story (Exod. 16) and the spy story (Num. 13—14), whereas the Deuteronomist chose a fresh retelling of these stories mixed with commentary (chaps. 8 and 1 respectively).
2. S. Dean McBride, Jr., "Deuteronomium/Deuteronomistisches Geschichtswerk/Deuteronomistische Schule," in *Theologische Realenzyklopaedie*, ed. G. Kraus and G. Mueller 8 (1981), 319.
3. Other examples within the introductory chapters are usually understood as explanatory "glosses" (2:10–12, 20–23; 3:9, 11, 13b–14; 10:6–7, [8], 9). Contrast Robert Polzin, *Moses and the Deuteronomist: A Literary Study of the Deuteronomic History* (Part 1: Deuteronomy, Joshua, Judges; New York: Seabury, 1980), 29–36.
4. Lev. 1:1–2a and *passim*. Cf. Num. 1:1; 2:1; 3:5, 11, etc., predominantly in chaps. 1—10; 26—36. In Deuteronomy, there is no direct speech by God until chap. 31, then at the end of chap. 32 and in chap. 34. The only divine speeches of any length are 31:16–21 and 32:48–52. (Of course, Yahweh often speaks *indirectly* in the narration of Moses.)
5. The cloud makes another brief appearance at the consecration of Solomon's temple (1 Kings 8:11), in a passage related to Exod. 40. On the torah of Moses

as guidance see immediately Josh. 1:7–8; cf. the role of the ark in the crossing of the Jordan in Joshua 3—4.

6. Cf. William Moran, "Deuteronomy," In *A New Catholic Commentary on Holy Scripture*, ed. R. Fuller et al. (London: Nelson, 1969), paragraphs 229e and f.

7. Ibid., 223c (4:44; 29:1; 33:1). For another division, see Plaut, *The Torah*,1289.

8. Including general commandments (chaps. 6—11), specific stipulations (chaps. 12—26), summons to witnesses (4:26; 30:19; 31:26, 28), deposit of the treaty document (31:24–26).

9. S. Dean McBride, Jr., "The Yoke of the Kingdom: An Exposition of Deuteronomy 6:4–5," *Int* 27 (1973): 288 and see n.30.

10. Gen. 47:29—chap. 49; cf. 27:1; Josh. 23—24; 1 Kings 2:1–4.

11. See 1:34–39; 3:23–28; 4:21–22; then near the end, 31:1–2, 14, 16. The Priestly tradition is maintained in 32:48–52.

12. See my previous study, "Theological Reflections on the Denial of Moses."

13. McBride, "Deuteronomium," 319.

14. See N. Lohfink, "Darstellungskunst und Theologie in Dtn 1, 6 —3, 29," *Bib* 41 (1960): 105–34.

15. The expression is an English translation of the title of a major work by Norbert Lohfink, *Das Hauptgebot*: *Eine Untersuchung literarischer Einleitungsfragen zu Dtn 5—11 (AnBib* 20: 1963).

16. Here (with vs. 45) and in 5:31 and 6:1, "commandment" probably refers to chaps. 6—11, while "statutes and ordinances" probably refers to chaps. 12—26 (cf. the concluding formula in 26:16).

17. Moran, "Deuteronomy," 226d.

18. On the former, see most recently Vermeylen, "Les Sections Narratives de Deut 5—11," in Lohfink, ed. *Das Deuteronomium*, 192; on Deut. 5:1–5 see Polzin's analysis in *Moses and the Deuteronomist*, 45.

19. The translation is McBride's, "Yoke of the Kingdom," 274.

20. Paul Ricoeur, *Essays on Biblical Interpretation* (Philadelphia: Fortress, 1980), 82–83.

21. Hallo in Plaut, ed. *The Torah*, 371; on the motive clauses in general, see Rifat Sonsino, *Motive Clauses in Hebrew Law* (SBL Dissertation Series 45; Chico, CA: Scholars, 1980), esp. 112–13.

22. *Systematic Theology*, 3 vols. (Chicago: University of Chicago, 1951–63), 2:174.

23. Norman K. Gottwald, *The Tribes of Yahweh: A Sociology of the Religion of Liberated Israel* (Maryknoll, NY: Orbis, 1979), 59 (emphasis added).

24. *Moses and the Vocation of the Jewish People* (New York: Harper, 1959), 97.

25. This assumes that the ceremony of first fruits (vss. 1–4) is to be an annual event, rather than once and for all. Cf., in context, Exod. 22:29; 23:19; 34:26; Lev. 23:9–14.

CONCLUSION

1. Indeed, in his study of the Pentateuch Clines has suggested that there is really *one* theme, namely "the partial fulfilment—which implies also the partial non-fulfilment—of the promise to or blessing of the patriarchs," *The Theme of the Pentateuch*, 29.

2. *The Sense of an Ending* (New York: Oxford University, 1967), 83.

3. "Deuteronomy," 238d.

4. Cf. Blenkinsopp, *Prophecy and Canon*, 89; and Polzin, *Moses and the Deuteronomist*, 19, 56–57, 72.

5. Cf. Clines, *The Theme of the Pentateuch*, 94–95, 99–100.

6. Ibid., 98.

7. Sanders, *Torah and Canon*, 51.

8. Stephen Crites, "The Narrative Quality of Experience," *JAAR* 39 (1971) 303; see 291–311, esp. 302–03. Cf. Gottwald, *Tribes of Yahweh*, 124: ". . . early Israel could read the vast assurance of the canonical history not as a finished story, giving security once and for all, but as a source of incentive and reinforcement to achieve in its own circumstances what its forebears had achieved in theirs."

9. Cf. Jan van Goudoever, "The Liturgical Significance of the Date in Dt 1,3," in Lohfink, ed. *Das Deuteronomium*, 145.

10. See Hauerwas, *Community of Character*, 148–49; and Clines, *The Theme of the Pentateuch*, 107–11.

11. See S. Dean McBride, Jr., "Polity of the Covenant People: The Book of Deuteronomy," *Interp* 41 (1987), 229–44.

Bibliography of Frequently Cited Sources

Alter, Robert. *The Art of Biblical Narrative*. New York: Basic Books, 1981.

Auerbach, Eric. *Mimesis: The Representation of Reality in Western Literature*. Princeton: Princeton University, 1953.

Blenkinsopp, Joseph. *Prophecy and Canon: A Contribution to the Study of Jewish Origins*. Notre Dame: University of Notre Dame, 1977.

Brueggemann, Walter, and Hans W. Wolff, eds. *The Vitality of Old Testament Traditions*. Atlanta: John Knox, 1975.

Childs, Brevard S. *The Book of Exodus: A Critical, Theological Commentary*. The Old Testament Library. Philadelphia: Westminster, 1974.

————. *Introduction to the Old Testament as Scripture*. Philadelphia: Fortress, 1979.

Clines, David J. A. *The Theme of the Pentateuch*. Sheffield: JSOT, 1978.

Coats, George. *Genesis, With an Introduction to Narrative Literature*. The Forms of the Old Testament Literature, vol. 1. Edited by Rolf Knierim and Gene M. Tucker. Grand Rapids: Eerdmans, 1983.

Cross, Frank Moore. *Canaanite Myth and Hebrew Epic: Essays in the History of the Religion of Israel*. Cambridge: Harvard, 1973.

Fokkelman, J. P. *Narrative Art in Genesis: Specimens of Stylistic and Structural Analysis*. Assem: Van Gorcum, 1975.

Fretheim, Terrence E. *Creation, Fall, and Flood: Studies in Genesis 1—11*. Minneapolis: Augsburg, 1969.

Frye, Northrop. *The Great Code: The Bible and Literature*. New York: Harcourt Brace Jovanovich, 1981.

Good, Robert. *The Sheep of His Pasture: A Study of the Hebrew Noun 'AM(M) and Its Semitic Cognates*. Chico, CA: Scholars, 1983.

Gros Louis, Kenneth R. R., ed. *Literary Interpretations of Biblical Narratives*. Nashville: Abingdon, 1974.

Halbe, J. *Das Privilegrecht Jahwes, Ex. 34, 10–26*. Forschungen zur Religion und Literatur des Alten und Neuen Testaments. Göttingen: Vandenhoeck & Ruprecht, 1975.

Hayes, John and J. Maxwell Miller, eds. *Israelite and Judaean History*. The Old Testament Library. Philadelphia: Westminster, 1977.

Mann, Thomas W. *Divine Presence and Guidance in Israelite Traditions: The Typology of Exaltation*. The Johns Hopkins Near Eastern Studies, vol. 9. Edited by Hans Goedicke. Baltimore: Johns Hopkins, 1977.

Olson, Dennis T. *The Death of the Old and the Birth of the New: The Framework of the Book of Numbers and the Pentateuch*. Brown Judaic Studies, No. 71. Chico, CA: Scholars, 1985.

Plaut, W. Gunther, et al. *The Torah: A Modern Commentary*. New York: Union of American Hebrew Congregations, 1981.

Rad, Gerhard von. *The Book of Genesis*. The Old Testament Library. Philadelphia: Westminster, 1961.

Redford, D. *A Study of the Biblical Story of Joseph*. Supplements to Vetus Testamentum 20. Leiden: Brill, 1970.

Rendtorff, Rolf. *Das Überlieferungsgeschichtliche Problem des Pentateuch*. BZAW, 147. Berlin: de Gruyter, 1977.

Ricoeur, Paul. *The Symbolism of Evil*. Boston: Beacon, 1967.

Sanders, James. *Torah and Canon*. Philadelphia: Fortress, 1972.

Speiser, E. A. *Genesis*. The Anchor Bible, vol. 1. Garden City, NY: Doubleday, 1964.

Van Seters, John. *Abraham in History and Tradition*. New Haven: Yale, 1975.

Wicker, Brian. *The Story-Shaped World: Fiction and Metaphysics: Some Variations on a Theme*. Notre Dame: University of Notre Dame, 1975.

Wiseman, D. J. and A. R. Millard, eds. *Essays on the Patriarchal Narratives*. Leicester, England: Intervarsity, 1980.